D1707610

SELF-KNOWING AGENTS

Self-Knowing Agents

LUCY O'BRIEN

OXFORD
UNIVERSITY PRESS

OXFORD

UNIVERSITY PRESS

Great Clarendon Street, Oxford OX2 6DP

Oxford University Press is a department of the University of Oxford.
It furthers the University's objective of excellence in research, scholarship,
and education by publishing worldwide in

Oxford New York

Auckland Cape Town Dar es Salaam Hong Kong Karachi
Kuala Lumpur Madrid Melbourne Mexico City Nairobi
New Delhi Shanghai Taipei Toronto

With offices in

Argentina Austria Brazil Chile Czech Republic France Greece
Guatemala Hungary Italy Japan Poland Portugal Singapore
South Korea Switzerland Thailand Turkey Ukraine Vietnam

Oxford is a registered trade mark of Oxford University Press
in the UK and in certain other countries

Published in the United States
by Oxford University Press Inc., New York

British Library Cataloguing in Publication Data
Data available

Library of Congress Cataloging in Publication Data
Data available

Typeset by Laserwords Private Limited, Chennai, India
Printed in Great Britain
on acid-free paper by
Biddles Ltd., King's Lynn, Norfolk

ISBN 978-0-19-926148-2

1 3 5 7 9 10 8 6 4 2

For Mark Sacks

Preface

It strikes me that philosophy will tend to be affected by the way we do it. The natural conditions of contemplation and thought have one alone, fairly still, staring out of the window, occasionally scribbling or typing. While not offering a serious piece of philosophical sociology, is it any wonder that the philosopher's self is autonomous, contemplative and generally passive? However, like Briony in McEwan's *Atonement*, it has always felt to me that the clue to ourselves, and our self-consciousness, must lie in our agency:

She raised one hand and flexed its fingers and wondered, as she sometimes had before, how this thing, this machine for gripping, this fleshy spider on the end of her arm, came to be hers, entirely at her command. Or did it have some little life of its own? She bent her finger and straightened it. The mystery was in the instant before it moved, the dividing moment between moving and not moving, when her intention took effect. It was like a wave breaking. If she could only find herself at the crest, she thought, she might find the secret part of herself, that part of her that was really in charge. She brought her forefinger closer to her face and stared at it, urging it to move. It remained still because she was pretending, she was not entirely serious, and because willing it to move, or being about to move it was not the same as actually moving it. And when she did crook it finally, the action seemed to start in the finger itself, not in some part of her mind. When did it know to move, when did she know to move it? There was no catching herself out. It was either-or. There was no stitching, no seam, and yet she knew that behind the smooth continuous fabric was the real self—was it her soul?—which took the decision to cease pretending, and give the final command. (p. 35)

It is a part of the ambition of this book to play a part in a project, already underway, which seeks to undermine the conception of the subject as passive. I want to stress the importance of the fact that we are active creatures, both psychologically and physically. This is a somewhat neglected aspect of our subjectivity which in fact has an important role to play in addressing some of the central problems that subjectivity presents us with. In what follows I argue that the fact that we are active creatures gives us a way of being conscious of ourselves, through participation in our own actions, which we simply fail to identify if we concentrate on our purely passive ways of knowing.

My strategy, however, will not be to start with our active natures in the effort to give an account of the ways we have of referring to and knowing ourselves. It will rather be to present problems we face in giving a satisfactory account of self-reference and self-knowledge and to consider existing solutions. The shape of the available solutions serves to bring out the way in which we have assumed that our relations to ourselves must either be perceptual or theoretical. It is in the face of the inadequacies of either of these options that the positive suggestions emerge.

It is very tempting in a preface to do the equivalent of what Woody Allan does in the film *Take the Money and Run*, when he jumps on and crushes his own glasses before anyone else can. I will resist the temptation, leaving critics their due. Nevertheless, let me say that this book offers opinions on a broad range of issues: on first-person reference, on our knowledge of our mental actions, on our knowledge of our physical actions, on physical actions and on bodily awareness, and of a number of other things along the way—and in doing so may well stretch the limits of space and author. However, my aim was not to supply a final statement, or defence, of the views proposed; rather it was to produce a work that brought together, in a relatively clear and fast moving way, a number of distinct elements of how we relate to ourselves as subjects.

A word about pronouns: I have elected to use female pronouns as a default throughout. I suspect that the sensible thing would have been to use plural pronouns also as neutral singular pronouns. However, such usage is not well enough entrenched for me not to want to correct it. 'A subject referred to themselves using the first-person', for example, still sounds too far off to my ear. There is an argument that the male pronoun is already neutral. It seems to me, however, that it might once have been, and might be again, but that it is not now. So, 'she, herself' it had to be.

The book draws together work that I have presented at a number of talks and graduate classes at the following institutions: Freie Universität Berlin, University of Birmingham, University of Bristol, University of Edinburgh, Université de Fribourg, Universitat de Girona, University of Liverpool, University College London, School of Advanced Study (University of London), University of Manchester, University of Nottingham, University of Sheffield, University of Sussex, Universität Tübingen, University of Warwick, University of Stirling. The comments from those audiences have resulted in many improvements; I thank them collectively.

A large number of colleagues have helped me with this project over a long time, and in a variety of ways: by written and verbal comments on individual chapters, conversation, encouragement, sympathy, and intellectual support of one kind or another. I want to thank David Bell, Jay Bernstein, Simon Blackburn, Tyler Burge, Quassim Cassam, John Campbell, Tim Crane, Annalisa Coliva, Miranda Fricker, Sebastian Gardner, Max de Gaynesford, Marcus Giaquinto, Andy Hamilton, Ann Higginson, Axel Honneth, Jen Hornsby, Keith Hossack, Eric James, E. J. Lowe, Gideon Makin, Mike Martin, Colin McGinn, Adrian Moore, Véronique Munoz Dardé, Paul Noordhof, David Owens, David Papineau, Sarah Patterson, Christine Pries, Sarah Richmond, Sydney Shoemaker, Barry C. Smith, Gianfranco Soldati, Peter Sullivan, Julia Tanney, Jerry Valberg, David Velleman, Jo Wolff, and Arnie Zuboff. Special thanks are due to Dick Moran for his helpful and insightful comments on the whole typescript. I also want to thank Bill Brewer, Brie Gertler, and Johannes Roessler who, I now know, were readers for OUP. I am extremely grateful for their work. Whatever inadequacies remain, the book would have been significantly worse off without the many changes prompted by their comments.

In any philosophical project there are a handful of people whose work is particularly influential in directing the nature and course of ones thinking. It will be obvious that I owe much to Anscombe and Evans. I cannot thank them for that. However, I am happy to be able to thank David Bell, Tyler Burge, John Campbell, Chris Peacocke, John Perry, Sydney Shoemaker, David Velleman, and Tim Williamson for giving us work to aspire to.

A collective thank you—for being such good colleagues—to those in the Philosophy department at UCL. Thanks also to UCL for authorizing and funding research leave. I am also very grateful to the Arts and Humanities Research Council, and to the British Academy, for funding periods of leave in which work on this project was undertaken.

I have benefited enormously from being around excellent students in London. I would, in particular, like to thank Alan Brown, Fabian Dorsch, Lin Fou, David Levy, Will McNeill, Guy Longworth, Joel Smith, Finn Spicer, Alex Stanciu, and Daniel Viehoff.

I owe a considerable debt to Peter Momtchiloff. It has been an embarrassingly long time since we first talked about my doing a book on these issues, and he has kept faith to a remarkable degree. Two children but no finished manuscript later, he was still asking how things were going. His continued interest has been essential to my having got this far, and his efficiency and judgment have made it much easier. Thanks also to Virginia Masardo for her copy-editing; to Jenni Craig and Nadiah Al-Ammar for their help and efficiency as production editors; to Mick Belson for his proof reading, and to Hong Yu Wong for his excellent work on the index.

I have relied, I suspect more than most philosophers, on support from family and friends in managing life and writing. My debts are too numerous to list but I want in particular to thank my mother, my sisters, Anna Fairbank and Val Pumfrey.

It is customary, at this point, to thank ones long suffering children for their forbearance in the face of absence and grumpy presence. There has been some absence, and I fear more grumpy presence. But instead I want to thank Ben and Maya for all the times they succeeded in keeping me cheerily *away* from my desk, to be with them doing the things that most matter. My final and greatest thanks are for my partner Mark Sacks. I have relied heavily on his philosophical input, to this book, and over the years. For the rest, he has helped me more, and in more ways, than it makes sense to begin to say.

L.F.O'B.

London, UK

ACKNOWLEDGEMENTS
Two of the chapters are based on articles that have appeared elsewhere. Chapter 3 is based on 'Evans on Self-Identification', *Noûs* 29. 2:232–47 (1995) but has been rewritten and extended. Chapter 9 is based on 'On Knowing One's Own Actions' in *Agency and Self-Awareness*, Roessler, J. and Eilan, N. (eds). Oxford: Oxford University Press (2003). Although Chapter 1 is new, it draws on 'The Problem of Self-Identification', *Proceedings of the Aristotelian Society* 95: 235–51 (1995) in the way the problem of first-person reference is set up.

Contents

PART I

First-Person Reference

1

Introduction to Part I

This book is concerned with central aspects of self-consciousness. The leading idea of the book is that our most basic awareness of ourselves is as performers of actions, mental and physical. The conviction is that such awareness can serve to play a central and similar role in an account of first-person reference and in an account of self-knowledge. However, the concern with first-person reference is not, as is often the case, dealt with separately from the concern with self-knowledge. Although the discussion of self-knowledge does go beyond that which is required to understand first-person reference, it is a central claim of the book that an adequate account of first-person reference needs to draw on an account of self-knowledge, in particular on an account of our knowledge as agents of our thoughts and utterances. The book divides into two parts. Part I is devoted to a consideration of the problem of first-person reference. The main concern of Part II is to throw light on our knowledge of our physical actions. Apart from offering a suggestion about how best to construe our knowledge of our physical actions, Part II also aims to incorporate our knowledge of our physical actions within the compass of what philosophers call self-knowledge: knowledge we have of ourselves as subjects.

1. FIRST-PERSON REFERENCE

My aim in Part I of the book is to consider the difficulties we have in explaining our capacity for first-person reference, and to go some way towards offering an explanation that avoids them. The positive account is motivated by attending to the problems with existing models. However, the strategy will be neither to consider all possible, nor indeed all known to be extant, accounts of first-person reference. Rather the aim is to provide an account that seems plausible given desiderata that emerge from the shortcomings of key alternative accounts. Given this, it is helpful to have, at the outset, both a succinct account of the features of first-person reference that *prima facie* make it difficult to explain, and to have something like a map of what I take to be the key approaches to first-person reference and the problems they face. It will be the aim of the first part of this introductory chapter to supply both of these. In doing so, I will also be able to indicate the structure of Part I.

First-person reference has particular features that make it hard to account for:

(i) First-person reference seems to be indexical and context-dependent.

(ii) First-person reference seems to be reference that is identification-free.

(iii) First-person reference, despite being identification-free, seems to have an irreducible cognitive significance.

(iv) First-person reference is guaranteed reference.

Let us go through these features in turn.

(i) First-person reference is, *prima facie,* indexical and so context-dependent. Traditional accounts of reference had it that the contents of our thoughts and utterances were given by propositions that were determinate, impersonal, absolutely true or false, and were context-independent. It was long ago brought to our attention by Casteñeda, Perry, and Kaplan that giving an account of indexical thought or language against such suppositions was going to prove problematic. In particular, suppose we assume that the first-person element of first-person thoughts and utterances can be explained with reference to a fixed content. If we assume that such a content characterizes the first-person thoughts and utterances of different subjects on different occasions of use, then we have to give up the idea that the contents of our utterances are in themselves true or false. If, on the other hand, we assume that a distinct first-person content characterizes the first-person thoughts and utterances of each individual subject, then have to give up the idea that contents are shared. Certainly, an explanation of first-person reference along the model of those given for names or other singular concepts seems unlikely to be successful.

(ii) First-person reference seems to be identification-free. That is, a capacity for first-person reference that is fully expressive of self-consciousness seems to be available to a subject even when she appears to have no access to a means of identifying herself, of picking herself out as one from others. My perceptual faculties can be obstructed and I can be in a state of radical amnesia and still think 'Where am I?' However, standard models of reference draw on an explanation of how a referring subject picks out the object of reference as one object among others. An attempt to provide either a descriptive or demonstrative explanation of first-person reference that involves any such self-identification, is *prima facie* going to prove problematic.

(iii) First-person reference seems to have an irreducible cognitive significance. First-person reference is not merely reference to a person: the person using it. It is also expressive of self-consciousness and involves a way of referring to oneself that seems quite distinct from the way we can refer to other selves. When Oedipus makes the first-person discovery that *he* killed his father and married his mother he undergoes a fundamental psychological change. However, no articulation of what it is that he discovered in any other terms captures what he has come to know. It is not learning that the solver of the Sphinx's riddle, or that the father of Antigone, did these things that shocks him and propels him to act against himself, it is knowing that it was *he, himself* that did. Standard accounts of reference appeal to descriptive or perceptual information to explain cognitive significance. Both, *prima facie*, seem unavailable to do such work in the case of first-person reference.

(iv) First-person reference seems to be guaranteed, and guaranteed in three ways. First, a subject always succeeds in referring when she refers using the first-person. Secondly, she also succeeds in referring to *herself* when she refers first-personally. Thirdly, she knows that she is referring to herself. First-person reference seems always to have a referent, seems always to be reflexive reference, and seems always to be *self-conscious* reflexive reference.

The challenge, then, is to provide an account of first-person reference that explains and preserves these features. The fourth feature, the feature of guaranteed reference, in particular, tends to mean that accounts of first-person reference prove either insufficient or circular. It will prove a common complaint made against accounts of first-person reference that they fail to secure guaranteed reference, either because they fail to ensure that the subject herself is always the referent or because they fail to ensure that the subject knows that it is *herself* that she is referring to; that is, that she refers to herself *as herself.* On the other hand, attempts to secure both these kinds of guarantee can easily result in the invocation of a pre-supposed capacity to refer first-personally, in order to explain first-person reference. The challenge is to provide an account of first-person reference that delivers genuine first-person reference without already assuming that very capacity in the explanation given.

There are two dominant and contrasting ways of approaching the problem of how we refer to ourselves first-personally. They are what I will call *the perceptual approach* and *the self-reference approach.* On the perceptual approach, it is assumed that an account of the way we are presented with ourselves will explain first-person reference. It is then very natural to adapt the central model we have of the way we are presented with other objects—that is, via perception—to try to provide a model for the way we are presented with ourselves. The resulting model will generally take one of two forms. Some claim that we are presented with ourselves via some 'inner' or 'introspective' sense. Others, eschewing the idea of a quasi-perceptual faculty of introspection capable of apprehending ourselves, and suspecting that only very enigmatic sorts of objects (Cartesian Egos and the like) will be apprehended by such a faculty, have suggested that the five familiar senses plus our capacity for bodily awareness can provide an account of the way we are presented with ourselves capable of explaining first-person reference.

Both forms of the perceptual approach lead to difficulties. As we have said, it is a notable feature of first-person reference that it seems, in a certain sense, to be guaranteed to be successful. Assuming that a subject is using 'I' comprehendingly, it seems that her uses of 'I' will always succeed in referring to something, and what is more, her uses of 'I' will refer to that thing the subject intended it to refer to—herself. The fact that a subject lacks information about herself—if, for example, she is in a state of sensory deprivation—does not seem to undermine the possibility of first-person reference. Nor does the fact of a subject having misinformation about herself lead to her failing to refer, or lead to her referring to some other person, in her uses of 'I'. This feature of first-person reference will tend to cause problems for any view which holds that when we use 'I' we identify ourselves by means of some kind of perception or quasi-perception as long as it is possible for us to use 'I' while failing to perceive ourselves in the relevant way, or for us to use 'I' while perceiving another in the relevant way. However, an account of self-perception that rules out such possibilities will require a faculty of perception that, as a matter of necessity, has at least one object, no more than one object and only ever that object in view. Such constraints tend to lead to the postulation of somewhat mysterious faculties of introspection which are fit only for apprehending special sorts of selves.

In summary, the perceptual approach seems to face the following uncomfortable choice: either it retains what seems to be a mark of first-person reference—the feature of guaranteed reference—but at the cost of postulating a mysterious capacity for transparent self-perception; or it provides a reasonably plausible account of the kind of perception that is thought to be involved in securing first-person reference, but at the cost of abandoning the feature of guaranteed reference. It is the business of Chapters 2 and 3 to try to make good the idea that a perceptual approach to first-person reference is unlikely to be successful. Chapter 2 comprises an extended discussion of Anscombe on the problem of first-person reference. This serves to introduce and criticize the internal perceptual model for first-person reference, and to introduce and undercut the motivation behind Anscombe's sceptical and unacceptable view that 'I' does not refer. Chapter 3 argues against the prospects of the external perceptual model of first-person reference, concentrating on Evans's hallmark development of such a model.

The main alternative to the perceptual approach is what I called the 'self-reference approach'. The perceptual approach faces the problem of explaining why it is that the user of 'I' is always the referent of 'I', given that there seems to be no guarantee that the subject need be in receipt of self-identifying information. Given that what we wanted to explain was how it is that 'I' always refers, and always refers to the user herself, it is natural to note that we have available a perfectly clear rule that identifies first-person reference as reflexive reference. The rule says that 'I' refers to whoever uses it. We can call this the self-reference rule. I will refer to it as 'SRR'. The claim will then be that anyone who uses a term or concept governed by such a rule will refer to themselves first-personally. It might be that an appeal to such a rule is all that is needed to give an account of first-person reference.

At this point the problem will be raised that there is an important gap between mere self-reference, that is mere reflexive reference, and self-conscious self-reference, and that it is the latter that is the essence of first-person reference. Thus, it may be said, we have not supplied an account of first-person reference simply by appealing to the rule that the first-person refers to the person referring. Appeal to the rule may be insufficient to individuate first-person reference, and even if it is sufficient, we still need to explain why first-person reference is expressive of self-consciousness. But the worry is that any attempt to supplement SRR in order to explain why first-person reference is expressive of self-consciousness, will lead to a re-introduction of the capacity for first-person reference that stood to be explained. If we explain the subject's consciousness that it is to herself that she is referring in terms of the subject knowing 'I am referring', we may seem to have gone full circle. As Anscombe puts it:

The explanation of the word 'I' as 'the word which each of us uses to speak of himself' is hardly an explanation!—At least, it is no explanation if that reflexive has in turn to be explained in terms of 'I'; and if it is the ordinary reflexive, we are back at square one. (Anscombe 1982: 23)

While it is natural for an analytical philosopher such as Anscombe to put the problem in linguistic form, it is important to emphasize that the essence of the problem arises even if our concern is not with language and the first-person pronoun.[1] The problem is an older and venerable one about first-person reference in general. In essence the problem is that any attempt to explain first-person reference as 'reflexive' reference runs into trouble, because reflexive reference can only be first-person reference if one knows that one is referring to oneself. However, that knowledge then also needs explication. It can seem obvious however that knowing that one is referring to oneself involves referring to oneself first-personally. But if that is so it seems one cannot give a non-circular account of first-person reference.[2] There are two broad strategies we might employ to meet these worries with the self-reference approach. Which strategy we adopt will, I think, depend upon how seriously we

---

[1] This general problem is discussed in O'Brien (1995). Bermúdez (1998) can be understood as devoted to solving Anscombe's version of the problem. In what follows I shall assume that 'I' can be used to refer to the first person in both language and thought: that is to indicate both the first-person pronoun and the 'I'-concept in thought.

[2] Essentially the same problem is considered, with temple-aching agonising, in the work of Fichte. Fichte argued that any 'reflexion' account of self-consciousness was in trouble because reflexive consciousness—being conscious of yourself, can only be *self-consciousness* if you are conscious of that consciousness of yourself. But then 'It [that consciousness] too becomes an object and requires a new subject and so on *ad infinitum.*' (Fichte 1964: 30, quoted in Henrich 1982: 22 and Neuhouser 1990: 73.) The underlying problem is that self-consciousness seems to be more than merely a capacity for reflexive consciousness or reflexive reference: to get self-consciousness we seem to need such reflexive consciousness or reference also to be self-conscious. But now our account threatens to be regressive or circular.

take the objection that self-conscious self-reference, rather than mere self-reference is required for first-person reference. How seriously we take the objection is likely to depend, to a large extent, on how optimistic we are about the prospects of avoiding circularity in explaining the element of self-consciousness assumed by the objection to be involved in first-person reference.

1.1 The reductionist strategy

It was claimed that there were at least two strategies one might take in response to the objection that appeal to the self-reference principle will be insufficient to explain first-person reference. The first strategy is, in effect, to undermine the main pre-supposition of the objection. The objection takes it that first-person reference involves something significantly more than reflexive truth conditions. The reductionist holds that first-person contents are nothing more than systematically reflexive contents, and that an attitude has reflexive content just if the truth or satisfaction condition of the attitude depends in a certain systematic way upon the subject of the attitude. In particular, first-person contents are seen to be functions from context to truth or satisfaction conditions such that the subject of the attitude is the object of the truth or satisfaction conditions. It is further argued that the ascription of such first-person contents, in the absence of capacities for mastering SRR or for other forms of self-identification, is required if we are to explain the actions of simple creatures on the basis of their desires. A creature, on the reductionist story, is taken to refer to itself first-personally not in virtue of any application of SRR with a prior capacity for self-identification, but in virtue of the role its attitude plays in action. Much of Chapter 4 is concerned with exploring the reductionist approach. It concludes that while we may concede that there may be a kind of basic reflexive reference that the approach explains, there is nevertheless an element of self-consciousness in the kind of first-person reference under consideration which the approach fails to capture. The kind of first-person reference with which we are concerned requires us not only to make sense of the subject referring to herself reflexively, but also referring to herself self-consciously, aware that she is both the subject and object of her reference. We have a reason to eschew the task of explaining that self-consciousness only if we are convinced that it must lead to circularity.

1.2 The two-tier strategy

A second strategy one might take in response to the objection that an appeal to SRR will be insufficient to explain first-person reference is to separate the problem of first-person reference in to two. On the two-tier strategy there are really two kinds of first-person reference. The suggestion is that we can explain our capacity to refer first-personally, using 'I', by appealing to SRR plus some further independent capacity for first-person reference in thought. Someone who uses the first-person as governed by SRR will refer to herself in the first-person way because she usually knows that she is the user. However, her knowledge that she is the user is supposed to be explained by an independent capacity for the first-person way of thinking, so avoiding circularity.

The two-tier strategy faces two challenges. The first comes from the fact that when we use 'I' as governed by SRR we seem to be directly expressing our first-person thoughts. There is the *prima facie* worry that the need for the user to identify herself as the user complicates the link between 'I' as governed by SRR and the first-person thoughts it is used to express. We might try to solve this problem by exploring the nature that a subject has that she is using 'I'. If this knowledge is such that the subject immediately knows that she is using 'I' when she is, we might be able to preserve the idea that all uses of 'I' involve self-conscious thought.

The second challenge the two-tier strategy faces arises from the simple point that the self-reference rule seems to govern *all* first-person reference. The two-tier strategy assumes a prior and independent capacity for first-person reference in order to explain why uses of 'I' as governed by SRR involve self-conscious thought. However, if we acknowledge that this prior capacity for first-person reference is equally governed by SRR we have as yet no way of explaining how such reference could be so governed. Either the two-tier strategist must deny that all first-person reference is to be explained by appeal to SRR, and so must provide an account of the prior capacity for first-person reference that does not appeal to SRR, or the two-tier strategist must live with a potential regress.

The challenge then, is to explain how we can avoid the problematic elements of the two-tier strategy while retaining its insights. The two-tier strategy is more fully set out and criticized in Chapter 4. Much of Chapter 5 is concerned with fashioning an account of first-person reference which draws on the insights of the two-tier strategy but which denies that first-person reference is equivocal. The two-tier strategy appealed to a prior form of first-person reference in order to explain the awareness a user of 'I' has that she is its user. To investigate whether there is a form of awareness that explains, but does imply, a capacity for first-person reference is the primary aim of Chapters 5 and 6.

Chapters 5 and 6 aim to provide an account that supplies the element that is missing from the reductionist account. However, the account follows the reductionist in seeking a form of self-consciousness that does not presuppose a capacity for mastery of SRR and that does not rely on a prior form of first-person reference. It rather aims to find a form of self-consciousness that does not presuppose, but rather explains, our capacity for first-person reference. The account also draws on the two-tier strategy in finding that an account of first-person reference requires a distinction between two forms of self-consciousness. However, the distinction is not taken to be one between two different kinds of first-person reference, as on the two-tier strategy, but between two different kinds of *self-consciousness*. A distinction is made between a primitive form of self-awareness—one that does not imply a capacity for first-person reference—and the kind of self-consciousness that is constituted by a capacity for full first-person reference. In further contrast to the two-tier approach, the account offered takes both forms of self-consciousness to be in play whenever a subject refers to herself first-personally. It also takes the capacity for first-person reference to be explained partly by the more primitive form of self-awareness. The more primitive form of self-awareness, which it is argued can serve in an account of our capacity for first-person reference, is seen to arise from the particular awareness we have of our intentional actions. I call such awareness *agent's awareness*.

Having drawn on the strengths of the alternative strategies in order to outline an account of first-person reference, two key tasks are undertaken. First, in Chapter 5, I aim to make it plausible that the *form* of the account offered, in terms of the joint operation of SRR and a primitive form of self-awareness we have as agents (agent's awareness) is of a kind that can explain first-person reference. Secondly, in Chapter 6, I aim to find an articulation of the kind of primitive self-awareness of our intentional actions that is invoked. This latter task leads us to a consideration of competing accounts of the awareness we have of our mental actions and to a suggestion as to how we might best set about construing such awareness. Again the strategy is not to consider all possible alternative accounts of agent's awareness but to locate and motivate the suggestion by an understanding of the function that account needs to play. Although the account offered of agent's awareness, particularly with respect to physical actions, is further filled out in Chapter 9, with these tasks attempted I leave explicit discussion of the problem of self-reference behind.

2. ACTIONS AND SELF-KNOWLEDGE

The investigation of self-reference leads us to an inquiry into self-knowledge, in particular to the knowledge we have of our mental actions. This inquiry is picked up and broadened in the second half of the book. The core idea behind the second half is that our knowledge of ourselves as subjects, that is widely acknowledged to be provided by our knowledge of our mental states and actions, is also provided by our knowledge of our physical actions. I aim to give an account of our knowledge of our physical actions which has many of the hallmarks of those sorts of knowledge—knowledge of judgements, beliefs and perceptions—generally thought of as sources for self-knowledge. The central chapter of this second half of the book is Chapter 9. There I offer a characterization of our knowledge of our own actions and try to provide an account which is true to this characterization. My strategy, again, is to consider alternative accounts in order to facilitate the construction and motivation of the positive account that is offered. A critical element of the account offered of our knowledge of our actions is that our perceptual faculties, including bodily awareness, should not be thought to be *direct* sources for our knowledge of our actions, or at least of our basic actions. We can call the account offered a non-perceptual account. Such an account stands in contrast to perceptual accounts which hold that current perceptions, via the five senses and bodily awareness, constitute a direct source or ground for our knowledge of our actions. There are two main obstacles to the acceptance of the non-perceptual view. One is that it does not fit well with the standard views of actions as dual component constructions, built out of purely mental phenomenon—intentions or tryings—on the one hand, and movements of the body on the other. If actions are part mental state or act, and part movement of the body, it is natural to suppose that our knowledge of our actions is part knowledge of our mental state or act and part knowledge of the movement of the body. And a perceptual account of our knowledge of the movements of our bodies can seem almost inevitable. However, it seems to me that the standard view of actions is implausible. In light of this, in Chapter 8, I try to set out the bare bones of an account of actions that takes them to be, at the personal level, primitive psychological phenomena. I articulate a view of actions that denies that they are composable into more primitive personal-level psychological events, such as intentions, willings or trying, and movements of the body. A proper treatment of the account described would require an enquiry into the metaphysics of actions that goes beyond anything I am able to attempt here. So, in Chapter 8, I aim to do little more than make the view of actions assumed in Chapter 9 seem a possible, and not obviously unreasonable, one. My interest is primarily to urge a certain view of the epistemology of our actions.

What of the second obstacle to the non-perceptual view? The essential elements of the view proposed about our actions is that we are authoritative about what we are doing, but that that authority is not due to perceptual evidence with respect to what our bodies are doing. Rather, that we know what we are doing in virtue of being agents of what we are doing and having agent's awareness. The claim that we know our actions without perceptual evidence meets very quickly with the objection that there are many cases in which it seems simply absurd to suggest that we know what we are doing without perceptual evidence. Suppose that I press a light switch unsure whether it is working. I clearly have to look to see whether I have succeeded in turning on the light. And in a contrasting case, suppose I tie my shoelaces. I may not know exactly which fingers I move without looking to see. In response to such objections I suggest a way we can identify a class of basic actions, actions which are procedurally basic, and which are such that we are authoritative with respect to them independently of any perceptual evidence.

The book ends, in Chapters 10 and 11 with a discussion of bodily awareness and self-knowledge. First, in Chapter 10, there is some clarification and defence of a perceptual view of bodily awareness. In Chapter 11, there is a discussion of whether bodily awareness, so understood, is rightly seen as a source of self-knowledge in the relevant sense of knowledge of ourselves as subjects. I argue that despite the fact that we can construe bodily awareness as immune to error through misidentification in a fairly robust sense, we should not take bodily awareness, in contrast to agent's awareness, to be a primary source of self-knowledge. I introduce a distinction between transparent and non-transparent immunity through misidentification and suggest that sources of self-knowledge are marked by transparent rather than non-transparent immunity. I argue that self-ascriptions made on the basis of agent's awareness, in contrast to those made on the basis of bodily awareness, can exhibit transparent immunity. Whereas, even if bodily awareness allows us to self-ascribe physical properties in a way that is immune to error through misidentification, it will not be able to do so in a way that secures transparent immunity. I suggest that if we are to look to any physical self-ascriptions as providing the 'antidote to Cartesianism' we should not look to those self-ascriptions offered by Evans, that is, those justified by our awareness of our bodies through bodily awareness. Rather we should look to those self-ascriptions of actions based on agent's awareness.

2

Arguments for the No-Reference
View of 'I'

1. THE INTERNAL PERCEPTUAL MODEL

Descartes, in common conception, thought of the subject of experience as being presented with herself through introspection, and construed introspection as a sort of inward perception. If we are indeed presented with ourselves in this way, then we might seem to have what we need to explain the basis of first-person reference. Everyone will be, as Frege puts it, 'presented to himself in a special and primitive way, in which he is presented to no-one else' (Frege 1977: 12) and that presentation can explain how we are able to refer to ourselves. We would then be able to think of 'I' as functioning as a kind of internal perceptual demonstrative. The idea that first-person reference is grounded in some internal perceptual self-presentation has been influential in recent decades, although perhaps more in its rejection than in its endorsement. There has been important work aimed at undermining the idea that we are aware of ourselves via some internal perception.[1] It is not my aim in this chapter to establish that there could not be a coherent account of internal perception, nor to provide criticisms of such an idea that go beyond those offered by others. Rather, my aim is to bring out the connections between the idea that 'I' refers via such internal perception and the view that 'I' does not refer. In particular, I want to urge that the common sense view of the first-person as referring to the human beings we are, or are constituted by, is not available if we adopt an internal perceptual model as the basis of first-person reference. I will carry out this aim by considering the role that the model plays in arguments presented by Anscombe for the, *prima facie* extraordinary, view that 'I' does not refer. It seemed to Anscombe that the internal perceptual

---

[1] See especially Shoemaker (1996).

model of first-person reference is the only one available if we are to take first-person reference to be guaranteed to refer. However, it also seemed to her that adopting an internal perceptual model of first-person reference committed one to taking the referent of 'I' to be a Cartesian Ego, or a stretch of one. She found the resulting view problematic, and so raised doubts about whether there is first-person reference of the kind that was the target of explanation.

2. GUARANTEED REFERENCE

One ready explanation for the fact that philosophers have had difficulties in accounting for first-person reference is that the attempt to provide such an account is misguided. Maybe it is difficult to provide an account of first-person reference because there is no such thing: maybe 'I' does not refer. The conclusion that 'I' does not refer is, I think, too counter-intuitive to be acceptable. How are we to escape the thought that 'I' refers to the person who uses it? And how if 'I' does not refer, are we to make sense of truth value links between first-personal statements? How, for example, are we to explain the fact that 'Lucy is cold' follows from 'I am cold' and 'I am Lucy' if we cannot appeal to the idea that 'Lucy' and 'I' refer to the same thing. However, given a certain faith in the good sense of philosophers, the very counter-intuitiveness of the no-reference view should alert us to the possibility of there being some fairly compelling arguments in its favour. I think that once we have considered arguments for the no-reference view we will begin to see what obstacles stand in the way of some very natural views about how it is that 'I' succeeds in referring.

The arguments for the no-reference view that are offered by Anscombe in her seminal article 'The First Person' (Anscombe 1981) strike me as containing the kernel of the objection against the view of 'I' as referential.[2] Although, in considering these arguments part of my aim is to honour her work, my interest is not, primarily, to achieve a definitive understanding of Anscombe's position. My interest is rather to identify a train of thought that I take her arguments to embody and that needs to be avoided if we are to give a satisfactory account of first-person thought. The discussion will then be to dual purpose. Negatively, it will show that we are not forced, by these arguments at least, to accept the conclusion

---

[2] Unless otherwise stated all page references in this chapter will be to this article.

that 'I' does not refer. Positively, it will demarcate potential pitfalls for, and place constraints on, a satisfactory account of first-person reference.

The arguments I am going to discuss proceed by arguing for the conditional that 'if 'I' refers then it refers to a Cartesian Ego'. They then argue for the rejection of the consequent in order to establish, by *modus tollens*, the negation of the antecedent. The important argument, for my purposes, is for the conditional. Once this has been established Anscombe is able to utilize well-known objections regarding the coherence of the notion of a Cartesian Ego to carry her to her desired conclusion. I am not here going to consider arguments for and against the coherence of a soul substance in the Cartesian mould in any detail. I will rather, as Anscombe does, merely indicate the kind of familiar problems that such a notion faces and on that basis conclude that an account on which 'I' comes out referring to a Cartesian Ego is one we want to avoid.

Anscombe employs the assumption that if 'I' refers it is guaranteed to refer, as the starting point for her arguments. It is for her a defining feature of first-personal reference, if there be any such reference. The claim that 'I' is guaranteed to refer is understood by Anscombe as follows:

1. That if 'I' is a referring expression and is used by a subject then it will have a reference.

2. That if 'I' is a referring expression it will refer to that object that the subject intended it to refer to, which is the user herself.

3. If 'I' refers, a comprehending user could not doubt that it refers and refers to the user herself.

At the heart of Anscombe's arguments is a suspicion, in line with Wittgensteinian tradition, of the idea of guaranteed reference. The general suspicion of terms whose purported function it is to refer, while being guaranteed to do so successfully, is fuelled by the thought that the function of a referring term is to select one object from others. Given that there will be a case of selecting the right object, the thought is, there must be the possibility of selecting the wrong object. Where there is guaranteed reference there is no such possibility, and says Anscombe:

The suggestion of getting the object right collapses into absurdity when we work it out and try to describe how getting hold of the wrong object may be excluded. (31)

If 'I' is guaranteed to refer then it must be that the user picks out the object referred to in a way that excludes the possibility that no object, or the wrong object is picked out. It is Anscombe's view that such reference is impossible unless we postulate a special sort of object as the referent, the sort of object that cannot fail to be present to the subject when the subject is referring.

2.1 The argument from real presence

So what arguments does Anscombe offer us? Anscombe's paper tends to the obscure and suggestive, so the task of coming to see exactly what the arguments are that she intended to utilize is not a straightforward one.[3] There are, *prima facie*, at least two discernible arguments for the conditional, though it is not at all clear that Anscombe conceived of them separately. Both arguments employ the, now famous, sensory deprivation tank:

And now imagine that I get into a state of 'sensory deprivation'. Sight is cut off, and I am locally anaesthetized everywhere, perhaps floated in a tank of tepid water; I am unable to speak, or to touch any part of my body with any other. Now I tell myself 'I won't let this happen again!' If the object meant by 'I' is this body, this human being, then in these circumstances it won't be present to my senses; and how else can it be 'present to' me? . . . Am I reduced to, as it were, 'referring in absence'? I have not lost my 'self-consciousness'; nor can what I mean by 'I' be an object no longer present to me. This both seems right in itself, and will be required by the 'guaranteed reference' that we are considering.

Like considerations will operate for other suggestions. Nothing but a Cartesian Ego will serve. Or, rather, a stretch of one. (31)

This passage both introduces the sensory deprivation tank and contains the kernel of the first argument to be isolated from Anscombe's article. I will call it the argument from real presence. It has something like the following form:

1. If 'I' is a referring term, it has guaranteed reference.
2. If the referent of 'I' were not 'physically or really present' to my consciousness, 'I' would not be guaranteed to refer.

---

[3] Hamilton (1991) isolates a number of arguments for the no-reference view that can be found in Anscombe's paper. Although we differ to some extent in what we take these arguments to be, and about which we take to be more successful, I have been very much helped by his article.

3. 'I' is a referring term.

4. So, the referent of 'I' is physically or really present to me.

5. In a sensory deprivation tank I am still capable of self-conscious thought, i.e. if 'I' refers, 'I' refers in a sensory deprivation tank.

6. In a sensory deprivation tank the object meant by 'this body, this human being' is not really present to me. The only thing that could be really present to me is a Cartesian Ego, or a stretch of one.

7. So, 'I' refers to a Cartesian Ego, or a stretch of one.

If we are to assess the argument we must understand what is meant by 'real presence' and consider what reasons there are for accepting that it is a demand of guaranteed reference in this case. Anscombe is not particularly helpful in this respect, although we are provided with some clues. In the paragraph before introducing the notion of something's being present to consciousness Anscombe asks how, if it is the function of 'I' to refer, the reference of 'I' is accomplished, how it catches hold of its object: 'If "I" is not an abbreviation of a definite description, it must catch hold of its object in some other way—and what way is there but the demonstrative?' (28)

It is Anscombe's view that any attempt to answer this question will lead us to claim that the referent of 'I' is really present to the referring subject. For a Fregean, as Anscombe is (see p. 23), to ask how reference is accomplished is to ask after a term's sense, its mode of presentation. The demand that the referent of 'I' be really present to the subject is, I want to suggest, seen by Anscombe as a necessary component of an account attempting to give us the sense of 'I'. Something like the following reasoning seems to be in play: as the sense of 'I' cannot be given by a definite description, someone attempting to give an account of the sense of 'I' will inevitably be led to construct an account along lines analogous to that for demonstratives that refer to objects other than ourselves. Now, an account of the sense that accompanies a demonstrative will, at least in part, be given by an account of the way in which the referent perceptually presents itself to the referring subject. The presentation must be such that the subject is able to isolate and identify the individual object. If we are then to attempt to give a similar account of the first-person mode of presentation, we will be led to given an account of the way in which the referent of 'I' is present to the referring subject so that the subject is able to discern, isolate and identify the object referred to.

However, in the case of demonstratives there is the possibility of reference failure. In certain cases, the subject can take herself to be presented with the object she is trying to refer to without there being any such object. This possibility is explained by Anscombe in the following way:

It used to be thought that a singular demonstrative, 'this' or 'that', if used correctly, could not lack a referent. But this is not so, as comes out if we consider the requirement for an answer to 'this what?' Someone comes with a box and says 'This is all that is left of poor Jones'. The answer to 'this what?' is 'this parcel of ashes'; but unknown to the speaker the box is empty. What 'this' has to have, if used correctly, is something that it *latches on to* (as I will put it): in this example it is the box. In another example it might be an optical presentation. Thus I may ask 'What's that figure standing in front of the rock, a man or a post?' and there may be no such object at all; but there is an appearance, a stain perhaps, or other marking of the rock face, which my 'that' latches on to. The referent and what 'this' latches on to may coincide . . . But they do not have to coincide, and the referent is the object of which the predicate is predicated where 'this' or 'that' is a subject. (28)

Thus there must always be something that a singular demonstrative 'latches onto', something which, unlike the referent, must be present transparently to the referring subject. However, since whatever the demonstrative latches on to may not coincide with the referent, a demonstrative can fail to refer. Now, if it is the case that the referent of 'I' is guaranteed to refer either the term must latch on to the referent itself due to the referent itself being present to the referring subject, or the term must latch on to something that necessarily and transparently coincides with the referent. It is not possible to refer to the referent of 'I' by means of latching on to something that may be distinct from the referent, or that may seem to the subject to be distinct from the referent. For it is that which opens up the possibility of reference failure. Thus the way in which the subject is presented with herself must be such that it guarantees the existence and presence of the subject: the referent of 'I' must be 'physically or really present' to the subject.

If 'I' refers, it is secure against reference failure. Therefore, the way reference is accomplished must entail this feature. That, on Anscombe's view, demands that the referent is really present to the subject. Now, even the subject immersed in the sensory deprivation tank is able to refer to herself first-personally. So, however the subject is presented with herself, it cannot be via those perceptual sources that are unavailable to her in such a situation. It seems that just thinking 'I' guarantees successful reference. If that is so, then if 'I' refers, the referent is presented to the subject via thought alone. As Anscombe puts it:

Just thinking 'I . . .' guarantees not only the existence but the presence of its referent. It guarantees the existence because it guarantees the presence, which is presence to consciousness. (28)

An objection may now strike us: would it not be sufficient to explain the guaranteed reference of the first-person by adducing only the fact that thinking guarantees the existence of the referent? We can then claim that there is no need for the subject to be presented with anything in order for the guaranteed reference of 'I' to be secured. It may be true that thinking itself guarantees the existence of the thinker, but in that case thinking anything, 'the sky is blue' for example, guarantees the existence of the thinker. However, on my reading of Anscombe, in order for such thought to function as the basis for first-person reference, it must be that the thinking provides the mode of presentation of the referent. As such it must be that the thinking itself presents the subject with the reference, that is with herself, and in such a way that the subject takes herself to be so presented. These considerations, I hope, explain both the nature of, and the reasons for, Anscombe's claim that the referent of 'I' must be 'really present' or 'present to consciousness'. The account of the former stages of Anscombe's argument hinges on taking her to be thoroughly Fregean about reference in demanding a mode of presentation. She thinks that no descriptive account of the mode of presentation involved in first-person reference is available, and so thinks we must look to an account based on that for perceptual demonstratives. However, as 'I' is guaranteed to refer whenever the subject is thinking, it must be that thinking itself presents the referent of 'I' to the subject. Thus a thinking thing, really present to the thinker, is the only candidate for a reference for 'I'.

Surely, she has not however, reached her desired conclusion. For it seems that we may admit the above without admitting that this thinking thing is a Cartesian Ego. Why could it not be that the thinking thing that is really present to the subject using 'I' is also an embodied thing, perhaps a human being? The justification for the Cartesian conclusion is contained in premise (5) of the argument above. Because 'I' is guaranteed to refer the referent of 'I' must be really present to the subject on every occasion of use, even in the sensory deprivation tank. But no body or human being is really present to the subject in the tank. Therefore, it cannot be body or human being that 'I' refers to.

Is this the case however? Can it not be that thinking is a way of being presented with oneself as an embodied being? And if embodiment is essential to thought, does it follow that being presented with oneself as a thinking thing is also being presented with a body? Perhaps, it may be said, a human being can be really present to herself in two distinct ways: through perception and through introspection.

Anscombe would reject this suggestion. To see why she would we must remind ourselves of what was demanded of the notion of real presence. The justification we gave for the claim that the referent of 'I' must be really present to the subject was that it was via this presentation that the subject is able to demonstrate the object she is referring to in such a way that preserved guaranteed reference. We saw that, if the guaranteed reference of 'I' is to be respected, the identification of the referent must be based either on the object itself being really present to the subject even in the sensory deprivation tank, or on the subject latching on to something that necessarily and transparently coincides with the referent. Anscombe demands the 'physical or real presence' of the object because this is what is required if we are to ascribe to the subject a mode of presentation by means of which she is able to identify demonstratively the referent of 'I'. However, in the tank, the subject is not presented with a body or human being. She has no means of discerning the boundaries of any body or human being she is supposed to be and no mode of access that could underwrite a direct demonstrative identification. On the basis of what is available to her she is unable to identify directly any particular physical body or human being. If the subject is 'presented' with anything in the tank it is only thought.

Thus we face two options. First, we could say that thinking is itself sufficient to present you with the referent of 'I' in such a way that will underwrite direct demonstration. Secondly, we could say that in the tank we latch on to a property of the referent of 'I' which necessarily and transparently coincides with the referent. We are, therefore, able to refer to the referent of 'I' via that which we latch on to being immediately present. To take the first option is to take the referent of 'I' to be a thinking thing, or a stretch of one, which is itself present through thought alone. This is to adopt the Cartesian option of taking the referent of 'I' to be 'the thinking which thinks this thought' (31).

Suppose it is suggested that being presented with thought alone gives us a way of identifying the referent of 'I' just in so far as the thought is, perhaps necessarily, the thought of a particular body or human being. The claim that 'I' is able to refer to a particular body or human being in virtue of the fact that the thinking of 'I' is the thinking of a particular body or human being would, on Anscombe's view, commit us to holding that the subject was in some way 'referring in absence'. It is a possibility she recognises and rejects. As she puts it:

> It may be very well to describe what selves are; but if I do not know that I am a self, then I cannot mean a self by 'I'. (29)

For Anscombe this would be a move that ignored the essential concern with the *way* the referent of 'I' is given to the referring subject. While it may be that the tank subject is a body or human being it cannot be a body or human being that she is referring to when she uses 'I'. In fact, even if embodiment is taken to be an *a priori* knowable necessary condition of thinking, the subject cannot be said to be referring to that particular body using 'I'. While we might want to say that a subject can know that she possesses some body or other in the tank she will not know what sort of body—small or large, or how many bodies—over time or at a time. Thus she cannot be said to have identifying knowledge of the referent, in the sense required, in order to be referring to that body using 'I'. It is for these reasons that, if we are to think of first-person reference as mediated by thought alone while not wanting to adopt the conclusion that that thinking is itself the reference, we have to suppose that the thought is necessarily and *transparently* a property of a body or human being. This was the second option identified above. But in fact the second option either assumes that we already have a way of referring to ourselves using the first person, and so is circular, or it collapses into the first option. If it is supposed that the subject is able to refer, not to her thoughts using 'I', but to a distinct thing that her thoughts are a property of, then the subject must be supposed already to have some knowledge of the relation between this property and what she is. She will only be able to use 'I' to refer to herself on being presented with a thought if she knows that *this* thought is *her* thought. But that assumes that she has an independent capacity for first-person reference.[4]

---

[4] The argument is drawn from a very similar one offered by Shoemaker:

'Obviously, however, the introspective observation of a self being angry is not going to yield the knowledge that I am angry unless I know that that self is myself. How am I supposed to know this? If the answer is that I identify it as myself by its perceived properties, we have to point out that this requires that I already know that I have those properties' (Shoemaker 1996: 13).

Note that if the subject were to identify herself as 'the bodily thing having this thought' either the thought will present itself as a property of the subject *herself,* or there seems to be room for the subject to doubt that the bodily thing having *this* thought is her.

If instead it is insisted that the subject need have no such knowledge because the thought *itself* is both a property of the self and transparently presented to the subject as so, the second option falls back in to the first.

It thus seems that if we take 'I' to function as a kind of demonstrative that succeeds in referring by being directly presented with its referent in thought we are bound to be led in to taking the referent of that to which 'I' refers to be a Cartesian Ego, or 'a stretch of one'. However, we cannot, as Anscombe points out, rest contented at that point. If 'I' is to succeed in referring to a Cartesian Ego we must justify the assumption that a single thing is referred to by a single 'I'-thought, and by different 'I'-thoughts. But we have no reason to hold that there be a single thing which is 'the thinking of this thought'. What rules out the token thought being the thinking of multiple thinkers? As Anscombe puts it 'How do I know that 'I' is not ten thinkers thinking in unison'? And we have no reason to think that the same thing is re-identified in different 'I'-thoughts, that we have no unnoticed substitution. Kant famously makes this point particularly vividly:

An elastic ball which impinges on another similar ball in another straight line communicates to the latter its whole motion, and therefore its whole state . . . If, then, in analogy with such bodies, we postulate substances such that the one communicates to the other representations [thoughts] together with the consciousness of them, we can conceive a whole series of substances of which the first transmits its state together with its consciousness of the second, the second its own state with that of the preceding substance to the third, and this in turn the states of all the preceding substances together with its own consciousness and with their consciousness to another. The last substance would then be conscious of all the states of the previously changed substances, as being its own states, because they would have been transferred to it together with consciousness of them. And yet it would not have been one and the same person in all these states. (Kant 1933: 34–A364)

The only way to avoid the Cartesian conclusion and its ensuing 'intolerable' difficulties is, urges Anscombe, is to give up on the idea that 'I' refers. However, I hope it is clear that we need not follow Anscombe to this point. If we take 'I' to function as a kind of demonstrative which succeeds in referring in virtue of its referent being directly presented to the referrer in thought, Anscombe is probably right in thinking that we are bound to be led to unacceptable Cartesian conclusions. However, the mistake is to think of 'I' as such an internal demonstrative.

2.2 The argument from doubt

Let us now turn to Anscombe's second argument. We may call it the argument from doubt. It can be seen as a generalized form of the first—whereas the first argument insists upon the mode of self-knowledge which would have to underwrite self-reference being based on the real presence of the subject to herself, the second argument makes no such specific demands. We might hope that in not being committed to the problematic notion of real presence the argument stands to be more acceptable. It turns out not to be. The removal of the demand for real presence results in the argument obviously failing to go through.

The argument from doubt proceeds along the following lines:

1. If 'I' is a referring term it has guaranteed reference.
2. If 'I' is a referring term a subject in a sensory deprivation tank can refer to herself using 'I'. The conditions for successful reference are met in the tank.
3. The subject in the sensory deprivation tank can doubt whether she is embodied. ('I shall perhaps believe that there is such a body. But the possibility will perhaps strike me that there is none.' (34))
4. 'I' is a referring term.
5. So, the referent if 'I' being embodied is not one of the conditions of successful reference.
6. So, 'I' refers to a Cartesian Ego.

The argument is clearly flawed. Why should it not be that the conditions for successful first-person reference are fulfilled in the sensory deprivation tank and the subject not know what she is? The argument as it stands does not rule out the possibility that being embodied is one of the conditions of successful reference of which I know that, whatever they are, they are satisfied.[5]

Let us, as we did with the first argument, attempt to bolster the argument by looking at Anscombe's presuppositions about the nature of the reference involved. What is required on the part of the subject in the sensory deprivation tank, given the assumption that she is able to use 'I', is that she has available in that situation some identifying

---

[5] This criticism of Anscombe is given in Hamilton (1991: 43).

knowledge by means of which reference is secured, and is guaranteed to be so secured. Therefore, if while in the sensory deprivation tank, the subject is able to doubt that she is a human being or body, whilst succeeding in referring to herself, it cannot be essential that the subject's identifying knowledge includes knowledge that she is a human being or a body. The subject can doubt these things without doubting that she is successfully referring to herself. The subject can, quite generally, wonder whether most of the beliefs she has about herself are false, wonder whether she is hallucinating or the victim of deception or illusion. And she can do so without losing her ability for first-person reference. If 'I' is to be understood as requiring identifying knowledge, then whatever identifying knowledge is required for the subject to be in a position to refer using 'I' must be available in the face of either the absence of information, or the distortion of information, about herself. What the subject seems always in a position to know is that she is a thinking thing, so it must be a thinking thing she refers to using 'I'.

However, while it may be admitted that what 'I' refers to must be identified as a thinking thing, that admission is not sufficient to rule out the possibility that what 'I' refers to is also a bodily thing. For we can say that I do identify a body when I use 'I' it is just that I do not realize that that is what I am doing. This point strikes me as fatal to the argument as it stands. The opacity of propositional attitude states renders Anscombe's transition from the epistemological state of her subject to her ontological conclusion impermissible. The only way to stave off the objection would be to reintroduce some correlate of the 'physically and really present' requirement, which would take us back to the first argument discussed. Merely requiring identifying knowledge, without any demands being made on the source of such knowledge, is not enough to make the transition from conclusions about the epistemic state of the subject to conclusions about the nature of that which she refers to using 'I'.

We might think that, in fact, Anscombe cannot even get going with this argument. If the notion of a Cartesian Ego is an incoherent one, as Anscombe goes on to claim, can the tank subject coherently doubt that she is embodied? If the possibility of thought without embodiment can be ruled out *a priori* then even the subject who knows only that she is thinking, and whatever necessarily follows from that, is in a position to know that she is embodied. Given the claim that it is incoherent to suppose that there can be thoughts without embodiment, it seems that the threat of reference failure if 'I' is supposed to refer to a body by latching on to its thoughts is not a real one.

In response to this, Anscombe is likely to claim that all the coherence of a Cartesian Ego is going to get us is that thought must always be instantiated in something physical. So, even if the tank subject is not in a position to doubt that she is, embodied, she is in a position to doubt that she is a human being, or that she is a biological organism, or even that there is one physical thing that her thoughts are instantiated in, either at a time or over time. The bare fact that where there is thought there is embodiment does not give the thinking subject identifying knowledge of the body or bodies that her thoughts are thoughts of.[6] However, can the subject not refer to the body or bodies that she is, using the identifying knowledge 'the body or bodies having these thoughts'? I think that the objection goes through as long as all that is required is some kind of descriptive identifying knowledge, and as long as we do not adduce something like the 'physically and really present' requirement. So, again, we move back to the first argument.

What has emerged from the above discussion is the extent to which Anscombe's arguments rely on a particular view of how 'I' must refer, it if it is to refer at all. In order to show that if 'I' refers it refers to a Cartesian Ego, or a stretch of one, her arguments rely on a view of first-person reference as demanding that the referent of 'I' is 'really or physically presented' to the referring subject. This demand comes from the assumption that 'I' must function as a kind of demonstrative that is guaranteed to refer, even in circumstances in which the subject is in receipt of no external or bodily information of a kind that could underwrite such reference. As long as we thought of a subject as currently receiving information relating to her size, location, position, movements, and so on, then we can make some sense of 'I' functioning as a kind of demonstrative to refer to a single presented human being. But it was then noted that 'I' refers even in the sensory deprivation tank when no such information is available and when no human being or body is 'really present'. Thus, if 'I' refers it must refer to something that is 'really presented' through thought alone.

We are, as a result, pushed either towards accepting that 'I' refers to a Cartesian Ego or towards accepting Anscombe's conclusion that 'I' does not refer. However, if it is possible to give an account of first-person reference that avoids the requirement that the subject be 'really or phys- ically presented' with the referent of 'I', then Anscombe's arguments pose no threat to the view that 'I' refers. Rather they have served to

---

[6] See Lowe (1993).

provide some guidance as to what needs to be avoided by a satisfactory account.

A really present requirement on first-person reference demands that there be a presentation of the referent—that is the subject herself—which is such that if the subject accepts the presentation and refers on the basis of it alone, she will be *guaranteed* to knowingly refer to herself. Anscombe's discussion suggests that we should avoid such a requirement.

3

Perceptual Models of First-Person Reference

1. EVANS ON FIRST-PERSON REFERENCE

I have argued that Anscombe holds that if 'I' refers, the referent must be 'really present' to the subject when referring. I have also suggested that we should avoid attempting to ground first-person reference on any such requirement. The assumption that we have met that requirement in a sensory deprivation tank leads to the assumption that 'I' refers to a Cartesian Ego. In this chapter I want to consider the suggestion that we were looking in the wrong place for the kind of self-presentation that is required to ground first-person reference. In particular, I want to consider the suggestion that we can give a satisfactory account of first-person reference by appealing only to ways we are presented with ourselves through our ordinary perceptual faculties. An account of first-person reference that appeals to our ordinary perceptual faculties was somewhat brushed aside earlier, as being incompatible with the guaranteed reference characteristic of first-person reference. The assumption was made that if any kind of self-presentation was to underwrite first-person reference it must be internal self-presentation. However, I want to look at the alternative possibility with more care.[1]

1.1 Evans's account

It is very plausible to suppose that an account of demonstrative reference will draw heavily on the perceptual relations that obtain between the referrer and the object referred to. With demonstrative reference

---

[1] The central conclusion of this chapter is argued for in Campbell 1994, (chs 3 and 4). Campbell does not discuss Evans in detail, and there are significant differences in argumentation, but I owe much to his work.

such perceptual information can be seem as providing us with the epistemological basis that will explain how demonstrative reference is accomplished. My concern here is whether anything like the parallel treatment is available in the case of the first person. As we saw in Chapter 1, the challenge is to give an account of the epistemological basis that can underwrite first-person reference in a way that explains how the referent is fixed. We might call it Anscombe's challenge:

We seem to need a sense to be specified for this quasi-name 'I'. To repeat the Frege point: we haven't got this sense just by being told which object a man will be speaking of, whether he knows it or not, when he says 'I'. Of course that phrase 'whether he knows it or not' seems highly absurd. His use of 'I' surely guarantees that he does know it! But we have a right to ask *what* he knows; If 'I' expresses a way its object is reached by him, what Frege called an 'Art des Gegenbenseins', we want to know what that way is and how it comes about that the only object reached in that way by anyone is identical with himself. (Anscombe, 1981: 23)

As we have seen, Anscombe thinks the challenge is not one that can be met. However, Gareth Evans, in *The Varieties of Reference*, somewhat tentatively suggests an account of first-person reference that seems designed to meet the challenge. Of it he says:

Chapter 7, on 'I', represents something of a detour from the main line of argument. To a certain extent all the chapters on modes of identification are the result of an interest in them for their own sake; but I wish it to be clear that, in Chapter 7, it is this interest, rather than a concern to exemplify the general picture, that predominates. I regard the chapter as a presumptuous, and obviously incomplete, first attempt on a very difficult topic. (Evans 1982: 137)

In subsequent presentation of the account Evans raises specific elements of first-person reference which he acknowledges to be missing from his account, and which, if the criticisms of Evans that are presented below are right, are probably inconsistent with it. Thus there is every reason to suppose that Evans himself would have acknowledged some of the problems that are to be raised for his account. However, with Evans's qualifications duly marked, I will, in what follows, briefly characterize the account that Evans's general framework leads us to and criticize the account so characterized. Having found Evans's account of first-person reference unsatisfactory I will aim to generalize the result by considering alternative versions of a perceptual based account for first-person reference. In general terms, Evans sees first-person reference as based on ways in which a subject is presented with herself. He eschews the idea that 'I' functions as some kind of internal demonstrative securing its reference via introspection. He also remarks that 'the self-reference principle [the principle that the object of an 'I' thought is its subject] cannot by itself be regarded as an adequate account of self-conscious thought' (Evans 1982: 261). Rather, 'I' is understood roughly on the model of that applied to demonstratives. That is, 'I' refers to a particular human on the basis of information had, or liable to be had, about that human being by the referring subject. His account aims to take first-person reference to be conditioned by information we receive about the object of reference in something of the way other singular reference is:

> Despite the important differences, then, between 'I' and 'this' and 'here', the general structure of our account of these Ideas is the same. In particular, a subject's self-conscious thought about himself must be informed (or must be liable to be informed) by information which the subject may gain of himself, in each of a range of ways of gaining knowledge of himself. (Evans 1982: 212)

Evans offers us a general framework for singular reference in to which first-person reference is to be incorporated. It is a framework that is informed by two key principles that he takes to govern singular reference. The first of these is 'Russell's Principle'. Russell's Principle states that in order to refer to an object one must know which object it is; and to know which object it is, is to be able to distinguish that object from all other objects. The second principle is 'The Generality Constraint'. The Generality Constraint holds that it is a constraint on being able to understand a thought '*a* is *F*' that one be able to understand what it is for other objects to be *F*, and understand what it is for *a* to instantiate other properties. Meeting Russell's principle is needed for securing conformity to the Generality Constraint.

Evans claims that an account of a given type of thinking that respects these principles will have two interconnected elements. There will be an account of the role that thoughts of the relevant kind play. In particular, of the relation of such thoughts to the ways we have of gaining knowledge of them, and to the way in which the thoughts are manifested in action. But there will also be an account of the way in which the subject, in thinking a thought of that type, can be said to know which object is in question. These two elements in an account of our thoughts are reflected in a distinction Evans makes between two levels of thought: 'fundamental' and 'non-fundamental' levels. At the fundamental level of thought, reference is secured using 'fundamental identifications' of the object referred to. Having a fundamental identification of the object is having knowledge of the fundamental ground of difference of that object. And the fundamental ground of difference of an object is that which distinguishes the object from all others. Thus, fundamentally identifying an object is thinking of the object as the possessor of the fundamental ground of difference that the object in fact possesses. When the object referred to is material, fundamentally identifying it is identifying it *as* an object of a certain kind with a given spatio-temporal location. However, we do not always identify objects thinking of them as the possessor of the fundamental ground of difference that they in fact possess. We can also identify them using 'non-fundamental identifications'. Nevertheless, Evans argues, Russell's Principle and the Generality Constraint demand that the non-fundamental level of thought be dependent upon the fundamental level. For, in order to know which object is the object of one's thought—and therefore in order to think of that object as the bearer of properties beyond those we currently have the grounds to ascribe to it—we must be able to identify that particular object as an element of an objective order.

Evans spells out this dependence by the claim that I can be said to identify an object non-fundamentally only if I know what it would be for that object to be identified fundamentally. I can think '*a* is *F*' only if I know what it is for some propositions '$\delta = a$' and 'δ is *F*' to be true, where δ is an arbitrary fundamental identification of an object, and *a* a non-fundamental identification for the same object. So, I can non-fundamentally identify a *material* object only if I know what it is for '$\delta = a$' and 'δ is *F*' to be true, where δ is an arbitrary identification of it as an object of a certain kind with this or that spatio-temporal position.

Applying this general framework to the case of first-person reference, we can say that in order to refer to myself as 'I', I must know which object I am referring to. It is not exactly clear what such knowing consists in but it is clear that such knowing depends, on Evans's view, on the capacity to identify and keep track of myself as an element of an objective world. This capacity depends upon the various ways I have of gaining knowledge of myself as a spatio-temporal object that is an element of that objective causal order. On the basis of my perceptions, I am able to form a cognitive map of my surroundings and am able to locate myself as an object with a certain position and orientation within the map. I also have the capacity to gain knowledge about my condition, my boundaries and position without direct reference to where I am in relation to other things. We have, Evans says:

a general capacity to perceive our own bodies, although this can be broken down into several distinguishable capacities: our proprioceptive sense, or sense of balance, of heat and cold, and of pressure.

Together these different capacities for knowing myself enable me to identify fundamentally the object which is me. When these capacities are crucially lacking there can be no first-person reference because there can be no question of the subject knowing which object in the objective order of things she is referring to.

1.2 Reference without information

Evans's account, in making the various ways we have of gaining knowing of our location and position essential to successful first-person reference, faces problems. First of all, it strikes us straight away that our capacity for first-person reference, in contrast to demonstrative reference, seems to be independent of the various ways I have of gaining knowledge of my location and position. We can easily consider being deprived of all information relating to the external environment while continuing to have a fairly rich self-conscious mental life. As Melville puts it:

No man can ever feel his identity aright except his eyes be closed; as if darkness were indeed the proper element of our essences, though light be more congenial to our clayey part (Melville 1972: 149)

Further, as we saw in our discussion of Anscombe, we are inclined to think that our capacity for first-person reference will also survive the removal of bodily awareness. Consider again Anscombe's victim in the sensory deprivation tank, all his senses anaesthetized, still able to refer to herself first-personally.

And now imagine that I get into a state of 'sensory deprivation'. Sight is cut off, and I am locally anaesthetized everywhere, perhaps floated in a tank of tepid water; I am unable to speak, or to touch any part of my body with any other. Now I tell myself 'I won't let this happen again!' If the object meant by 'I' is this body, this human being, then in these circumstances it won't be present to my senses; and how else can it be 'present to' me? . . . Am I reduced to, as it were, 'referring in absence'? I have not lost my 'self-consciousness'; nor can what I mean by 'I' be an object no longer present to me. This both seems right in itself, and will be required by the 'guaranteed reference' that we are considering. (Anscombe 1981: 31)

Evans claimed that my kinaesthetic knowledge, my sensations of the positions of my limbs, and my knowledge of my location in my environment, all contribute to the ability I have to think of myself as an object in the world with a certain orientation standing in relation to others. He claims, further, that it is this knowledge wich serves to distinguish me as an object in the world from all other objects in the world, and thus enables me to satisfy Russell's Principle and refer to myself. However, the claim that we can consider a subject who gains no such information without thereby considering her to be incapable of first-person thought, seems to give us a reason to doubt that such information plays the role in first-person reference that Evans supposes it to.

However, Evans accepts that a subject can refer to herself first-personally in conditions such as Anscombe's bath, and indeed worse: even in conditions where the subject is an *amnesiac* as well as suffering current total sensory deprivation (215). He denies that his account requires that the subject actually have information deriving from herself in order to meet his key principles. Although 'I' is subject to the same broad conditions as perceptual demonstratives such as 'this', it is not information-dependent in the same way. Evans claims that 'here' provides a better analogy than 'this'. A subject can clearly think of a place as 'here' without having any information deriving from that place. If one is taken, senses obstructed, to a place one knows not where, one can still wonder what it is like 'here'. Equally subjects can be in a position in which all (or some) of the usual channels from which they gain information about themselves are blocked, and yet be able to have self-conscious thoughts in this state. There is no doubt that extending the ability to 'I' and 'here' in these information free circumstances accords with common sense. There is however a question about how Evans's account allows him to permit it. How, in particular, on Evans's view, are we able to know which object we are referring to when we have none of the kinds of information that enable us to locate the object referred to?

Evans's suggestion is that, in order to be credited with knowledge of one particular place or person it is not necessary for subjects to be actually receiving information from the object, rather they need to 'be disposed to have such thinking controlled by information which may become available to them in each of the relevant ways' (Evans 1982: 216). He adds:

It is not surprising that 'I' follows the model of 'here' rather than 'this. The explanation is somewhat similar to the explanation for here (see 6.3). A subject does not need to have information actually available to him in any of the relevant ways in order to know that there is just one object to which he is thus dispositionally related. (Evans 1982: 216, n. 21)

Evans's suggestion is that, with certain types of identification, the subject can know which object is the object of her thought (and so satisfy Russell's Principle), even in the absence of actually receiving information. She can know this because she is disposed to have her thinking controlled by that object in these cases and she can know that there is just one object to which she is so related. To assess the suggestion we need to know two things. First, we need to know what account is being offered of what gives the subject such knowledge in these cases. Secondly, we need to know how the subject can have such knowledge about her dispositions which does not already pre-suppose a capacity for first-person reference that is independent of the disposition to receive information. The suggestion that the subject knows that there is just one object to which she is so related, *prima facie*, involves the first-person knowledge that 'I am dispositionally related to one object'. Such knowledge seems to invoke a capacity for first-person reference that does not rely upon such knowledge but rather precedes it.

Before looking to see what Evans has in mind, let me set one suggestion aside. We might wonder whether Evans needs the claim that a subject must *know* that there is one object to which it is dispositionally related, or whether simply being so related would be sufficient for his purposes. I think it is clear that Evans's construal of, and commitment to, Russell's Principle makes it impossible for him to be contented with the weaker claim. A subject could be disposed to have her thinking controlled by an object located in front of her. But if she has no memory, and no information from that object, we would not credit her with knowing which object she is thinking about if she is struck by the thought that there is an object in front of her. We would not credit her with such knowledge because as Evans puts it:

it is not, in general, possible to *know* that one is dispositionally so related to an object—still less to know that one is remaining dispositionally so related to the same object over a period of time. (169)

So, returning to our question, what is it that explains a subject's capacity to know, even in the absence of information, that there is just one human being to which she is dispositionally related? In the case of 'here'-thoughts, Evans explains the disposition, and our knowledge of it, in the following way:

Places, however, being—how shall we say?—so much thicker on the ground than objects, a subject cannot fail to have a single place as the target of his 'here' dispositions at an instant; and, since it is possible for a subject to know whether or not he is moving (relative to the earth's surface, or something comparable which provides the framework for identifying the place), a subject can know that his 'here' dispositions over a period have concerned the same place, without needing to have perceived the place during that period. (169)[2]

But, what is it that explains the capacity to refer to *oneself* independently of actually receiving information? How does a subject know that there is one object to which she is dispositionally related, to which she is identical? It seems clear that an explanation analogous to that given for 'here'-thought is not what is required. It may be, given that places are so thick on the ground, that there is one place at any given time to which I will be dispositionally related. Further, given my capacity to know whether I am moving relative to a framework, I may know that I am thus dispositionally related despite there being no perception of the place in question. But human beings are not so thick on the ground, and in the tank I am in receipt of no information at all about the location of the object which I seek to identify with my 'I'-thoughts. It seems that, unlike in the case of 'here'-thoughts, the claim that first-person thought can be independent of actually receiving information is not supported with reference to the kind of thing referred to—in this case a bounded object. Nor is it supported by available alternative information that enables one to keep track of the referent.

A natural move at this point may be to link a subject's capacity for first-person reference in the tank to a prior capacity to identify herself on the basis of information gained in the relevant ways. This link might be made in two ways. First, it may be suggested that the subject use her memories of her spatio-temporal identity to refer to the same thing now. However, this suggestion proves powerless if we take our subject to be an amnesiac, as Evans does (215). Secondly, it might be suggested that the subject relies not on her memories, but rather in an abiding conception of herself as a spatio-temporal object built up on the basis of past information gained in the relevant ways. On this suggestion 'I' might be thought to function somewhat as a name rather than a perceptual demonstrative. However, Evans is explicit about

[2] Note that Evans is here concerned with how we refer to one place understood as the immediate environment of the subject as opposed to the street, city or country etc. in which the subject is located. Evans clearly takes it that in the basic case 'here'-thoughts involve reference to the space of action and perception—the egocentric space—surrounding the subject.

claiming that we can refer to ourselves first-personally without having a current conception of ourselves (Evans 1982: 249). And note that if Evans is to maintain the requirement on first-person reference that the subject be currently disposed to gain information about themselves in the relevant ways, he *must* maintain the independence of first-person reference from both memories and conceptions based only on past experiences. Further, setting aside Evans's claims on the matter, it is not clear what use a conception based on past experience will be in securing current knowledge of which object is being referred to. Since, in the tank we have no way of assuring ourselves that we have not lost track of the object that our conception applied to. Thus it looks as though the subject's knowledge of existing dispositional relations is going to have to do all the work.

This then takes us to our second question, as to why Evans is not in fact relying on an unexplained capacity for first-person reference that has been smuggled in at the foundations of the account. Unless we have either past or current information to rely upon, it is hard to see how our knowledge that we are disposed to have our thinking controlled by information of a certain kind can avoid the assumption that there is a form of identification of ourselves that has not been explained.

It appears that Evans's account of first-person reference is unable to explain how dispositions to receive information secure a capacity to know which object one is referring to. Given that such knowledge is a requirement of reference it will be unable to explain how the tank subject is able to refer to herself first-personally. It is worth noting at this point that even if Evans *had* been able to meet the explanatory demands we placed on him with respect to the tank case, there would remain cases in which it is highly intuitive to suppose that there can be first-person reference but where Evans must deny it. I have in mind cases where a subject suffers not only a current perceptual information block, but also loses her *disposition* to receive the kind of perceptual information that Evans assumes is needed for her to be credited with a capacity for first-person thought. Consider the case of a mature subject who as a result of an accident suffers amnesia along with a permanent loss of her perceptual faculties, or at least sufficient of those faculties for her to be unable to keep track of her body. It is highly intuitive to think such a subject could at least for a while, bemoan *her* loss and wish that she knew where *she* was. Certainly, it does not seem that any inability for her to do that would have a conceptual or semantic source. But according to Evans, her capacity to refer to herself in the first-person lapses, as a matter of conceptual necessity, with her disposition to gain information about herself in the relevant ways.

Before moving on to a different kind of objection to Evans's account, it is important to stress one thing. I do not, and could not, take the arguments above to show that Evans is wrong to think first-person thought depends in some way on a subject's information-based ability to conceive of herself as a spatio-temporal object located in the world. It may well be that the subject having, or having had, such an ability is a necessary condition on first-person thought, perhaps on any thought at all. But Evans was not exclusively in the business of articulating general pre-conditions of this kind, and if that is what he is doing, we were wrong to take his account in the way we have. That is, we were wrong to take it as constituting a response to Anscombe's challenge to provide an account of the way in which we determine the referent in first-person thought. Denying that perceptual information plays a critical role in explaining how first-person thought reaches its referent does not imply that it may nevertheless be a broader necessary condition of such thought.

1.3 Reference and misinformation

I now want to turn to a further problem that Evans's account faces. When a capacity to refer depends upon information from, and about, the referent we can expect two sorts of failure. There may be failure through there being no information forthcoming and there may be failure through misinformation. Given the fact that first-person reference seems peculiarly immune from failure we need to look at how Evans's account deals with such possible failures. We have considered cases in which there is no information. I want now to consider cases where there is misinformation.

Armstrong supposes that:

> We can conceive of being directly hooked-up, say by transmission of waves in some medium, to the body of another. In such a case we might become aware e.g. of the movements of another's limbs, in much the same sort of way that we become aware of the motion of our own limbs. (Armstrong 1984: 113)

Let us, following Armstrong, imagine a case where I am for five minutes wired up in such a way that I am disposed to receive information from someone else's body as if it related to my own. In such a case, I might find myself thinking on the basis of that information that 'I have crossed legs', say. How are we to think of such a thought? Well, we will surely take it that I am thinking, probably falsely, about myself, rather than thinking truly about the person who was the source of the information. This feature of 'I', what Ayer called its 'adhesive quality', has been noted commonly enough. But it is not a feature of 'I' that Evans's account has a ready explanation for. For him such information is reference-determining, by which I mean that such information constitutes the means by which the subject is able to identify herself as the referent of 'I'. This case seems to show us that, if we take the referent of 'I' to be determined by the information received, we will get the wrong result. 'I' will refer to the source of the information and not to the receiver, as it seems it should. I will refer to this as 'the problem case'.[3]

What the problem case serves to show is that the relation between information from which we gain knowledge of ourselves, and our capacity for first-person reference, is fundamentally different from the relation between the information received from an object, and our capacity to think of it demonstratively as 'this' or 'that'. It seems plausible to claim in the case of demonstratives that, if they succeed in referring, then the reference follows the source of information. If there are two sources of information, then either reference will fail, or it will switch from one object to another with the referent determined by which object was the source of the information underwriting the token. However, even if there are two sources of the kind of information that Evans takes to underwrite first-person reference, it does not seem plausible to say, either that there is reference failure, or that the reference of 'I' follows the source of the information. On the account presented above 'I' seemed to function in fundamental respects like other demonstratives. The main difference between 'I' and 'this' seemed to lie in the fact that it is more difficult, and is therefore rarer, to use 'I' thinking that one is meaningfully using it, while failing to do so, than to think one is referring to an object using the term 'this', but failing to do so. It is rarer because the kind of information that underwrites the first-person is usually available and comes from a wide variety of sources, and also because successful reference for 'I' is supposed to rest on knowledge we have that we are disposed to receive information from one body. On the account it is not because of the special logic of first-person reference that reference failure is rarer than for perceptual demonstratives. It is

---

[3] I owe the thought that such a case causes a problem for Evans to John Campbell. It appeared in a paper 'Self-Consciousness and "I"'. (MS).

just easier for things to go wrong in the demonstrative, rather than first-person, case.[4]

It is important to stress again that the problem case should not be taken to show that Evans was wrong to think that the ability to conceive of ourselves as spatio-temporal objects is a precondition of first-person thought. Nor that he was wrong to think that we might not have such a capacity if we were generally disposed to have our thinking controlled by information from more than one source. Such general pre-conditions of first-person thought is not what is at issue. Rather the question is whether we can take such information as the basis by means of which we fix the referent of 'I'.

Can Evans's account cope with the problem case? Evans treats certain possibilities that are similar to the problem case. It is incumbent upon us to consider whether his treatment of them contains the basis of response to the criticism raised here. The possibilities Evans considers arise in response to his account of 'here'-thought. (164–168). We are asked to imagine a subject knowingly receiving information via television pictures sent back from the seabed. Evans imagines the subject becoming engrossed in the pictures and the environment they depict: 'It is getting dark and dingy here' she says. Evans argues that 'here' does not occur in its normal use in such a situation. In contrast to its normal use, such a use of 'here' requires the addition of a conceptual ingredient on the part of the subject, the identification of the place as 'the place

---

[4] Note that Evans is not insensitive to the fact that there are significant features of first-person reference that set it apart from other reference. In particular, he states that:

'the essence of "I" is *self*-reference. This means that a subject of thought and action is thinking about him*self*—i.e. about a *subject* of thought and action . . . Equally, I do not merely have knowledge of myself, as I might have knowledge of a place: I have knowledge of myself as someone who has knowledge and who makes judgements, including those judgements I make about myself.' (Evans 1982: 207)

and

'It is true . . . that the essence of self-consciousness is self-reference, that is to say, thinking, by a subject of judgements about himself, and hence, necessarily, about a subject of judgements. (This means that we shall not have an adequate model of self-consciousness until our model provides for the thought, by a subject, of his own judgements. Without that, no matter how much it mimicked our own use of "I", the model would always be open to the sceptical challenge: how can it be guaranteed that the subject is referring to himself?' (ibid.: 213)

However, despite the acknowledgement no account is given of how this feature is explained and made compatible with the account that is offered.

where these pictures are coming from', for example. This identification is not involved in ordinary 'here'-thoughts, and is not needed because the subject is able to know which place is in question without any such descriptive component. Can we imagine a similar case for 'I' and will we be tempted to say the same sorts of things about it? It is more difficult to produce such a case for first-personal thoughts. This may be precisely because the case envisaged for 'here' depended on breaking the link between the thoughts 'It is F here' and 'It is F in the place where I am'. In these non-ordinary uses of 'here' the referent is identified as 'the place where these places are coming from'. That place is precisely not where I am; I am where the pictures are.

We can perhaps imagine using 'I' in such circumstances if 'I' is used to indicate some sort of possession relation, as when we refer to a counter on a board game as 'I'. We can also imagine a subject who was controlling the camera starting to identify herself with the camera: 'I have reached a dark and dingy place'. In such cases 'I' seems to refer to something distinct from the subject, the camera, via something like the conceptual component 'the thing that I possess or control'. Or we might imagine a subject playing back pictures she had been at the locus of, dropping the continued use of the past tense. We might have Jacques Cousteau talking over his programme in which he does not appear before the lens: 'And here I am under the seemingly lifeless surface of the water.' 'I' here does seem to refer to the subject himself while 'here' refers to the place where that person was in the past. It says something like 'the place where these pictures are coming from is the place where I was under the seemingly lifeless surface of the water.' It is less natural to suppose that I would use 'I' to refer to the camera without any possession or involvement, but merely by thinking of it as 'the source, or focal point, of these pictures'. There seems to be some dis-analogy with 'here' on this point. If 'I' did function as 'here' does, we might expect it to be as easy to cast the reference of 'I' on to another object or person, as it is to cast the referent of 'here' to another place. However, perhaps the dis-analogy can be explained by Evans. In any case, I will not discuss such cases further here. As such cases are not relevantly similar to the problem case not much turns on whether what has been said of them is right.

The important case to consider is that in which the subject takes herself to be receiving information *in the usual way*, to relate to her egocentric space. It is this case which mirrors the problem case. So let us imagine a subject receiving information from the seabed in such a way that the subject is unaware that there is anything amiss; the subject takes the information to relate to her immediate environment. Evans argues that a subject's 'here'-thoughts in such a situation are ill-grounded and so do not refer. They are ill-grounded, in Evans's view, because the subject does not know *which* place is in question and thus the conditions on successful reference are not satisfied (165). Evans's treatment of 'here' in such a case provides good evidence that he would take the view that the subject's 'I'-thoughts would be similarly ill-grounded in the problem case. That conclusion, however, seems simply wrong. 'I' has a propensity to succeed in referring partly due to its insensitivity to the content of the information received. To say this, is not to be committed to the view that 'I' can never fail to refer, but only to the view that a token 'I'-thought does not appear to be rendered ill-grounded simply because for a period the information which a subject receives, and takes to relate to herself, in fact relates to something else. This point about 'I' has often enough been made in relation to cases in which the information I receive, and take to relate to myself, is observational. I might, for example, see a reflection of a woman in a mirror, a reflection I take to be myself, and judge 'I am wearing red boots' (see Rovane 1997). My judgement is taken to say something that is false about me, and not something ill-grounded or something true about the woman who is the source of the information. But if the point can be made for such cases why should it not be applicable to the problem case?

It seems that Evans's discussion of 'here'-thoughts serves only to confirm the counter-intuitive conclusion of the problem case. It is not going to help him meet the problem we had with his account. In fact, rather the reverse seems to be true. Evans claims an important link between 'I'-thoughts and 'here'-thoughts. He rejects the suggestion that one is more primitive than the other, and so the suggestion that we understand 'here' as 'the place I occupy', but holds that the thought 'p is here' is the same as the thought 'I am at p' (153.) They are the same thought roughly because the subject conceives herself to be at the point of origin of egocentric space, which is the space the subject identifies as 'here'. The identification of both requires the subject to be able to identify that space. However, if we are right about 'I', but accept Evans's story for 'here', we are in the surprising position of holding that 'here'-thoughts can fail of reference in a way that 'I'-thoughts seem not to be able to. If there is such a close interdependence between 'I' and 'here' how is that possible? If we accept what I take to be data about 'I'-thoughts, then we cannot both hold that the thoughts 'I am at P'

and '*P* is here' are equivalent and that a subject's use of 'here', which is occasioned by information from a distant source which she takes to relate to where she is, is ill-grounded. If the equivalence holds, and if the subject in the problem case can refer to herself, she should also be able to refer to the place she is as 'here'. In fact I think that it is plausible that 'here' often functions as a kind of perceptual demonstrative. ('Please sit down here.') But in that case it is not plausible to claim that 'I am at p' and 'p is here' express the same thought. To sustain that claim we seem to need a use of 'here' that is not a more or less demonstrative use.

2. ALTERNATIVE PERCEPTUAL MODELS OF FIRST-PERSON REFERENCE

The above discussion aimed to show that the Evans's account of first-person reference was unsatisfactory. We might however wonder how general the problems raised against Evans's account are, and how they would relate to alternative perceptual models of first-person reference. I hope it will not prove hard to show that the problems are likely to affect any account that aims to explain first-person reference as reference to ourselves effected, in the standard case, via perceptual information.

2.1 Dominant source models

Suppose it is suggested that we can get around the problem case by adopting a broadly perceptual model of first-person reference according to which 'I' refers to whichever object is the dominant source of the information (of the relevant kind) being received. Of course, we can take 'being received' here to mean either 'currently being received', or to mean 'having been received' and which we choose will lead us to different accounts. However, on either account the referent of 'I' will be determined as that which is the source of *most* of the information being received in the relevant sense. In this way we might think that the presence of information from another person is allowed for and that such information would not be sufficient to bring about a failure to secure the correct referent of 'I'.

The first thing to note is that this is not a revision that Evans himself could accept. For Evans, the capacity to refer requires more than that there be an information received from the object by the referrer. He requires that the information be of a kind that enables the subject to satisfy Russell's Principle. In so far as the reference of a term is fixed by information received, even a small amount of mis-information can undermine the subject's knowledge of which object she is referring to. It is for this reason that Evans in general takes cases that have the form of the problem case as cases where the reference is ill-grounded. For Evans, in order to conform to Russell's principle, the dominant source view would have to rely on a descriptive component such as 'the object which is the source of most of the information received'. But the suggestion that in first-person thought the subject identifies herself as the thing which is the source of most of the information received, is hopeless. For one thing, it involves a conceptual element that is surely not involved in normal uses of 'I'. Further, the identification cannot underwrite first-person reference because it already involves the subject thinking about herself, in a first-personal way, as the receiver of information: 'most of the information received' must mean 'most of the information received *by me*'.

However, even if we set aside the general dependence on Russell's Principle, I think it is clear that the dominant source model does little better than Evans's in respecting the particular nature of first-person reference. First, it has problems similar to Evans's in explaining how reference is fixed in the absence of information. Even if it can explain reference in the absence of information, the dominant source model still leaves room for reference failures that do not accord well with our intuitions about the guarantees attached to first-person reference. In the problem case, the subject herself has no way of determining which object is the dominant source of the information she is receiving. This threatens to leave her in ignorance of which object she is referring to. While reference combined with such ignorance might be plausible in other cases, as we have seen, it does not fit well with first-person reference. When a subject uses 'I' it is guaranteed both that the subject succeeds in referring to herself and that she knows that it is herself that she is referring to. Further, it is not even clear that, on the dominant source view, a person other than the subject herself could not be the dominant source of the information she is receiving. Certainly, if we adopt the account on which the referent is fixed by the dominant source of information *currently* being received it seems that in the problem case itself the other person could be the referent of 'I'.

Note also that, even if the dominant source model allows for successful reference in cases that Evans took to be ill-grounded, it too will have to admit of the possibility of reference failure. There will be cases where the reference is indeterminate because the same amount of information is received from two objects. The subject will be able to resume referring to herself only given a little more information from one source rather than another. However, *ex hypothesi*, the subject will be unable to detect which information comes from which source. So, it will be opaque to the subject whether she is successfully referring and which person she is referring to using 'I' if she is. But this seems an absurd view of first-person reference.

Even if it were argued that in fact no person other than the thinker could be the dominant source of information, this fact does not seem to be something that is transparent for the thinker. The possibility of referring in ignorance, that the dominant source model leaves room, seems to conflict with the fact that in first-person reference the subject knows that it is herself she is referring to.

2.2 Bodily awareness as a single object faculty

I have suggested that Evans must hold that in cases such as the problem case the subject's 'I'-thoughts are either ill-grounded or that they refer to the wrong thing. However, there is some evidence that Evans is drawn to holding that in cases such as the problem case, what we have is rather successful reference to the ascribing subjects, with the assumption that they are subject to illusion resulting in false belief. How might he claim the latter? In order to do so he would need to render information gained through the sort of channels that are operating in the problem case as irrelevant to our ability to refer first-personally. One suggestion might be that genuine bodily awareness of the kind being invoked to secure first-person reference is a form of perception that necessarily delivers information from just one object—that is the subject herself. If bodily awareness is a single object faculty in this way, then we might claim that we do identify ourselves by using information from our faculty for bodily awareness, but that what the subject is receiving in the problem case cannot properly be said to be information from her faculty for bodily awareness. Thus, it can be set aside as not germane to the subject's attempts to identify herself.[5]

The thing to note about this suggestion is that, while it may be a view that Evans is drawn to, it cannot I think be ascribed to him. Evans does hold that we are immediately disposed to take information

---

[5] See Martin (1995, 1997a) for the suggestion that we take bodily awareness to be a single object faculty.

from bodily awareness to be information about ourselves. However, Evans also explicitly acknowledges the possibility of getting kinaesthetic information from another (250) and this acknowledgement is of a piece with his discussion of information in Chapter 5. Further, even if Evans were to hold that the mis-information coming from another person in the problem case was not information from bodily awareness but from some other source, I think it is clear that he would take such information as nevertheless sufficient to make the subject's 'I'-thoughts ill-grounded. In his discussion of 'here'-thoughts Evans is quite explicit that information about places can come through abnormal channels, and that when a subject is receiving and using such information, thinking it is coming from normal channels, her 'here'-thoughts are ill-grounded. Given the close analogy between the cases, and the claim he makes for the close relations between 'I'-thoughts and 'here'-thoughts we would expect the cases to be treated similarly.

However, even if Evans himself did not adopt the suggestion that first-person reference is determined by bodily awareness understood as a single object faculty, such a suggestion does offer us a perceptual model of first-person reference that might seem to meet the problem case. The idea would be that we have information from bodily awareness which determines the reference of a subject's 'I'-thoughts. In the problem case, we have quasi-bodily awareness which is not the basis on which first-person reference is determined. Therefore, there is no possibility of the person who is the source of such abnormal information being determined as the object of first-person reference.

I think the basic problems remain for this version of the perceptual model of first-person reference. The account has still to account for first-person reference in cases where the subject has no information of the relevant kind at all. Consider if, in the problem case, the subject is not only receiving information from another's body but is also anaesthetized with respect to her own body. In such a case, our theorist would have to claim either that 'I' does not refer, or try to ground first-person reference in dispositions of the kind Evans appealed to. However, the idea that a subject's being disposed to have her thinking controlled by genuine bodily awareness is sufficient to secure reference is, if anything, more problematic in this case than in the case where the subject is receiving no information. For in this case, it is clear that the subject is also both actually having, and is disposed to have, her thinking controlled by quasi-bodily awareness. Thus, the theorist will have to explain why such quasi-information does not interfere with a subject's capacity for first-person reference based on a mere disposition.

But the problem that is most damaging for the current account arises from the fact that it is, by hypothesis, opaque to the subject whether the information she is receiving is from genuine bodily awareness or from an abnormal source. Given that it is opaque to the subject what the basis for her use of 'I' is, and given that only genuine bodily awareness can ground first-person reference, the subject will not be in a position to know whether she has succeeded in referring to herself or not. This seems to be an unacceptable conclusion. Construal of bodily awareness as a single object faculty may be used by a perceptual model of first-person reference to argue that any successful use of 'I' by a subject must refer to the human being she is. However, we will be left with an account of first-person reference which although guaranteed to refer to the user, if it refers, has the subject not knowing whether her use was a successful one or not.

In order for the proponent of this version of the perceptual model to meet the guarantees we have taken to be the hallmark of first-person reference, they are going to have establish not only that first-person reference is determined by information from bodily awareness, and that bodily awareness is necessarily a single object faculty or set of faculties, but also that bodily awareness being a single-object faculty is sufficient to make the kind of misinformation present in the problem case unable to undermine the subject's capacity to refer to herself using 'I'. Perhaps it can be argued that such information is not sufficient to undermine the first kind of guarantee that attaches to first-person reference, that is, that it refers to the referrer. However, it will be very much harder to show that it does not undermine the second kind of guarantee, that the subject knows both that she is referring and that she is referring to herself.

3. CONCLUSION

There are no doubt alternative perceptual models that I have not considered. However, we are now, I think, in a position to generalize the conclusions reached in relation to those we have considered. To the extent that an account of first-person reference assumes that the referent of 'I' is fixed by perceptual information, which is the essential claim of a perceptual account, the account will be subject to the possibility of coherent and comprehending uses of 'I' surviving the absence or disturbance of such information. In order to block such a possibility we would need a tight conceptual dependence between our currently being able refer to ourselves and our having available accurate perceptual information to identify the person we are. Even if the ability to refer to ourselves first-personally depends in some more general way on an ability to identify oneself perceptually, it is implausible to suppose that every exercise of the former ability implies an exercise of, or disposition to exercise, the latter. But this is what is required if we refer to ourselves first-personally by identifying ourselves perceptually, which is what the perceptual model contends.

That there is not such a tight connection between our capacity for first-person reference and our capacity for perceiving ourselves is not surprising. It is in the nature of perception to allow for the possibility of a rational subject suffering from 'blindness' and mis-perception. The problem with attempting to fashion a perceptual model of first-person reference comes, in essence, from the fact that we take the subject who suffers such perceptual disruption to be able, nevertheless, to express herself, as herself, using the first person. To conclude, even though there may very well be general perceptual conditions that are required for the existence of a rational subject, it is implausible to suppose that perceptual information is the means by which we fix reference to ourselves in the first-person way.

4

The Self-Reference Rule

Let us suppose that we are convinced that it is a mistake to model first-person reference on demonstrative reference underwritten by some introspective or perceptive self-presentation. Such accounts gave us a model of how we might construe first-person reference, but seemed unable to explain how it is that when we think first-personally it is always, and without exception, ourselves that we are thinking of.

The thought that it is a constraint on first-person reference that it always be reference to the person referring suggests we might do better to build our account of first-person reference on the familiar rule which identifies first-person reference precisely as reflexive reference. The self-reference rule (SRR) states that 'I' refers to the subject who produced it. It is very plausible to think that this rule gives us the meaning of the first-person pronoun and governs correct usage of the first-person concept. Perhaps this rule is all we need to explain first-person reference? As Barwise and Perry put it in relation to the first-person pronoun:

Let us begin with the word 'I'. A reasonable thing to say about this expression is that, whenever it is used by a speaker of English, it stands for, or designates that person. We think that this is all there is to know about the meaning of 'I' in English and that it serves as a paradigm rule for meaning. (Barwise and Perry 1981: 670)

It is, I think, clear that such a rule is bound to play a central role in any adequate account of first-person reference. However, it is less clear exactly what role the rule will play. The fundamental idea that first-person reference should be understood in terms of reference in accordance with SRR is common to very different accounts. The accounts tend to be separable from one another in terms of two basic parameters.

The first parameter concerns how we should understand what it means to claim that a subject is referring in accordance with SRR. In particular, the claim that a subject is referring in accordance with SRR may be understood to imply that the subject has, in some sense, mastery of the rule that 'I' refers to the subject who uses it, which she utilizes in order to refer to herself. Or the claim may be understood in such a way that a subject can be said to refer in accordance with the rule with no mastery of the rule. Rather the capacity for reference in accordance with the rule may be taken to be secured by other factors, such as the role of belief contents in bringing about action.

The second parameter which separates accounts that appeal to SRR concerns whether one should take the capacity for reference in accordance with SRR as sufficient to explain the nature of first-person reference. Should we consider all systematically reflexive reference as first-person reference, or should we distinguish between kinds of reference which are systematically reflexive and full first-person reference?

However, before addressing these questions, I want briefly to consider whether first-person reference need even be reflexive. This will detain us for the next section. I will then return to explore the suggestion that SRR proves the best basis for an account of first-person reference.

1. NON-REFLEXIVE FIRST-PERSON REFERENCE

1.1 Fiction

It might be objected that the self-reference rule cannot be a critical element in an account of first-person reference since it is not always true that a use of 'I' refers to the person who produced it. If that is so, conformity with the rule is not even necessary for first-person reference. Hence, we might be doubtful about the prospects for the self-reference principle providing a satisfactory account of first-person reference.[1] Let me consider the sorts of cases in which it can seem that a subject refers to others using the first-person pronoun, and the sorts of cases where there are thought contents that would be naturally expressed using 'I', but that are not about the subject who is thinking.

In fiction, 'I' may seem to refer to someone other than subject who uses it. Whether in speaking the lines of a play or writing a fictional

---

[1] See Velleman (1996). There are a number of non-standard uses of 'I' which have received attention recently. (See, e.g., Corazza, Fish and Gorvett 2002; Predelli, S. 1998, 2002; Romdenh-Romluc, K. 2002; Sidelle 1991.) I treat here what I take to be the most significant kinds of case and hold that all non-standard uses are derivative of the fundamental use, and indeed have to appeal to its fundamental use as reflexive to be properly explained.

text, the actor or author can use tokens of 'I' intentionally, and knowing its full meaning, without it seeming to be the case that they thereby refer to themselves. In using 'I' they seem to refer to the character they are playing or creating. However, this is not the only way to describe what is going on in these cases. We could equally say that, in fictional contexts, 'I' *does* refer to the person using it, but that the fictional context determines who that person is. Let us take the case of an actor playing Ophelia. The actor has been assigned to the role of Ophelia, and so stands for Ophelia within the fictional context. In that context when the actor uses the first-person normally to refer to herself, the reference gets shifted on to Ophelia as the character who is supposed to be speaking. Thus, in pretending to be Ophelia, and producing the first-person pronoun within that pretence, the actor brings it about that within the fiction we have Ophelia using the first-person pronoun to refer to herself. Thus, within the fiction, 'I' does refer to the person who is using it: Ophelia refers to Ophelia. We can equally say that, viewed from outside the fiction, we have the actor using the rule she normally uses to refer to herself. Indeed, using 'I' as governed by SRR is the means by which she brought it about that Ophelia *referred* to herself using 'I'. In order to make it the case that within the fiction Ophelia referred to herself, the actor need only do what she normally does to refer to herself. Does this mean that there is a double referring here—a reference of the actor to herself and a reference by Ophelia to herself? Yes, but in a way that is quite intuitive: the actor knowing she is acting a part uses the term she normally uses to refer to herself to bring about an act of reference by Ophelia to Ophelia.[2] There are two acts of reference—one fictional and one not—in the way that there are also two people—the actor and Ophelia.

It might be responded that as the actor is not really Ophelia, indeed no one is, there are in fact neither two people and nor can Ophelia be the user of 'I'. If Ophelia cannot be the user of 'I', it cannot be that we have a case of Ophelia using 'I' to refer to herself. If this is meant to suggest that there is no real act of reference in such cases, then we have no counterexample to SRR, and so it need not worry us. But perhaps the suggestion is rather that since Ophelia cannot refer to anything what

---

[2] This is not to say that the actor cannot slip out of the fiction and declare in her own voice 'I can no longer stand this depressing play', even while being still taken by her audience to be Ophelia self-referring. This raises nice issues with respect to speaker's reference and hearer's reference in the case of the first-person which I will not go in to. It can be assumed that I am concerned primarily with the speaker's reference.

we must have is a non-reflexive use of 'I' where the actor is the user of 'I' while Ophelia is the referent. However, if one is to insist that it is really the actor, not the character, that uses 'I', then can we not also insist that it is really the actor, not the character, who is being referred to. What seems to be happening in such a case is that we take an actor's act of first-person reference as if it were an act of self-reference by another. That is, we are taking 'I' to be governed by the rule that it refers to whoever is using it, but we, in make-believe, re-assign the identity of the user. That this is the most natural account of what is going on is evidenced by the fact that the actor cannot bring about this kind of first-person reference to a character from *outside* the fiction. The actor cannot in her own voice refer to Ophelia using 'I'. It is only in so far as she is within the perspective of the character that it is possible for her to bring it about that the character is referred to using 'I'. In so doing, she brings it about that the character refers to herself. Of course, given the kind of double reference seen to be in play, there is a good sense in which the actor refers to Ophelia in her use of 'I'—but it is a sense that needs to appeal to SRR in its explanation. Further, to refer to another, in that sense, is to use 'I' in just the kind of derivative way we would expect from fiction creating creatures like ourselves who understood 'I' as a term or concept governed by SRR.

If this is the right thing to say of the actor's use of the first-person, there is good reason to suppose that we can say it of the writer's use of the first person. The writer who writes her characters in the first person, much like the actor, brings it about that her characters refer to themselves first-personally by re-assigning to her characters, via pretence, imagination, or some fictional device, her normal acts of first-person reference.

1.2 Oration and dictation

Setting aside cases of fiction, let us consider the cases of someone reading out, or writing out, a letter on behalf of someone else, as for example, when I read out an absent colleague's text or take a dictation. The speech or text I produce may be peppered with uses of the first-person pronoun that do not refer to me, the person who is producing them. Does this mean that the principle that 'I' refers to the subject using it does not necessarily hold in cases of first-person reference?

The first thing to note about such cases is that, while the user of the first-person pronoun might produce it, fully knowing its meaning, such knowledge is not required for the producer to carry out her task of being the mouthpiece for another. Suppose that the text is in a language that the speaker can read or transcribe without understanding (as many people can read and transcribe Hebrew or Latin). This does not detract from the speaker's or dictation taker's capacity to communicate the author's words to the audience. As long as the author and audience understand the words used, and the audience have notification of who the author is, all that is required for successful communication is that the speaker or writer be a reliable mouthpiece (or handpiece), able to reproduce a syntactically accurate copy of the original text or speech. Given this, I think it turns out to be implausible to suggest that the speaker or writer, in such cases, is using 'I' in the relevant sense. She is uttering or writing the term, but she is not using it to refer to anything. Rather the author is using the term 'I' to refer to herself, and because of a distance between herself and the audience, is using another subject to duplicate her words.

Of course there are more complex cases than the straightforward oration and dictation cases raised above. Consider the case of Cyrano, reading and writing the love letters on behalf of Christian.[3] Cyrano is, in this story, both the author of words produced on behalf of someone else, the mouthpiece (or 'handpiece') that communicates those words, and the expresser of his own thoughts and feelings by use of those words. As such, the case involves elements of the fictional case, the oration/dictation case and the normal case. Nevertheless, despite the complexity, we can unravel what is going on in such a way that it remains plausible that the basic principle to be adhered to is that 'I' is a device of reflexive reference. Use of 'I' by an author to make it seem to refer to someone else is brought about not by giving up the rule, but by a reassignment of the identity of the user in that context. So, for example, Cyrano writing to be understood to be referring to Christian, writes as if he were Christian. So Cyrano writes pretending to be Christian referring to himself. When he writes expressing his own feelings he uses the first-person in the normal way—he refers to himself, and when he writes out the words of another he acts as a mere scribe. The interest of the case is that all this happens at once—the texts Cyrano produces are ambiguous and we are able to slip in and out of the fiction he is trying to produce and finding hard to sustain. But what explains the ambiguity in his use of the first-person is the central rule

---

[3] Thanks to Barry C. Smith for raising this wonderful example.

that 'I' refers to the user. By playing in imagination, and with his audience, with the identity of who the user is, he can play with who the referent is.

Such cases are endlessly fascinating, and there is much to be said about the way in which fictional elements mesh with each other. We have, for example, said nothing about the fact that the story of Cyrano is a *play*. 'I' is not written by Cyrano pretending to be Christian, it is written by the actor playing Cyrano, who is pretending to be Christian—to be read out later, not by Christian, but by the actor playing Christian, pretending to have authored words that are not his own. However, I hope enough has been said to make it plausible that these cases do not pose any real threat to the view that first-person reference involves reference in accordance with the rule that 'I' refers to its user. In fact, the little work we have done to unpick what is going on in these cases suggests that, on the contrary, such cases only arise given an understanding of 'I' as a device of reflexive reference and the possibility of pretending or imagining the user of 'I' being other than who she in fact is.

1.3 Imagination

We have so far discussed putative cases of non-reflexive reference where we have a public token of 'I'—written or spoken. There may be a remaining worry about non-standard uses of the first-person concept in thought, uses that typically occur in imagination. In fact, however, the treatment of the cases raised above, suggest a way of dealing with uses of the first-person in imagination that philosophers have found perplexing. What is going on when I imagine that I am Napoleon? I imagine being Napoleon and imagine myself as Napoleon thinking 'I wish I was not so short' or 'Able was I 'ere I saw Elba' and so on. Clearly it is hard to take such thoughts as straightforwardly reflexively referential. I do not seem to be referring to myself, who I know to be LOB. I am not imagining that I, LOB, am short, or am on Elba. I am imagining that I am Napoleon who is short, or is on Elba. Thus, my use of the first-person in these thoughts seems to refer to Napoleon, rather than to me the thinker. We seem to have a way of shifting the reference of 'I' in thought that is very similar to the way we have seen that we can shift it in language. It is natural to suppose that such reference shifting can be treated in very much the same way in both cases. We set up the imagined scenario with the thought 'I am Napoleon'. In so doing we imagine Napoleon to be the user of the first-person concept, that, as a device of reflexive reference, refers to Napoleon.[4] Thus when I think the thought 'I wish I was not so short' while engaged in imagining being Napoleon, I imagine Napoleon referring to himself, by referring to myself.

Non-standard cases of dictation, fiction and imagination do not *prima facie* stand to undermine the suggestion that we should understand first-person reference in terms of self reference. In fact, we have the beginnings of an explanation of how we seem to be able to refer to others by use of 'I' if we keep it in mind that 'I' is fundamentally reflexively referential. Once we fix for our audience what the pretence is and what role has been assigned to the speaker or writer, then the standard use of 'I' as reflexively referential will explain how they are able to take that person or character as the referent. Cases, in which we seem to refer to others first-personally in thought, where we imagine being someone else, do not undermine the fundamental reflexivity of first-person thought, but rather rely on it.

In fact putative counterexamples to the claim that 'I' is governed by SRR seem to fall to the following thought.[5] Imagine a community of speakers and thinkers that, by hypothesis, use a term and concept for which SRR gives the rule for correct usage. Would we not expect them to come on occasion to use such a term, in their pretences and short cuts, in precisely the sort of non-standard ways we saw above. By pretence, convention or specification, speakers are likely, on a given occasion, to use their device of reflexive reference expressive of first-person thought, to produce a speech act that allows their audience to pick out someone else.

2. THE SELF-REFERENCE APPROACH

With the above concern set aside let us return to the suggestion that SRR is able to provide a satisfactory account of first-person reference. SRR states that 'I' refers to the subject who uses it. We have said that it is plausible to think that correct usage of the first-person pronoun and the first-person concept abides by this rule. The question is, how does this

---

[4] This account of the matter is similar to that found in Velleman (1996).

[5] The thought uses a kind of test due to Kripke (1977). Kripke discounts certain putative counter-examples to Russell's theory of descriptions by considering how a community of users who speak 'Russell-English', a language for which Russell's theory of descriptions is assumed by hypothesis to give the right semantics, might come to use such definite descriptions.

help us to explain a subject's capacity to refer to herself first-personally? *Prima facie*, reflexive reference need not be first-person reference. A subject may self-refer, that is refer reflexively, without knowing that it is herself to which she is referring; she may refer to herself without knowing that she, the subject, is also the object. Since the latter knowledge seems to be a key component of genuine first-person reference we may doubt the ability of the self-reference principle to capture the nature of first-person reference. This concern is most famously voiced by Anscombe (1981: 22). She claims that understanding 'I' as a device of self-reference is not sufficient to characterize the meaning of 'I' because the claim that 'I' is the word each one uses in speaking of himself involves the locution 'speaking of himself' that can be applied to cases of merely reflexive reference which are not first personal. A subject, for example Oedipus talking of the killer of Laius, can be described as speaking of himself even when he does not know that it is he, himself that is speaking of (where he, himself indicates thought of himself in the first-person way). Anscombe considers the suggestion that the cases of non-self-conscious reference can be ruled out if the rule be amended to:

'I' is the word each one uses when he knowingly and intentionally speaks of himself.

The modified version is given equally short shrift on the same grounds—does not Oedipus knowingly and intentionally speak of that person who is in fact himself? The general point seems to be that 'I' cannot be understood merely as a device of reflexive reference because reflexive reference is possible in the absence of genuine self-conscious self-reference. Anscombe suggests that the only way that the gap of insufficiency can be plugged is at the cost of circularity. If we demand that the 'himself' be read as a self-conscious himself, as what she calls the 'peculiar indirect reflexive', our explanation will prove circular since that reflexive has to be explained in terms of 'I'. Her view is that there is no non-circular statement of SRR that can be used to individuate first-person reference.

However, Anscombe's arguments do not succeed in showing that a non-circular statement of the SRR is insufficient to identify first-person reference.[6] The claim being made by the self-reference approach is not that whenever one has a subject using a term (knowingly and intentionally) to refer to herself one will have first-person reference. The

---

[6] See O'Brien (1994) for a fuller response to Anscombe's treatment of SRR.

claim is rather that when a subject uses a term *governed by* the rule that it refers to the subject using it, it will be expressive of first-person reference. Oedipus may use 'The killer of Laius' knowingly and intentionally to refer to himself but the reference of 'The killer of Laius' is not governed by SRR. Anscombe introduces an example of society in which speakers use a term 'A' to refer to something that falls under their observation in a particular way. It happens that the speaker itself is the only thing that falls under its observation in quite that way. Thus, 'A' is used by each speaker to refer itself. However, this need not worry the self-reference theorist either: although 'A' refers to its speaker it does not do so of necessity and the rule governing 'A' is some observational rule rather than SRR.[7] The speaker who comprehendingly uses 'A' uses it as a device that refers to that thing, whatever it is, that falls under its observation in a particular way. In contrast, the person who comprehendingly uses 'I' uses it precisely as a device of self reference. The self-reference theorist can claim that it is as a device governed by SRR, rather than merely in accord with SRR, that 'I' is expressive of first-person reference. There is therefore no threat to the view that SRR is sufficient to secure first-person reference without involving any circularity in the statement of the rule.

However, there are two worries the self-reference approach might be concerned with here. One worry is whether SRR is sufficient to individuate first-person reference. Call this the *individuation problem*. The other worry is that, even if SRR individuates the first person, it fails to explain how it is that 'I' expresses self-consciousness. We can call this the *explanation problem*.[8]

I will argue in what follows that a term used by us *as* a device of reflexive reference will in fact be sufficient to individuate first-person reference. A subject who uses 'I' as governed by SRR will inevitably succeed in self-referring self-consciously, because of an awareness she has of her own thoughts and utterances. If it is given that a subject is aware of using a term when she is, then any term governed by SRR will in fact be used by comprehending subjects to refer to themselves in the first-person way. The conditions of use will provide us with the elements that Anscombe feared would render the rule either insufficient or circular. However, this way of meeting the individuation problem suggests that we need to do more than appeal to SRR to explain why a term governed by SRR is expressive of self-conscious self-reference.

---

[7] See Campbell (1994: N 132–4) and O'Brien (1994: 278–9).

[8] Thanks to Johannes Roessler for suggesting this way of dividing things.

Why we may need more than mastery of SRR can be further brought out by use of an example. Consider Lewis's example of two gods (Lewis 1983: 139): one lives on the tallest mountain and throws down manna and one lives on the coldest mountain and throws down thunderbolts, both are omniscient with respect to propositional knowledge. Neither god knows which god he is. We can also take it that the gods know that 'I' is governed by SRR and that they know for any utterance of 'I' who made that utterance. So if the god on the tallest mountain utters 'I am throwing down manna' they both know that the 'I' refers to the god on the tallest mountain.

Similarly, if the god on the coldest mountain utters 'I am throwing down thunderbolts' they both know that the 'I' refers to the god on the coldest mountain. Thus, both gods know that 'I' refers to whoever produces it, and are guaranteed to refer to themselves when they use it. But it is not plausible that either god succeeds in referring to himself first-personally. Each god is guaranteed to refer to himself using 'I' but he is not guaranteed to refer to himself, knowing that it is *himself* that he is referring to. Thus it seems that the gods' use of 'I' understood as governed by SRR is insufficient for them to be able to use it to achieve self-conscious self-reference. However, notice that taking the case this way hinges on taking the gods to be in some peculiar way estranged from their own utterances—they do not know, as we do, that they, themselves are uttering when they are. In fact this estrangement seems to me to rule out the possibility that the gods are genuine speakers or thinkers. But in any case, the case suggests that if SRR, as used by us, is sufficient to individuate first-person reference it is because of something we have that the gods lack. In what follows I explore the suggestion that it is the self-conscious awareness we have of our own thoughts and utterances that enables us to self-consciously self-refer when we use 'I' as governed by SRR. Thus, while an appeal to SRR (given our natures as speakers and thinkers) may be sufficient to solve the individuation problem, a full explanation of why it is sufficient, and how of 'I' is expressive of self-consciousness, has to go beyond a simple appeal to SRR. That is, an appeal to SRR is not sufficient to meet the explanation problem.

There seem to me to be two broad ways in which we may respond to the latter insufficiency worry. The first strategy is—as suggested above—to appeal to further features that are in play when we use 'I' as governed by SRR that explain why the use of 'I'—as so governed—is sufficient to secure self-conscious self-reference. The second strategy is to try to deny the force of the explanation problem. Before considering how we might develop the first strategy, let me deal with the second.

2.1 The reductionist approach to first-person reference

According to the explanation problem a simple appeal to SRR is not sufficient to explain first-person reference because it has not been explained how a term of reflexive reference is expressive of self-consciousness. If first-person reference involves not only a subject referring to herself, but also involves a subject self-consciously referring to herself then, the claim was, we have to invoke something further than SRR to explain first-person reference. I suggested we might appeal to a subject's mastery of SRR and awareness of her acts of reference. However, there is a view according to which there is a very basic form of systematically reflexive reference that is properly call first-personal, but that does not involve self-consciousness (except in some equally reduced sense) and requires no explanation beyond an appeal to SRR. The view can be called the reductionist approach to first-person reference.[9]

The reductionist argues that we have good reason to postulate a capacity for first-person reference that is very basic: if we are to explain actions in simple creatures we need to be prepared to ascribe first-person beliefs to creatures for whom there is no question whether they have mastery of any self-reference rule or awareness of referring, and so on. How else do we explain why the dog ducks because he sees the ball coming now towards him?

Consider the simplest creature to which one can envisage ascribing desires and actions. Suppose the creature to be hungry, to be facing food, and coming to eat the food it is facing. Further suppose that we should explain the creature's action as the result of a belief state that leads, from the creature's desire to eat, to the action of eating the food it is facing. But now what belief can explain the appropriateness of the action of eating the food facing it, given its desire to eat? The belief ascribed needs to allow us to explain what motivated the creature to eat the food it was currently facing, given that the creature desired to eat. A belief that will explain *that* is a belief that, if true, would mean that the

---

[9] The following discussion is guided by a number of views extant in the literature, but especially by those expressed in Mellor (1989). O'Brien (1993, ch. 4) in 'Who Mellor?' deals in detail with Mellor's account, raising essentially the same criticisms as are raised here. Perry can also be thought of as something of a reductionist. (See Perry 1986, 1990.)

action of eating satisfied the creature's desire for food. The belief that
meets that condition is the belief that is true just if the creature believing
is currently facing food. A belief that has such systematically reflexive
truth conditions is a belief with systematically reflexive content. That is
the belief we represent as 'I am now facing food'. Thus the creature must
have first-person beliefs and, thereby, be credited with a capacity for
first-person reference. On the basis of this, the reductionist concludes
that the explanation of the actions of simple creatures requires us to
ascribe a capacity for first-person reference to them.

Let us allow the reductionist to assume that such a creature will
have beliefs, as well as desires and actions, if it is motivated to act. We
might still object that the line of argument presented fails to distinguish
between very different belief contents that may have similar causal
roles. Consider a distinction made by Campbell between structured
and unstructured thoughts.[10] A thought is structured if it is composed
of separable elements that can be put to work in other thoughts.
Thus, it is a necessary condition of a subject having a thought with a
structured content that the subject has distinct capacities for thinking,
that correspond to the separable elements of the thought. Consider,
to take Campbell's example, a child who utters 'Rain' in response to
rain. We cannot take such an utterance as expressive of a structured
thought with a content given by such expression as 'It is raining here,
now' or 'It is now raining where I am' as long as we have evidence that
the child is unable to think separately about rain and about here, as
opposed to there, or about herself, as opposed to another. However, it
seems quite obvious that even if the child has no such abilities, and can
only be credited with the unstructured thought of 'Rain!', her thought
might nevertheless motivate her to act. The reductionist's argument
that we can only explain her action if we attribute to her a belief with
the content 'It is now raining here' or 'It is now raining where I am'
looks to have established too much. The ascription of such contents to a
creature who could not understand what it would be for it to be raining
where someone else is seems unwarranted. The content of the creature's
attitudes seems better conveyed by the expressions 'Food!' or perhaps
'Food here' rather than by 'I am facing food'.

Perhaps the reductionist will respond that first-personal beliefs are
required for explaining action because of the nature of desire. The

---

[10] Campbell (1994: 138). I owe the heart of the argument presented here to
Campbell's discussion.

suggestion might be made that we need to construe the contents of desires as first personal, and construing the contents of desires as first personal requires as to construe the contents of motivating beliefs as similarly first personal. Consider the assumption made earlier that the subject can have a desire for food, the content of which is most naturally expressed as 'Food' or perhaps as 'Eat Food'. It might be argued that such contents cannot be motivating contents since motivating contents need to match the conditions under which the desire will be satisfied.[11] Since the satisfaction of the desire to eat requires not just that there be food, nor just that food be eaten, but that the desiring subject eat food, it might be argued that the content of the desire cannot be just for food, or for food to be eaten, but must be for 'me to eat food'. If it is legitimate to read off the content of a desire from the conditions required to bring about its satisfaction, then it might be argued that even the most simple desires must have first-personal content. And if desires are first personal in this way, then the beliefs that motivate actions on the basis of such desires must also be first personal. Thus, action explanation requires a capacity for first-person reference.

It will, I think, help clarify matters if we identify four distinct claims on which the reductionist conclusion rests:

1. The truth (veridicality) or satisfaction conditions of motivating states depend systematically on who the subject of the attitude is, even though the subject may lack any representation of herself, or any knowledge that she is referring to herself. Such conditions, therefore, need to be specified reflexively.

2. States of mind with truth or satisfaction conditions that need to be specified reflexively are states of mind with systematically reflexive *content*.

3. A creature is a state of mind with systematically reflexive *content* has a capacity for systematically reflexive *reference*.

4. The capacity for systematically reflexive reference is a capacity for first-person reference.

---

[11] Mellor's strategy is to determine belief content by its utility conditions. Starting with the idea that desire content is determined by its satisfaction conditions makes it easier to bring out the fact that the argument for reflexive belief content depends upon assuming reflexive desire content. As long as it is assumed that a desire simply for 'food' is motivating, it is not clear why it needs anything more than an unstructured representation of 'food' to result in an action apt for satisfying it.

A natural response at this point is that we need not, and should not, accept conclusion 2. We may reject the equation of desire content with satisfaction conditions precisely because we can imagine a subject, with no capacity to take itself, rather than another, as the object of an ascription, seeming to have a simple unstructured desire that is satisfied by something coming to be true of it. The reductionist argument can, I think, be seen as based on a supposition that we need to choose between taking our simple creature to have an attitude with a content that is first personal or one that is entirely general. Given that, it is certainly implausible to take the merely existential belief 'There is food' or the desire 'That there be food eaten' as immediately motivating, we seem forced to take the content of our desires and beliefs to be first personal. But this is a false choice. It is not that our creature is motivated either by existential or referential contents. The view is rather that for the simplest creatures there is only the possibility of their having representations of properties in relation to *them*. The explanation of why those will be effective in motivating will indeed by specified reflexively. However, given that there is no possibility of such creatures ascribing such properties of the environment to other creatures, there is no need for us to assume they have the capacity for ascribing such properties to *themselves*. Any representation with the content 'food' or 'food here' will be sufficient to motivate eating given hunger, thus reflexive satisfaction conditions need not imply reflexive contents.

However, the reductionist may insist, that there must be a *kind* of desire and belief content that the story in terms of unstructured contents leaves out. It has been allowed that our creature has a desire that is satisfied if and only if the desiring creature eats food, and has a belief that is true if and only if the believing creature is facing food. But, to allow that, our reductionist may claim, is *thereby* to allow a notion of content as given by those satisfaction and truth conditions. And on that notion of content our creature has beliefs and desires with reflexive content.[12]

Suppose we agree, that the satisfaction conditions of a desire that brings about action needs to be reflexively specified, and that desires have a kind of content that is reflexively specified, that we might call reflexive content. Suppose we further agree that this means that the beliefs that

[12] Note that Perry in fact allows for distinct notions of belief content. He argues that primitive first-personal beliefs require no representation of themselves by their subjects and will accept that, on a notion of belief content as constituted by representations, a creature has unstructured content, rather than first-personal content.

motivate actions, given desires, have a kind of reflexive content and that there is therefore a notion of content on which conclusion 2 is true. Such allowances seem to do little to obviate the need for an account of first-person reference. To establish that there is a kind of content that is reflexive is not yet to have established that the creature whose attitude is characterized by such content has the capacity for reflexive reference, never mind the capacity for first-person reference. To establish *that* the reductionist needs to establish that the elements of all contents of the kind determined by satisfaction or truth conditions, correspond to capacities of the subject whose attitudes they characterize. However, the notion of content that the reductionist is suggesting seems precisely to outstrip the capacities of the subject whose beliefs and desires it is supposed to capture. Our creature may be thought to have belief contents that are reflexively specifiable, but without the creature having a capacity to master a rule reflexive reference it is a stretch to suppose that it also has a capacity for systematically reflexive reference. Perhaps the reductionist will claim that a creature has a capacity to refer to itself, in some sense, *simply in virtue* of the fact that the satisfaction conditions of its belief are reflexively satisfied. That means that the subject is assumed to have the capacity to reflexively ascribe a property even though it is agreed that it has no capacity to ascribe the property, assumed to be self-ascribed, to another subject, and it is therefore agreed that it has the capacity to self-ascribe the property without there being any meaningful sense in which the subject can be said to know that it is reflexively referring, and that in doing so it is referring to itself. I think it now becomes clear that even if we allow the reductionist to claim that the subject can be said to be reflexively referring, simply in virtue of acting on desires with reflexively specified satisfaction conditions, the nature of the capacity being ascribed to the subject cannot be the capacity for first-person reference that has been the focus of our concerns.

I have allowed that the reductionist has good reason to hold conclusion 1. In so far as we take content ascription to be constrained by the capacities of the subject, we saw reason to worry about 2. It is not clear why 1 implies the need for reflexive contents rather than simply indicating a fact about certain representations. But, whether we have these worries will depend upon what we want our notion of content to do. So, I suggested that we allow the reductionist that there is a kind of content determined by truth or satisfaction conditions, taking content ascription to be not so constrained. We then saw reason to worry about conclusion 3. What capacity for reflexive reference on the part of the creature could be assumed by having attitudes with content of that sort? It is agreed that the creature does not know that it is reflexively referring and does not know that in doing so it is referring to itself, rather than another. The capacity can only amount to one the subject has, by definition, in virtue of having desires and beliefs whose satisfaction and belief conditions are reflexively specified. However, if that is what the capacity for reflexive reference amounts to it is a very different capacity from the capacity for first-person reference that we initially set it our aim to explain. Such first-person reference was expressive of self-consciousness, involving a subject referring to herself as object, knowing that it is herself, rather than another, that she is referring to. Neither the reflexively specified contents, taken to be ubiquitous by the equation of desire content and satisfaction conditions, nor the unstructured desires for food, seem to involve first-person reference in that sense.

While all this is true, there in fact need be no genuine dispute with the reductionist as long as we restrict the scope of her approach. We can allow the reductionist to claim that there is a kind of systematically reflexive content that is implied by no more than having desires with reflexively specified satisfaction conditions. Although such use would I think be reformative of our normal use, we can even call such content first-person content, if we like. We can further allow a notion of reference according to which being in a state characterized by such reflexive, or supposedly first-person content, implies a capacity for reflexive or first-person reference. Indeed it seems very plausible that there are, what we might call, self-indicating contents that are more primitive than first personal contents. A reductionist account of such contents, in terms of reflexive satisfaction and truth conditions, may very well be the right one.

However, it also seems clear that there is a distinctive phenomenon of self-conscious reflexive reference—as when Oedipus realizes that *he* is the killer of Laius—that is not reducible to the reductionist's minimalist conception of first-person reference. Such a capacity for first-person reference involves elements that the reductionist will acknowledge that his simple creature does not exhibit. Most importantly, as we characterized first-person reference at the beginning, first-person reference is guaranteed to refer in three ways: a subject using 'I' is guaranteed (i) to refer, (ii) to refer to herself and (iii) to refer to herself, *as herself.* To think of oneself in the first-person way involves thought of oneself as both the subject and object of reference. An adequate account of what it is to think of oneself in that way is still to be given. However, the reductionist denies that such an account is even needed. The reductionist approach allows that a simple creature can think first-personally despite having no capacity to ascribe a predicate to itself, in contrast to another, and despite lacking any self-consciousness or, indeed, consciousness of its mental states. The creature cannot, therefore, be granted any knowledge of the rule governing first-person reference, nor any awareness of its thoughts or utterances.

That the normal understanding of first-person reference is not captured by the reductionist account is, I hope, plausible. Given this, it seems that, with the reductionist approach to the explanation problem, the individuation problem in fact re-emerges. *If* all it takes for a creature to be credited with the capacity to use the concept 'I' in accord with SRR is that it carry out actions on the basis of desires, despite lacking any capacity to refer to itself self-consciously, then an appeal to SRR will not even be sufficient to individuate first-person reference in the non-reductive sense. Thus, the task of explaining why 'I', as governed by SRR, is expressive of full self-conscious self-reference has not been avoided by the reductionist strategy.

2.2 The two-tier strategy

We indicated that there were two strategies one might adopt for dealing with explanation problem. We have dealt with the reductionist strategy. The other strategy—a version of which I will recommend—is to acknowledge that to appeal to SRR on its own is inadequate, and but show that appeal to further features that are in play when we use 'I', as governed by SRR, is sufficient to explain self-conscious self-reference.[13]

---

[13] There is further more a 'top-down' strategy. One might hold that we need to explain why 'I' is expressive of self-consciousness, but deny, as Campbell (1994) seems to, that the explanation of why 'I' is expressive of self-consciousness lies in facts about how 'I' refers. Campbell takes there to be general demand that the conceptual role of a singular term be in concord with what fixes its reference. In particular, 'the bases on which judgements using a singular term are made must yield knowledge of the object assigned as the reference' (137). Perhaps the fact that 'I' is expressive of self-consciousness can be explained by pointing out that given (i) the general demand, and (ii) that 'I' is governed by SRR, the bases on which judgements using 'I' are made are such that they must yield knowledge of the particular person judging.

Such an explanation may tell us why 'I' must be expressive of self-consciousness. It does not, however, tell us how 'I' meets the condition of being expressive of self-consciousness. It may be that in the end we conclude that the best explanation we can give of why 'I' is expressive of self-consciousness is by appeal to certain general norms. However, in what follows I consider attempts to provide a more substantial, 'bottom-up' answer, in preparation for an attempt to offer one.

In *Sense and Content*, Peacocke presents a version of the second strategy. He argues that if I understand any expression in my language as a device governed by the rule that the expression refers to whoever uses it, then in using that device I will be referring to myself in the first-person way. This is because:

> Each person usually knows of the utterances he intentionally produces that it is indeed he who is producing them. (Peacocke 1983: 137)

This means that given that we have the capacity to know that we are uttering when we are, we can give an account of our use of the first-person pronoun by identifying 'I' as a device of reflexive reference, in accord with SRR. Why is such an account not blatantly circular? If our knowledge that we are uttering when we are is first-personal it might seem that we are explaining first-person reference by assuming a capacity for first-person reference. Peacocke avoids such circularity, however, by distinguishing two different kinds of first-person reference: first-person reference in language and first-person reference in thought. We *can* give an account of the first-person pronoun by appealing to SRR. However, such an account rests, according to Peacocke, on an independent, and distinct, capacity to think of ourselves first-personally in thought. Thus, for Peacocke, a complete account of first-person reference will involve both SRR applied to 'I' in English, and an independent account of the first-person way of thinking, that is expressed in the user's knowledge that *she* is the producer of her utterances. It is clear that the account would face blatant circularity unless it held that there are two different kinds of first-person reference in operation, each amenable to different explanation. Let us call the strategy of solving the problem of first-person reference by assuming a distinction between first-person reference at two levels (in his case, between first-person reference in language and in thought) the two tier strategy.

This form of the two-tier strategy seems to face a problem: the problem comes from the fact that when we use 'I' in language we seem to be directly expressing our first-person thoughts. What is *prima facie* worrying about spoken first-person reference needing the speaker to identify herself as the speaker, as is claimed on Peacocke's two-tier account, is that the link between the term 'I' and the first-person thoughts it is used to express begins to look over-complicated. Use of SRR, on this account, determines the first-person way of thinking of oneself and so any expression that is governed by such a rule will express first-person thoughts. However, we will not have a satisfactory account if this determination, and so the link between uses of 'I' and the first-person thoughts they express, relies merely on the fact that speakers usually know that it is *they* who are speaking, as they might usually know that others are speaking. If it is the case that the realization required on the part of the speaker is frequently not forthcoming, that the speaker can mistakenly identify someone else as the speaker, or even that the speaker can be in a position to know that 'the speaker is using 'I'' without being sure that she is the speaker, then it is hard to see how we can suppose the term governed by SRR rule can be used for the direct expression of self-conscious thoughts. It seems plain that the subject of such thoughts, and thus of the direct articulation of them, cannot be said to have a problem about knowing who her first-personal remark is about, as if awaiting the adjudication on whether or not she is the speaker.

We might try to solve this problem by exploring the nature of the knowledge that a subject has that she is speaking. If this knowledge is available without the need for the subject to identify the speaker as herself, but it is of kind that in speaking the subject immediately knows that *she* is speaking, then we might be able to preserve the idea that 'I' is a direct articulation of self-conscious thought.

Suppose it is suggested that we can preserve the idea that 'I' is a direct articulation of self-conscious thought by pointing out that a subject's belief that she is speaking is normally based on grounds that render the belief immune to error through misidentification. That is, for the subject to have grounds of a certain kind for the belief that someone is speaking is just for her to have grounds for the belief that *she* is speaking. Thus, if a subject forms the belief that she is speaking, on such grounds, then there is no possibility of her belief being mistaken as a result of there being someone speaking that the subject mistakes for herself. This might seem to close the gap that threatened to emerge between the subject's thought of 'the speaker' and the subject's thought of herself.

The suggestion might seem to provide a partial answer to the problem raised. But, as yet, what is being offered is rather the shape of a solution rather than the solution itself. It may indeed be the case that what we need is the possibility of identification that is immune to error through misidentification, but the nature of the phenomenon needs careful characterization. In particular, we need to be clear about what precisely the grounds are which are said to support the belief that is immune to error through misidentification, and not beliefs of a certain type *tout court*. In this case, it does not seem sufficient, for example, to say that it is the simple motions of speech, of which the subject is aware, that explain the appropriateness of SRR governing that term by means of which we directly express self-conscious thought. It is essential that what is known is an act of speaking that the speaker intentionally produces. This is so, because we can make limited sense of a functioning human body acting as a mere mouthpiece for a distinct subject. Suppose a super scientist were to use another human being as her mouthpiece by appropriately stimulating her victim's vocal cords and so on. Then in order for the victim to be the referent of any 'I'-utterances that issue from her mouth, we need to make sense of them being in some sense *her* utterances. However, what is going to determine whose utterances they are is who has intentional control over them.[14] As long as the speech produced by the victim is not under her intentional control we cannot take her to be referring to herself. Rather, the utterances will refer to the scientist. The 'intentional control' spoken of by Peacocke is essential to the account. 'I' refers to whoever has the control over its production.

Therefore, even if a subject were in a position to know, on grounds that were immune to error through misidentification, that there were certain motions in her head and throat and that certain noises were being emitted from her mouth, as one might know in a way that is immune to error through misidentification that one's hair is blowing in the wind, this would not be sufficient for a token of 'I' that issued from the subject's lips to refer to her. Nor, of course, would such a subject be properly thought of as the speaker. Thus what seems to be important is that what is known in a way that is immune to error through misidentification is an intentional act on the part of the subject.

The second issue that the two-tier strategy faces is that it replaces the demand for an explanation of first-person reference at one level by a demand for an explanation of first-person reference at another. We might now understand why the first-person pronoun as governed by SRR is expressive of self-conscious self-reference, but we now also need an explanation of the kind of first-person reference at the level of thought. And it is important to note that if it is to be first-person reference at all, first-person reference at the level of thought must also

---

[14] If I utter 'I am cold' as a result of brainwashing or hypnosis we might think that I am not a mere mouthpiece, but that nevertheless my utterances are not under my intentional control. It seems to me that in such a case whether the speaker is genuinely referring to herself in the first-person way is correlated with whether she has any control over the production of her utterances. If she really has none, then while hearers might take her to self-refer in virtue of understanding the term 'I' she in fact does not.

be self-conscious reflexive reference: it must involve the subject referring to herself, aware that she is doing so. What explains the latter kind of self-conscious self-reference?

The two-tier strategy used a prior capacity for first-person reference in thought, to explain how we use 'I' in language to express self-consciousness. However, if we acknowledge that this prior capacity for first-person reference is equally subject to SRR and the associated guarantees, we have as yet no way of explaining such reference. And we clearly face a problematic regress if the explanatory demand at the level of thought is met in the same way as the demand at the level of language; that is, by postulating a yet further capacity for first-person reference.

Peacocke's own suggestion seems to be that we give an account of first-person reference, in thought, in terms of a capacity of a subject to refer demonstratively to her own conscious states.[15] The subject's capacity to think of herself in the first-person way is explained by her capacity to think of herself as the thinker of 'these' conscious thoughts. It seems, however, that such an appeal to demonstrative reference will prove either redundant or inadequate. Suppose we are able to give an account of a kind of demonstrative reference, 'THESE' say, for which it is true that if a person identifies someone as the thinker of 'THESE' thoughts they are, *thereby*, guaranteed to think of themselves in the first-person way. It seems that such an account would be able to serve *directly* to ground reference to the thinker's thoughts as 'mine', and so to ground reference in the first-person way making the appeal to the demonstrative redundant. Any grounds that are adequate to explain the application of the demonstrative 'THESE' would be sufficient to explain the application of 'my'. If, on the other hand, the capacity to refer using 'THESE' is not sufficient to guarantee that the subject thinks of 'THESE thoughts' as 'my thoughts', but is nevertheless supposed to explain first-person reference in thought, the claim that all first-person reference is necessarily and transparently reference to the referring subject looks in danger of contravention. The subject might refer to herself as the thinker of 'THESE' thoughts without, thereby, knowing that she is referring to herself.[16]

---

[15] I say 'seems' because Peacocke does not quite *analyse* the first-person way of thinking in terms of 'the thinker of these thoughts. He takes them to share the same rational role, and takes the first-person way of thinking to be illuminated by appeal to the demonstrative identification.

[16] Note also that it seems to be a consequence of the suggested account of first-person reference that it make 'I' equivocal between its use in utterances and thoughts. It

For these reasons I am sceptical of the idea that there is a capacity to refer demonstratively to one's own mental states that is both more primitive than the capacity to refer to them—even in thought—as *my* mental states, and that is nevertheless adequate to secure first-person reference in thought. This is not to rule out an account of first-person reference that appeals to a way in which we are aware of our thoughts that is prior to any capacity to refer to them or self-ascribe them. (Indeed, as will become clear, I hold that there is such awareness and that an adequate account of first-person will need to appeal to it.) Further, it does not to rule out a kind of awareness of our thoughts that *is* capable of grounding a sort of demonstrative reference that is independent of our capacity to self-refer. However, if we were to try to base first-person reference in thought on such latter awareness we would face a problem in securing the self-consciousness that accompanies such reference. Suppose that a subject has as a kind of immediate access to a thought that grounds a demonstrative identification. Now suppose that that demonstrative identification is distinct from any first-personal identification. If the thinker were to identify herself descriptively as 'the thinker of that thought' using the demonstrative as a fixed point it need not follow that the speaker think of herself in the first-person way. In fact this maybe exactly what happens in cases of 'thought insertion'. Suppose a schizophrenic subject demonstratively identifies what are in fact her own thoughts presented to her in a particular way. If she then identifies someone as the thinker of this thought it does not follow that she thereby identifies it as *her* thought. This, I think, shows that if there is a kind of awareness that we take to underlie our capacity to refer first-personally we should think of first-person reference as being directly and immediately warranted by such awareness, without any need for a mediating demonstrative reference. Furthermore, given the nature of brute perceptual connections if the kind of awareness we have of our thoughts is a quasi-perceptual awareness, in which our thoughts are presented to us as input of a certain kind, there will always be the possibility of demonstrative identifying them in a way that is not immediately and directly sufficient for a first-person identification. If we are to appeal to an awareness of our thoughts in an account of first-person reference, we should appeal to a kind of awareness that is non-perceptual and that immediately grounds first-person identification.

retains something like Frege's distinction between the 'I' of soliloquy and the 'I' of communication.

In what follows I will argue that it is only as the agents of our thoughts that we have the kind of awareness suited to an account of first-person reference.

Before leaving discussion of the two-tier strategy let me note that we have so far been considering a two-tier strategy within which the separation between the two tiers is marked by the separation between language and thought. However, we could take the separation to be one between conceptual and non-conceptual identifications.[17] The claim might be that there is a kind of first-person reference at the conceptual level that is explained by the subject's mastery of the principle that 'I' refers to its user. When it is objected that such mastery will allow the subject to refer to herself first personally only if she knows that she, herself is the user, the reply might be that there is a capacity for first-person reference at the non-conceptual level that enables her to have the required knowledge without rendering the account circular. On this strategy there are again postulated two kinds of first-person reference, both operative in thought and language and one more primitive than the other. The more primitive kind of non-conceptual first-person reference is supposed to explain the capacity to refer to ourselves at the conceptual level, given our mastery of the self-reference principle.

As will emerge in what follows, I take this version of the two-tier strategy to be right in appealing to the non-conceptual level: there is a non-conceptual awareness that is involved in first-person reference. However, this two-tier strategy does not only appeal to the non-conceptual level, it appeals to first-person reference at the non-conceptual level. Even if there is non-conceptual first-person reference this construal of the two-tier strategy will face challenges similar to the earlier one. If something like SRR governs all forms of first-person reference we need to know what it is for a representation to be governed by SRR at the non-conceptual level. Perhaps it is for there to be a non-conceptual representation, call it 'I_{nc}', that non-conceptually represents the subject in which it occurs. But we again need to explain why a subject's representing something as 'I_{nc}' constitutes a representation of it that expresses the subject's self-consciousness. This two-tier theorist again faces the prospect of appealing to a regress of distinct kinds

---

[17] Bermúdez (1998) endorses such a view. However, he also claims close dependency between conceptual abilities and linguistic ones, claiming that mastery of the concept 'I', in contrast to the capacity for non-conceptual first-person referring, requires mastery of the semantics of the first-person pronoun (44). His version of the two-tier strategy is, therefore, not dissimilar to Peacocke's.

of first-personal reference, or of grounding first-person reference at the non-conceptual level in some other kind of identification.

3. CONCLUSION

In the following chapter I will turn to my own suggestion as to how we should explain first-person reference. However, before doing so, let me briefly summarize where we have got to so far. This will enable me to gather together constraints and desiderata that will structure how we proceed.

1. *Appeal to our use of SRR to meet the individuation problem*
Lewis's gods fully understand SRR but are unable to refer first personally. The reductionist's simple creatures are claimed to have a capacity to refer in accordance with SRR independent of any capacity to understand the rule, or be conscious of the thoughts characterized by it. But, they are unable to refer first-personally in our sense. However, it seems that SRR is able to individuate first-person reference in our case because of features of our use of 'I', that are absent in the case of gods and simple creatures.

2. *Appeal to SRR plus further features to solve the explanation problem*
The explanation problem was not met by a simple appeal to SRR. The most promising approach to the explanation problem seems to be to show how the further features present in our use of 'I' operate with the use of SRR to give us self-conscious self-reference.

3. *Which further features?*
Lewis's gods are supposed to understand SRR and be able to use 'I', but they lack a capacity to self-consciously self-refer. On applying SRR the gods still do not know that they, themselves are the objects of reference. That seems possible because the gods lack awareness that they are also the subjects of reference; the gods lack awareness that they, themselves are using 'I' when they are. The reductionist's simple creatures are supposed to have thought contents governed by SRR, but they seem to lack a capacity to self-consciously self-refer. That seems possible because they are credited with thought contents governed by SRR despite having no understanding of SRR, and despite not being conscious of using 'I'.

This suggests that an adequate account of first-person reference ought to appeal to a subject's mastery of SRR and her awareness of using 'I' when she does.

4. *Avoid appealing to a prior capacity for first-person reference*
From the discussion of the two-tier strategy it emerged that an explanation of how an understanding of SRR enables a subject to refer to herself first-personally faces threats of circularity, regress or insufficiency. It seems sensible to aim to give such an explanation in a way that does not invoke a capacity for first-person reference: either of the same kind or of an alternative kind.

5. *Avoid appealing to prior capacity for demonstrative reference*
We saw that the two-tier strategy, which aims to ground first-person reference in demonstrative reference to the thoughts of the subject, faces either redundancy or insufficiency. Either the grounds of such a demonstrative would be sufficient immediately to ground first-person reference, in which case our account should identify such awareness and appeal to it immediately. Or the grounds of such a demonstrative will make it possible that the subject fails to know that it is her, herself she is referring to via use of such a demonstrative.

6. *Non-first-personal self-consciousness*
If we are to, as I have suggested we should, appeal to the awareness we have of our uses of 'I' while avoiding appeal to a prior capacity for first-person reference, we must identify a form of self-consciousness that is prior to, and independent of, our capacity for first-person reference.

7. *Non-perceptual self-consciousness*
If we are to appeal to an awareness of our uses of 'I' that is sufficient to ground genuine first-person reference we should avoid perceptual models of such awareness, on pain of failing to meet the guarantees involved in first-person reference. I will try to show that in the awareness an agent has of her own actions (agent's awareness) we find a primitive, non-conceptual, non-perceptual form of self-consciousness that will play a key role in explaining first-person reference.

5

The Agency Account

In the previous chapter we concluded that SRR is not on its own sufficient to provide an *explanation* of what makes first-person reference self-conscious self-reference. We considered the two-tier strategy according to which our mastery of SRR is sufficient to secure first-person reference because of an underlying and distinct capacity for first-person reference. This seemed problematic. On the two-tier strategy, first-person reference is taken to be equivocal and to come in two different forms at different levels. On pain of blatant circularity this faced the two-tier theorist with a choice: either of embracing a regress of kinds of first-person reference, or of providing an alternative explanation of the underlying capacity for first-person reference in terms that did not appeal to SRR. The suggestion considered was that of basing the underlying form of first-person reference on a capacity for demonstratively identifying one's own thought. An explanation of first-person reference in terms of demonstrative reference was criticized and seemed to fail to acknowledge the fact that all first-person reference is essentially both reflexive and self-conscious.

Nevertheless, we should retain much of the two-tier strategy. First, it is right to claim, with the two-tier strategist, that first-person reference at the linguistic or conceptual level is governed by SRR. Secondly, it seems right to take the explanation problem that survives appeal only to SRR seriously. First-person reference is *self-conscious* self-reference and we need to explain why a term or concept governed by SRR is used by a subject to refer to herself, as herself. Thirdly, in meeting the explanation problem it is plausible to appeal to a subject's *understanding* of SRR. When we refer to ourselves using the term or concept 'I' it is not just that we bring it about that we satisfy 'x is referring to x', we also refer to ourselves intending for it to be the case that 'x is referring to x'. When a person comprehendingly uses 'I' as governed by SRR she uses a term or concept knowing that its function is to bring about reflexive reference.

Fourthly, it is surely right to think that a comprehending use of 'I' is *sufficient* to give us first-person reference, understood as self-conscious reflexive reference, given that a subject knows that she is referring, when she is. Of course, it is in the explication of this knowledge that regress or insufficiency threatens. Nevertheless, it is plausible to think that the self-consciousness involved in first-person thought arises from a joint operation of our understanding of 'I' and our awareness of our acts of reference.

If we are to retain these key features of the two-tier account we need to provide a suitable account of what is involved in the claim that a subject is aware that she is referring when she is. However, whatever account we give will need to attend to the threats of insufficiency or regress. On the one hand, we want to avoid the two-tier strategy's commitment to a prior capacity for first-person reference whose conformity to SRR has not been explained. But equally, we want our account of the subject's awareness that she is thinking or uttering to be *sufficient* to explain why a subject who refers to herself first-personally knows that in reflexively referring she is referring to *herself*. How can we explain such knowledge, which is naturally expressed by use of the first person, without assuming a prior capacity for first-person reference?

I want to explore the suggestion that we can give an adequate account of first-person reference if we take the central cases for explaining first-person reference to be those in which the subject can said to be an agent. Much of our mental lives are active. When we think, judge, question, imagine, suppose, decide, deny, reflect, and so on, we are *prima facie* involved in mental actions or activities. Less contentiously, when we express our judgements, questions, and so on, in utterances we function as agents. I want to consider what account of first-person reference is available if we take it as given that our thoughts and utterances are actions or activities of a subject functioning as an agent. I am going to explore the idea that we can put together a satisfying account of first-person reference if put together our capacity to operate with SRR with an awareness of ourselves that we have through participating in our own actions. I want to argue however, *pace* the *two-tier account,* that the kind of awareness of our actions that is involved need not be thought to involve first-person reference. Nevertheless, I will claim that such awareness is sufficient to explain why a subject who uses SRR can be said to believe that *she* is the referrer. Such awareness is sufficient to ground first-person beliefs when it is awareness by a subject who has a capacity for mastery of SRR.

Note that it is natural to look to our awareness of actions in our attempt to develop an account of the kind of awareness that, when combined with mastery of SRR, will deliver an account of first-person reference. Our awareness of our actions has features that suggest that it is suited to playing a particularly crucial role in characterizing the nature of self-conscious thought. It promises to give us a way of being aware of ourselves as a subject, rather than an object. Central to the account to be offered is the thought that there is a vital asymmetry between the way we stand to what may be called input, and the way we stand to our controlled output. We have seen, in earlier chapters, that accounts of first-person reference that seek to explain how we identify ourselves on the basis of information received are likely to be unsuccessful. The possibility of information failing to come from the source that we take it to come from means that such accounts fail to secure guaranteed reference. Our relation to our controlled outputs is quite different. We stand to our actions as agents, not as receivers, and I simply cannot stand to another's action as an agent. Thus, if we identify a kind of awareness we have of ourselves as agents it will be particularly well fitted to functioning as the grounds for self-ascriptions that are immune to error through misidentification. In what follows I will argue that there is a form of awareness had by creatures capable of controlling their actions, mental and physical, that is independent of any capacity of the creature to understand the term or concept 'I', that is both non-conceptual and non-perceptual in nature and yet that is capable of immediately warranting the self-ascription of the action that the creature is aware of in this way. However, before turning to the task of characterizing the awareness we have of our use of 'I', I want to consider the structure of the account of first-person reference in which such awareness is supposed to play a key part.

The form of the account to be offered is this: The first-person pronoun and first-person concept can quite generally be characterized as reflexively referential. 'I'-thoughts and utterances are thoughts and utterances that refer to the subject thinking and uttering them. And in a way this is all that needs to be said about first-person reference. The reason that this is sufficient to give us *self-conscious* self-reference is that our use of a term or concept governed by SRR is such that, at the same time as reflexively referring, it can give us knowledge that we are referring, when we are.

We can set things out more clearly if we identify three elements that play a role in the account:

A. Mastery of SRR: A subject who is able to refer first-personally uses the term or concept 'I' as governed by the rule that it that refers to its user.

B. Knowledge of use of 'I': A subject who is able to refer first-personally must have a capacity to know that she, herself is using 'I' when she is.

C. Agent's Awareness: A subject who is able to refer first-personally must have a capacity to be aware of her own acts of thinking and uttering that does not imply a prior capacity for first-person reference.

The suggestion is that if these three components are in place then we have a subject who is capable of first-person reference. The three components are not independent, however. Suppose a subject meets condition A—she uses 'I' as governed by SRR, and meets condition B—she is able to know that in so using 'I' that she is referring to herself. That seems to be sufficient for her to be said to be able to refer first-personally. However, condition B—the knowledge that a subject can have that she is referring to herself—while plausibly a condition of first-person reference, is itself first-personal and so not going to be able to explain that capacity. This was the blatant circularity that 'reflexive' account of first-person reference seemed to meet. We, therefore, need to appeal to something more primitive than condition B. The suggestion is that meeting condition C and meeting condition A enables one to meet B, and thus meet the conditions on first-person reference.

The central idea is that a subject who uses 'I' in accordance with SRR, and who has agent's awareness of what she is doing, thereby simultaneously refers to herself first-personally and is able to know that she is so referring. We can call this the agency account.

The outline of the agency account comes from adapting the two-tier strategy in an attempt to avoid circularity or regress. As yet, it has little substance of its own. There are two key tasks that need to be undertaken if we are to give it any.

First, we need to make it plausible that an account of this *form* is of a kind that can explain first-person reference. When we asked how it is that mastery of SRR is sufficient to secure self-conscious self-reference, given that it is a principle of reflexive reference only, the two-tier strategist claimed that it is because the speaker or thinker knows 'I am speaking or thinking' when she is. Invoking such a prior capacity for first-person reference may have proved to have the costs either of circularity, or regress but it answered the question. We might now worry that the attempt to ground that account in a form of awareness that is supposed not to be first-personal may avoid such problems only at the cost of not being able to answer the question at all. Thus, we need to explain how a non-first-personal awareness of our thoughts and utterances can coordinate with knowledge of SRR to produce a capacity to refer first-personally, and with it the capacity to know that one is so referring.

Secondly, we need to say something about agent's awareness. We can perhaps see what it must not be, if we are to avoid the pitfalls of the two-tier or perceptual-demonstrative accounts, but we need to say a bit more about what it is.

1. THE FORM OF THE ACCOUNT

We identified two tasks that need to be undertaken if any substance is to be given to the outline of the account offered. Let me now turn to the first of them: to make it plausible that our account has the proper *form* to explain first-person reference. There is, *prima facie*, a problem with the account. The supposition is that there is a form of awareness we have of our own uses of 'I', in speech and thought, that is not itself first-personal, but that is nevertheless capable of explaining why a use of 'I' as governed by SRR gives the user knowledge that she is referring to *herself*. There is a concern that such awareness would be able to play the role required of it only if it were assumed to be first-personal awareness, involving first-personal reference. But that would then render the account circular or regressive.

We might imagine the objection being put as follows. We formed the account offered above as a response to the thought that SRR cannot explain first-person reference without invoking a prior, and therefore unexplained, capacity for self-reference. The thought that we need such prior self-identification rested on the claim that in first-person reference I am not just referring to myself reflexively, rather I must also be aware that in reflexively referring I am referring to myself. That is we need more than knowledge that 'I' refers to its producer in order for it to be the case that I know that a particular token of 'I' refers to me. The answering suggestion was that the missing element was provided by the fact that I have a certain kind of awareness of my actions. Moreover, it was suggested, we can avoid circularity or regress here by pointing out that the awareness of my actions, that I create by acting, thinking and uttering, is of a different and more primitive kind than the self-awareness constituted by a capacity for first-person reference. It is non-conceptual and non-first-personal.

But now, it may be said, we can avoid the threat of circularity or regression only by the self-awareness invoked being of a kind that then proves insufficient to turn the knowledge that I am reflexively referring into knowledge that I am referring to *myself.* The worry will be that we are trading on an ambiguity in awareness.[1] Suppose that a capacity for first-person reference requires the subject to know SRR and to know that she is using 'I', and that the latter kind of knowledge is first-personal propositional knowledge. If it is also claimed that we have a non-conceptual awareness of using 'I', we might then wonder how that is supposed to help explain the kind of propositional first-personal knowledge we assumed was needed.

The worry might be developed as follows: the account suggests that a subject is able to refer to herself first-personally only if she knows 'I' is governed by SRR and knows that for any use of 'I' in accordance with SRR that 'I' refers to herself. The claim is then made that she is able to come by the latter knowledge, given the former, because she knows that she is the producer of her uses of 'I'. We can, the objector might propose, present the suggested progression of the subject's knowledge as an inference of the following kind:

1. 'I' refers to its producer.
2. I am the producer.

Therefore:

3. 'I' refers to me.

Prima facie, however the subject is entitled to her conclusion only on the assumption that there is no equivocation. Suppose that the conclusion 3 expresses the subject's first-personal knowledge that she, herself is the referent of 'I'. It seems then that the second premise of the argument must be a proposition of identity with the first-person on one flank. In which case, it will be claimed, the first-person is being used to explain the first-person. If instead the second premise is taken to express something other than an identity statement involving the first-person, say a subject's non-first-personal awareness of producing 'I', then the claim will be that there is an equivocation between 'I' as it appears in

---

[1] Thanks to Johannes Roessler for putting the point in this way.

the second premise and 'me' as it appears in the third. In which case, the argument would not be valid.[2]

Dealing with this objection will enable us to bring out the way in which the distinct aspects of the account are supposed to work in concert. The first point to make is that the objector seems to take it that the situation is properly captured in the form of a deductive propositional argument. But this is a mistake for a number of reasons.

1.1 The normative role of non-conceptual elements

The account offered draws on a non-conceptual awareness that a subject has of her own thoughts and utterances. Therefore, it cannot be assumed that the normative role of such awareness can be represented in the form of a propositional argument. If we were to try to represent the normative role of such awareness in an argument form, perforce requiring conceptual articulation, we would be bound to end up with an argument that appeared circular or ambiguous.

There is needed an acknowledgement that normative connections can outstrip our standard representations of them in impersonal inferential schemata. This acknowledgement is in fact widespread. Indeed, we accept that in order to take an instance of the argument like the one presented above as valid, we already need to assume that the premises are held roughly contemporaneously, by a single person speaking one language. (We do not take 3 to follow from 2 if we hold 3 and 2 to be uttered or thought by different subjects.) The demand that such conditions be stated within the argument leads to regress. More pertinently, it is also widely held that our warrants for our perceptual beliefs are not well represented by such schemata. Suppose that my warrant for holding that 'The door is ahead' is simply my seeing that it is. The schema:

1. I see that the door is ahead

therefore:

2. The door is ahead

importantly misrepresents the nature of my warrant.[3] I want to claim that such schemata are in a similar way insufficient to represent the role of agent's awareness in first-person reference. We have supposed that a

---

[2] I owe this objection to John Campbell.
[3] See Burge (2003); Pryor (2000, 2005).

subject's awareness of her use of 'I', with mastery of SRR, immediately warrants knowledge that *she* is using 'I', and in so doing warrants knowledge that she is referring to herself. The explanation of such a warrant is something we will come back to. Roughly, it lies in the fact that an agent's actions are determinations by a person for herself.

But perhaps the problem is not that we are supposing that a form of awareness can itself warrant knowledge. Perhaps the problem is supposed to come from the fact that the non-conceptual awareness is asked to play a role in giving an account of a capacity for reference that is *itself* used in the expression of the schema. Let us consider how the problem fares in relation to a more widely accepted story about the way in which a capacity for non-conceptual awareness may ground a capacity for reference.

Suppose it is held that 'this' refers to an object of perceptual attention and held that one cannot refer to an object using 'this' unless one knows which object one is attending to. Suppose, further, that it is claimed that one's knowing which object one is attending to is grounded in a certain kind of non-conceptual perceptual awareness of the object. It would be a mistake to suppose that such an account is either circular, or trades on an ambiguity on the grounds that the following argument is either circular or equivocal:

(i) 'this' refers to the object being attended to
(ii) this object is the one being attended to

therefore:

(iii) 'this' refers to this object.

It seems true that if I refer to an object as 'this' then I must know that 'this' refers to this object. It is also true that this knowledge rests on my knowledge that 'this' refers to the object being attended to, and my knowledge that this object is the one being attended to. It does not follow from this that the *account* is circular. Although the argument assumes a capacity for demonstrative reference in its expression, the subject's knowledge expressed by (ii) is assumed not to be basic but rather to rest on perceptual awareness of the object. Nor does it follow that the account is equivocal. If it is the case that a subject who knows (i) requires only a certain kind perceptual awareness of the object in order to know (ii) then she can be said to know (iii). So, as long as the account can explain why and how the knowledge expressed in (ii) is provided by a distinct awareness of the object then it avoids the objection.

The account of first-person reference that has been proposed can begin to meet the objection in a similar way: by denying that the argument schema properly represents matters and by showing why and how our awareness of using 'I' provides knowledge that we, ourselves are using 'I'.

1.2 Making sense

Consideration of the argument presented by our objector enables us to bring out a further feature of the account being offered. The account attempts to explain why use of a term or concept governed by SRR will result in a subject thinking of herself in a self-conscious way. It does so by suggesting that that way of thinking is *generated* by the joint operation of the application of SRR and agent's awareness. The full sense of 'I' is, on the account, best seen as a product of two components: the capacity to reflexively refer by use of SRR and agent's awareness. The objection, as set out, ignores this aspect of the account. Consider the objection that if we read step 2 of the argument as involving first-person reference, then the account is circular. It is true that, if we read step 2 as expressing the subject's knowledge that she, herself is the producer then she must already have a capacity for first-person reference. But given her mastery of SRR and her non-conceptual awareness of using 'I' she *does*, according to the account given, thereby attain a capacity for first-person reference and a capacity for knowing that she, herself is the producer. If we instead read step 2 as an expression of the subject's non-conceptual agent's awareness we can, on the account offered, nevertheless take the conclusion to involve genuine first-person reference. What we have is the subject knowing 'I' refers to its producer and the subject consciously producing 'I'. These provide sufficient grounds for the subject both to generate the content and to come to know that 'I' refers to me.

The above story implies that the contents of first-person utterances or thoughts can be generated by the subject setting out to make them. But there need be nothing mysterious or problematic about this. It is entirely expected that the content of indexical and demonstrative judgements should be a joint production of rule and features of use. Otherwise we might wonder what would make the utterance or thought an indexical one.

Consider accounts of the meaning of a token 'you'. It is plausible to think that part of the content of an utterance or thought expressed by

'You are tall' will be the joint upshot of a rule that governs 'you'—'you' refers to the person being addressed', say—and the awareness by the thinker of which person is being addressed. The latter is awareness that the thinker can have independently of a capacity to master the concept 'you'. Indeed what would be mysterious if the idea that there is a special and primitive presentation of the other ready and waiting, rather than one created by the use, one by one.

We can further note that in fact any Fregean or neo-Fregean view that takes there to be a way of thinking associated with each use of a referring term, and takes indexicals such as 'I' and 'you' and 'now' to be referring terms, is going to have to choose between either accepting that the use of the indexical creates the sense on that occasion of use, or accepting that in being used it is latching on to a sense that is ready and waiting. To think that the first person in part creates its associated sense on its occasions of use seems the less problematic option.

1.3 The psychological process

The objection represents the elements involved in first-person reference in the form of a propositional argument. As we have seen, in doing so it misrepresents the normative basis of a subject's knowledge that she is referring to herself when she refers first-personally. However, it also misrepresents the psychological process that is supposed to be required for first-person reference. The account holds that the capacity for first-person reference rests upon capacities for knowledge of the kind expressed in the argument presented by the objector. However, the suggestion is not that in order to refer first-personally a subject must run through a quick deduction. The exact psychological process will differ on different occasions. It will, for example, be only in certain conditions that the subject will form occurrent beliefs corresponding to the steps in the objector's argument.[4] The subject's knowledge of her concept, and the rules that govern it, will rarely occupy space in the progress of her thought. Nor will the subject often consciously conclude ' "I" refers to me' on using the first person. However, this is compatible with holding that the capacity to refer first-personally depends upon the subject's knowledge of her concept and her capacity to know that she is using it when she is. When

---

[4] Note that, for a start, the precise terms used in the statement of the argument may not be available to many subjects capable of first-person reference.

these capacities are realized, and the knowledge is given expression in deductive form, we might have something like the objector's argument.

Although, this is true, the argument offered does show that we need further clarification of the relation between the capacities identified and the psychological processes being assumed when a subject is said to refer to herself first-personally.

The intention is for the account to allow us to ascribe a first-person thought or utterance to a subject who uses 'I', just if she knows SRR and has the capacity for agent's awareness. We might, however, wonder what to say about the following cases:

(i) A subject has knowledge of SRR, uses 'I' and is currently agent aware of doing so, but does not form a belief that she is using 'I'.
On the account proposed a subject who is agent aware of using 'I' in accord with SRR is referring first-personally. Agent awareness is supposed to be able immediately to ground knowledge of what one is doing. I have so far said nothing about what I take knowledge that one is using 'I' to consist in. In particular, I have not said whether I take knowledge to imply belief. This is not, I think, something we need to decide here. If knowledge does not require belief then the subject's mastery of SRR and her agent's awareness will itself give her knowledge that she is using 'I'. Suppose knowledge does require belief. We can expect a subject who has mastery of SRR to have the capacities required to have the belief that she is using 'I'. Given that, in the case supposed, the subject is agent-aware of using 'I' and given that agent awareness immediately warrants knowledge of what one is doing, our subject will be able to know that she is using 'I'. Thus, on the account given, the subject will be referring first-personally.

(ii) A subject has knowledge of SRR, uses 'I' but lacks agent's awareness of doing so, and does not gain immediate knowledge that she is using 'I'.
There are two kinds of case at issue here. There is the case where we a subject who has mastery of 'I' but no *capacity* for agent's awareness. According to the account given there could be no first-person reference in such a case.

The second kind of case is that in which we have mastery of SRR, a broader capacity for agent's awareness, but a lack of agent's awareness on a particular occasion of use. However, in cases where we have a local lack of agent's awareness, we should remark on a further distinction between, what we might call, an *incidental* lack and a *structural* lack. There may be uses of 'I' where the agent could easily have been agent aware—had she not been distracted, or had she wondered what she was doing. In such cases the subject seems to have both a general capacity for agent's awareness and a capacity to be agent aware on the occasion of use, but was not agent aware due to incidental perturbations. In contrast, there may be uses of 'I' from which the agent is more robustly screened. Well-known pathologies that result in subjects producing thoughts and utterances that they take to be the thoughts and utterances of others, might produce such uses. Imagine a case in which someone utters or thinks 'I am angry', but insists 'I was aware of the utterance 'I am angry' coming out of my mouth, but it was not me speaking' or 'I was aware of the thought 'I am angry', from the inside, but it is not my thought'. Does the subject refer to herself first-personally in her original utterance? In such cases, the subject may have a general capacity for agent's awareness, but we have some evidence that she lacks the capacity to be agent aware on the occasion of use.

Neither of the above cases will constitute paradigm or canonical cases of first-person reference on the account offered, because in neither case is the ability to be agent aware actually being exercised so as to provide full self-conscious self-reference. However, given that the subject has a general capacity for first-person reference, and given that she is operating with a stable term 'I', the account allows us to view her thoughts and utterances that use 'I' as first-personal, in some sense.

Nevertheless, the cases under consideration will count as first-personal only in some derivative or secondary sense. Further, it is natural to treat the case in which we have an incidental lack of agent's awareness as a more central case of first-person reference than the case in which we have a structural lack. Where the subject has an incidental lack of agent's awareness she has the capacities—both generally and locally—that are required for her to refer to herself using 'I'. Where the subject has a structural lack—on a given occasion of use—she lacks a local capacity, the exercise of which would be required for a central case of first-person reference. It seems clear if we are to count a subject's utterance of 'I', when she thinks that some-one else is speaking out of their mouth, as a first-personal we must count it as a marginal and debased case of first-person reference. It counts as marginal because we deem it to be a case of first-person reference only in virtue of a general capacities that the subject cannot—for structural reasons—exercise on that occasion. It is debased, because had the subject been able to exercise the capacities in virtue of which her alien thought or utterance counts as first-personal she could not have formed the view of her alien thought or utterance that she does.

(iii) A subject, who understands SRR, uses 'I', lacks agent's awareness, but gains knowledge about who is using 'I' from observational sources other than agent's awareness.

The case here is much as it was with (ii). If the subject lacked the capacity for agent's awareness she would not, on the view advocated be able to refer first-personally. She would, rather like Lewis's gods, be able to refer to herself reflexively, know who is referred to, but not know that *she* is the person they referred to. If, however, she has the relevant capacities, lacking them only locally, then we can allow that her use of the term 'I' as governed by SRR is in some sense first-personal. The observational knowledge of who is uttering 'I' will neither help nor hinder.

(iv) A subject, who has no understanding of SRR, utters the sound 'I'—copying other speakers in her language—and has the more primitive agent's awareness of doing so.

Although such a subject would not, on the view advocated be able to refer first-personally, we might we inclined to think of her utterance as a primitive form of first-person reference. She has all that is needed for her to refer first-personally, once she comes to comprehend the rule that governs 'I'.

2. MASTERY OF SRR

The agency account has three components. Having said something about the form of the account, and the way in which the different components are supposed to work together, I now want very briefly to comment on the first component of the account: mastery of SRR. The account assumes that the term and concept 'I' is governed by SRR: the rule that it refers to its user. It also assumes that anyone who understands

'I' will use it as governed by SRR. Now, of course, we face the question of what 'using 'I' as governed by SRR' consists in. Does it, for example, require the subject to be able to articulate SRR? If not, what conceptual resources are required by the subject who masters SRR? Can young children and mature apes have mastery of SRR?

The account does assume that mastery of the first-person pronoun or concept requires further related concepts on the part of a subject. In particular, to understand a term or a concept 'I' as governed by SRR, a subject must have the concept of a user of 'I'—a thinker or speaker. In the case of embodied creatures, like us, this probably means that a subject will not be capable of first-person thought without some inter-subjective communication of some kind with others. The account also assumes that the subject must be able to follow, and not merely conform to, the rule set down by SRR in her use of 'I'. To answer the question properly as to what it is to do *that* would be to answer the question as to what it is to follow a rule. I am not going to attempt to do that here. Let me, instead, point out that we need not take mastery of SRR to imply that the subject needs to be able to articulate SRR as we have, nor that the subject needs to be able to think of SRR as a *rule*. Thus, while mastery of SRR will require some conceptual ability on the part of the subject we need not be unduly worried about the account being over-intellectualist. When exactly we develop those capacities that I have argued are required for first-person thought, is a matter for further study. But we can expect a full capacity for first-person thought, to develop in early childhood at the point when a subject has the concept of a thinker or speaker, and that of somethings being spoken or thought about. Prior to that we will have, on the account offered, forms of self-indicating thought, and forms of consciousness that are more primitive than the capacity for first-person reference. We can further acknowledge that it will be natural to use the first-person in ascribing such thought and forms of consciousness. We may usefully describe a simple creature's self-indicating thought as the thought that 'I am facing food' and we may describe a subject's non-conceptual aware-ness of her own action as the awareness that she, herself is acting. However, while such ascriptions will reflect important features of the thoughts and consciousness being ascribed, they will be using a capac-ity for first-person reference that the ascriber, but not the ascribee, need have.

2.1 Appeal to agent's awareness

In the following chapter, we will move on to discuss the nature of agent's awareness. However, first I want to clarify what role it is intended to play and raise some objections to the idea that agent's awareness can play that role. First, let us look at the role it plays.

(i) Agent's awareness is used to explain first-person reference and thought—so it must be more primitive than, and not invoke, the capacity for first-person reference and thought.

(ii) Agent's awareness is supposed to be capable of *immediately grounding* knowledge of our actions. Furthermore, it is supposed to be capable of immediately grounding first-personal knowledge of our actions. That is, given the relevant conceptual capacities a subject who is agent-aware of using 'I' must be able immediately to know 'I am using 'I''.

(iii) Agent's awareness is a form of awareness that a subject has of her own actions, and that precedes her capacity to conceptualize it. It is a form of non-conceptual awareness.

(iv) Agent's awareness must give the subject knowledge of action in such a way that guarantees that it is the agent's own actions she is aware of in that way. Therefore, it must be a non-perceptual or quasi-perceptual form of awareness of an agent's actions. Were it to be perceptual/quasi-perceptual there would be the possibility of its source not being the agent's own actions.

(v) Agent's awareness must accompany first-person thoughts and utterances.

The account offered hinges on the idea that in thinking and uttering we have a form of awareness of our thoughts and utterances that is non-first-personal, non-conceptual, non-perceptual or quasi-perceptual, and apt for immediately grounding self-knowledge. The suggestion to be offered is that our awareness of ourselves in acting provides the best candidate to fulfil the role required. The feature that makes agent's awareness particularly suited to play the role required is that—as I will argue—agent's awareness is awareness by means of *production* rather than *reception*. While one can mistake the source of information received, even if one is the source, one cannot similarly mistake the source of awareness one has of one's actions due to producing them.

2.2 Are all first-person thoughts acts?

Let us now consider an objection. We have suggested that we can account for first-person utterances and thoughts by appealing to a kind of agent's awareness we have in thinking and uttering. We can divide this claim up in to one concerning first-person utterances and one concerning first-person thoughts. It might be thought that the suggestion is much more plausible for the claim concerning utterances than that concerning thoughts. Most people will grant that most first-person utterances are acts of a subject. If there is an awareness we have of our own actions in virtue of being their agent, then it seems unproblematic to claim that we can have such an awareness of our utterances of the first-person pronoun. Suppose we can give an account of agent's awareness in physical actions—such as utterances—and show that it can play the role identified in the account of first-person reference. We may then conclude that we have an account of first-person reference in utterances.[5] However, we may nevertheless deny that we have an account of first-person reference in thought. Many will object that not all, if any, first-person thoughts are acts. They will, therefore, object to the idea that we have agent's awareness of them.

There are those who will deny that there are any mental acts. It is, however, usually agreed that there are at least some mental acts. The dispute comes in answering the question of how many? and how common? Most will agree that visualizing a rainbow, carrying out a complex mental calculation and trying to remember a name are mental activities that involve mental acts. There are others, including myself, who hold that mental acts are commonplace and, indeed, are the chief occupants of our conscious lives. In particular, judgements, questions, suppositions are held also to be mental acts.[6] I will assume the less restricted view. It should be noted, however, that there are objections to thinking of judgements, in particular, as acts. The worry is that to do so is to adopt an overly voluntarist conception of judgement. But it is important to stress that the assumption that judgements are acts is

---

[5] We will come back to the nature of agent's awareness in physical actions in ch. 8. Note that there is a view according to which thinking is the rehearsing of sentences. If such a view were true, the claim that most utterances were actions would lead fairly directly to the claim that most thoughts were actions of a similar type, involving not the physical uttering of a sentence but the mental rehearsing of it.

[6] For recent expressions of the view see Peacocke (1999); Moran (2001); O'Brien (2005).

not meant to imply that judgements are something that the agent can merely will to do. It is entirely implausible to suppose that it is within my power to choose to make it true that I am judging that P (although it may be in my power to make it true that I come to a view with respect to P). Rather my judgements are under my rational control. That is, my judgements are acts by virtue of their relation to my capacities to take rational responsibility for them.

However, even if we can agree that judgements, questions and suppositions are mental acts we face the following objection: while many of our first-personal thoughts might be mental acts, there are surely some first-personal thoughts that are not. If we can identify some thoughts as passive, even if there are very many that are active, how can the account offered explain such thoughts, given the appeal to agent's awareness?

There are two sorts of case that come to mind. First, we seem to have a large number of first-personal beliefs understood as dispositional states that are not sufficiently 'event- or process-like' to be counted as acts or activities of the mind. Secondly, a thought can seem to occur as something that happens to me, rather than as something under my rational control. Consider when it suddenly strikes me that 'I am supposed to be outside the school gates right now', or when I persist in thinking, despite myself, 'I am going fail to get this job' throughout an interview. Such seemingly uncontrolled and unbidden thoughts are conscious and event-like, but we might doubt that we can think of them as acts of rational agency, in contrast to a judgement made on the basis of deliberation for example.[7]

There are, roughly, three options we have in responding to each putative counterexample. First, we can try to deny that it is a counterexample. Secondly, we can restrict the scope of the account, arguing that there are distinct kinds of first-personal reference in active and passive cases, and that the agency account aims to explain only the former leaving a quite distinct account to explain the latter. Thirdly, we can argue that, while there are indeed first-personal thoughts that are not actions, their status *as* first-personal thoughts is dependent on what goes on in the case of thoughts that are active. The account offered is intended to leave room for the something like the third reaction in response to such examples, so let me say something in favour of it.

Consider an example of the first kind identified. Suppose we have a subject who judges 'I am 5 ft 5 inches tall' having measured herself. Let

---

[7] Thanks to Johannes Roessler for an example of this kind.

us assume that we can plausibly attribute to such a subject the belief that 'I am taller than 3 ft 7 inches'. Furthermore let us suppose that we can plausibly attribute such a belief even if the subject has not judged that she is taller than 3 ft 7 inches. The question we then face is how we can attribute to the subject the latter first-personal belief given that there is clearly no mental action involved and so no agent's awareness. The answer in the case of such purely dispositional beliefs seems to be fairly obvious. It is plausible to suppose that such a belief counts as a belief only if the subject is also disposed, in response to the appropriate stimulus, to assert or judge 'I am taller than 3 ft 7 inches'. We might similarly claim that it counts as a first-personal belief only in virtue of the same disposition. In asserting or judging that 'I am taller than 3 ft 7 inches' the subject will have the kind of agent's awareness I have claimed is a crucial element of first-person thought, and it is in virtue of the dispositional connection to such acts of assertion or judgement that the subject's belief is capable of being construed as a first-personal belief. If the subject had no such dispositions she would not be able to have beliefs with first-person content—indeed we might doubt whether she was able to have beliefs at all.

The second kind of counterexample is, *prima facie*, less easily dealt with. Here we cited the case of thoughts or judgements that are occurrent, but that seem to come to us unbidden, and that seem not to be under our control. In the case of merely dispositional states it is natural to suppose that they can inherit their features from the acts of mind with respect to which they are individuated. So they count as first-personal in content in virtue of being dispositions to make first-person judgements, say. However, when we are dealing with occurrent thoughts, it is not obvious why we would take our ascription of content to them to depend upon ascription to other occurrent thoughts.

The first thing to say in response to these latter cases is that even if a thought arises from nowhere, unbidden, it does not follow that it is not an act. Consider the case of physical actions. There are many cases of spontaneous, often unbidden and unwelcome actions. In the case of utterances, for example, we talk to ourselves or blurt out opinions, recoiling when we realize our lack of form or tack. We are often well aware of being the agent of these actions, despite their spontaneity, and we take responsibility for them.[8] There is no reason to suppose that

---

[8] There are also things we do which are spontaneous and unbidden, but also disjoined from our control to an extent we would not consider them actions. For example, subjects

the thoughts we have, or judgements we make, cannot be acts of mind despite arising in a similarly spontaneous manner. Further, we should remember that the claim that thoughts are active does not imply that thinking is something that the agent can merely will to do. A thought can be taken to be act of mind, and an act of which the subject is agent aware, even if it is not voluntary. In so far as the thoughts of a subject are objects of her rational agency—subject to her rational responsibility, revision and acceptance—we are entitled to take them as acts of mind of which the subject is capable of being agent aware. It does not follow from the fact that a simple act of volition might to be sufficient to bring about a given thought that the thought is not an act of the subject under her rational control.

The above response suggests that the objector might be underestimating the number of thoughts that are not also acts of mind. But it does not really get to the heart of the problem. Suppose it is insisted by the objector that while sudden realisations and uncomfortable judgements may well be acts of mind and under our rational control, there are cases of compulsive thought with first-person content that are pure impositions on the agent, and not in any way under her rational responsibility, or subject to her revision or acceptance. If such thoughts are not acts of mind, and so cannot be thoughts of which we are agent aware, how are we to explain their first-person content?

In responding, we ought to remember that in appealing to mastery of SRR and to the *capacity* for agent's awareness, the account allows a subject who has the concept-term or word 'I' in virtue of her mastery of SRR and has a capacity for agent's awareness in central cases, may be said to refer first-personally on other occasions when she uses 'I', even if she lacks agent's awareness on those occasions. (This came out in section 1.3 above.) The account allows us to acknowledge cases of first-person reference in the case of thoughts that use 'I', but are thoughts we are disinclined to treat as actions, and of which we are not agent aware. Notice that it also allows us to extend first-person reference to utterances arising from compulsive speech disorders, such as Tourette's syndrome, that we might similarly be disinclined to treat as actions. What it would not allow is that a subject who suffered only compulsive thoughts or utterances (if such a thing were possible) could refer to herself first-personally. The non-active compulsive thoughts or

---

suffering compulsive speech disorders, such as Tourette's Syndrome, make utterances that are spontaneous but which we might not be inclined to treat as actions.

utterances only count as first-personal due to their relation to a subject who typically has active thoughts and utterances of which she is agent aware.

The claim that compulsive non-active thoughts, and utterances, are first-personal in any secondary or derivative way might be resisted by our objector. Perhaps it will claimed that in such cases the subject can refer to herself first-personally without any reliance on her capacity for agent's awareness in other cases, because the subject can at the time of thinking be fully aware of her thought, and be immediately aware of it as her own, even though it is not an *act* of hers, subject in any way to her rational responsibility.

If it could be established that the subject's awareness of her thought in the passive case both gave immediate awareness of it as *hers*, and was indeed independent of the subject's capacities for active thought and her awareness of her thought as hers in those cases, then we may have to acknowledge that there are distinct kinds of awareness on which first-person reference depends. This, of course, would mean that the account of first-person reference offered above would be less comprehensive than suggested. Notice, however, that it would not mean—without a further argument in favour of a uniform account—that the account offered did not have extensive application, nor would it mean that the structure of the account, allowing for distinct kinds of awareness playing the same role, did not apply to all first-person reference. However, before the requirement to make any concession arises, the objector would need to establish three things. First, that the subject has no capacity for rational control in such cases of compulsive thought. Secondly, that the subject is indeed immediately aware of her thought as her own in such purely passive cases. Thirdly, that the awareness a subject has of her passive thought is independent of the awareness she has in the active case.

I think that a subject who had no capacity whatever for rational control over her thoughts or utterances would be inclined to think of them as impositions that were not her thoughts or utterances in a full sense. If that were so it would become plausible to think of them as cases in which only a marginal and debased kind of first-person reference operated. (See 1.3 above). Further, I suspect that our awareness of our thoughts in the passive case is dependent on the active case and that a subject who had no rational control or responsibility over her mental life would have no awareness of her thoughts at all. However, I do not take myself to have closed off the possibility that there are non-active sources of self-knowledge that may play a role in first-person reference. I just do not know what they are.

Let me conclude this chapter by suggesting that we accept that:

- there is agent's awareness
- it grounds knowledge of our own actions mental and physical
- it can, in principle, play the role described in an account—more or less comprehensive—of first-person reference.

We still need to say a bit more to characterize such awareness. This will be the job of the following chapter.

6

Agent's Awareness and Knowledge of Our Mental Actions

The account being offered claims that the key to understanding why a subject who sets about referring to herself using 'I' will succeed in referring to herself self-consciously, is that she has an agent's awareness of what she is doing—that is, thinking or uttering. We ought, therefore, to ask what account we should give of such awareness. For the remainder of this chapter I am going to concentrate on the question as it relates to thoughts rather than utterances. If we can give an account of first-person reference in thought, we are well positioned to extend it to first-person reference in language. Further, the extension of the account to utterances is, to a large extent, going to have to await our conclusions with respect to our knowledge of our physical actions in Chapter 9.

It is a distinctive feature of the agency account that it takes the capacity for first-person reference to draw upon a capacity to know our own thoughts and utterances. Thus, according to the account the problem of first-person reference and of self-knowledge with respect to our thoughts and utterances must either be solved together, or not solved at all. More particularly it claims that there is a form of awareness—agent's awareness—that is both an immediate and central source of self-knowledge and that explains our capacity for first-person reference.

Thus, in looking for an account of agent's awareness we can be guided by the following hypothesis:

(H) *Our agent's awareness of our own thoughts is an immediate source of our knowledge of our own thoughts.*

We can use H to test suggestions of how we might understand agent's awareness. There are a number of well-known suggestions as to how we should understand the awareness (or consciousness) we have of our own mental states. In what follows, I will proceed by considering such suggestions and evaluating asking whether they are adequate to giving an account of our awareness of our mental actions that is of a kind that can plausibly ground self-knowledge. In this way, I hope to move towards plausible characterization of agent's awareness.

1. THE HOT APPROACH TO AWARENESS OF OUR MENTAL STATES

A popular approach to psychological self-knowledge has it that there is, in essence, no distinction between our awareness of our thoughts and our beliefs that we have them. This is the *higher-order thought (HOT) approach.*[1] The idea is that psychological self-awareness *consists* in a subject coming to have the right second-order beliefs, where those beliefs are *not* grounded in any distinct non-conceptual awareness of the thoughts they ascribe.

The main motivation for such a view comes from the thought that to be committed to a form of self-awareness, as the grounds for the second-order belief, is to be committed to a perceptual form of introspective awareness. Let us call the view that our awareness of our thoughts is a form of internal perceptual awareness, *the perceptual approach.*

We have already found problematic the idea that there is a form of perceptual awareness of the self that serves to ground first-person reference. A form of perceptual awareness as the mode by which we know our mental states is also problematic, and is so for similar reasons. Apart from problems about characterizing the nature of a perceptual faculty of the relevant kind, it is hard to see how an account of the knowledge we have of our own thoughts, that is modelled on the perceptual awareness we have of objects through our senses, can deliver the specific features that characterize such knowledge. The primary worry is that in perceptual awareness the relation between that which is known and the knowing subject seems quite different in kind from the relation between a subject and her thoughts.

Perception allows for brute error of a kind that suggests no defect in the perceiving subject. Perception is such that we can misperceive, either because of something about the object perceived or something about the condition under which we perceive, without any malfunction

---

[1] See Rosenthal (1986); Carruthers (1992, 1998).

of the cognitive or perceptual systems. As Burge puts it: 'The objectivity of perception depends on the possibility of epistemically entitled misperception' (Burge 1996: 108). However, our knowledge of our thoughts does not seem to allow for brute error of this kind. The relation between the perceiving subject, and that which is perceived, also seems to allow that, at the extreme, a well-functioning subject can nevertheless receive no perceptual information at all. A subject immersed in a sensory deprivation tank, for example, experiences an almost total blindness with respect to the external environment. If our knowledge of our own mental lives were analogous to perceptually based knowledge we would have to acknowledge the possibility of a subject capable of psychological self-knowledge, nevertheless, due to some block, being totally self-blind with respect to their psychological states. Again, as Shoemaker has impressed upon us, this seems to get the relation between a subject and her psychological states wrong.[2] I do not intend to argue the case here, but think that we cannot make sense of a rational subject, capable of utilizing the concepts required for second-order judgements about her thoughts, simply not knowing anything of what she thinks.[3]

The HOT approach seems an attractive option if we take a perceptual model as the only alternative. If it is agreed that the perceptual model allows for an implausible disassociation between a subject's thoughts and her self-ascriptions, then it can seem a mistake to take self-ascriptions to be grounded in awareness of our thoughts. If we then remove the appeal to awareness from the story, we are left with just the higher-order thought itself. Thus, we come to adopt the HOT approach on which awareness of our thoughts is constituted by the ascription of them.

However it is hard to see how the HOT approach can be right. Possibly the main problem lies in the fact that we are inclined to take the awareness we have of our own mental states as the grounds for the judgements, or beliefs, about them. On the HOT approach we are forced instead to take such awareness as *constituted* by self-ascriptive judgements. Not only does this have the effect of seeming to get things the wrong way round, it also means we are left with no account of what grounds our judgements about our mental states and so with no account of why we are authoritative about our mental states. If my

---

[2] The problems here obviously mirror the problems we identified for the perceptual account of self-reference.

[3] Shoemaker (1996) and Burge (1996) constitute the key texts in support of the point that a perceptual model of introspection is implausible because it allows for a brute dissociation between the knower and domain known about.

judgement that I am in such-and-such a state is not supported by my being aware that I am in that state, then I need to provide an alternative explanation of why it is that my judgement can nevertheless count as knowledgeable. The simplest of such accounts has it that, as a matter of fact, agents like us, due to some mechanism, are disposed to self-ascribe certain of their mental states and only self-ascribe those states that they actually have. Given that a self-ascription of the belief that P is a reliable indicator of a belief that P, if we accept reliablism about knowledge we can accept that by such self-ascriptions, agents like us express knowledge of their beliefs.

However, such simple reliablist accounts are problematic in making the connection between the psychological phenomenon, and the knowing of it, seem entirely brute. Thus part of the problem that was identified in relation to perceptual accounts seems to re-emerge. There seems to be room for the kind of disassociation between the subject's mental states and her self-ascriptions that does not respect the nature of the phenomena. Could not the underlying mechanism break down and so leave the judging subject susceptible to widespread error in her self-ascriptions: judging, for example, that she believes that P when she does do not, and judging that she does not believe P when she does? Further, even supposing that there is no possibility of break down, and even if pure externalism is plausible in general, it is hard to accept that our warrant for our self-ascriptions lie merely in external reliable, non-rational connections being in place.

Such accounts tend, therefore, to be embellished in such a way that the relation between the phenomenon and the knowing of it is a rational relation, either because it is partly constitutive of the *relata* or is taken to have some wider rational significance. So Shoemaker argues, for example, that it is not just a matter of fact that certain psychological states are self-intimating (that they normally give rise to the possibility of self-ascription); it is rather a conceptual, and so necessary, truth that they are. It is such a conceptual truth because it is partly constitutive of what it is to be a belief that a creature with the belief and capable of self-ascription, will normally be able to self-ascribe it. Burge argues that what makes the connection between our psychological states and our self-ascriptions capable of sustaining knowledge is the role such a connection plays in our nature as rational beings. He argues that our nature as critically rational subjects depends upon the obtaining of such a relation and takes this to confer a kind of warrant for the self-ascription. Such moves serve to bring out the necessity and consequences of being authoritative about one's mental states, and in so doing they serve to introduce a kind of 'top-down' warrant for our self-ascriptions. However, we may doubt that it provides all that is needed to underwrite or explain such authority. Rather, we might expect the appeal to the necessity and consequences of being authoritative about one's mental states to presuppose an independent warrant for our self-ascriptions.[4]

A simpler, but more familiar criticism of the HOT approach is that it makes awareness of our mental states a relatively complex cognitive achievement. It thus puts the ability for such awareness beyond the reach of creatures that we might take to be conscious of their mental states, even if they are unable to make judgements about them.

Such observations are not sufficient to establish the falsity of the HOT approach. However, they do suggest that the approach, whether it takes there to be a merely reliable connection, or some sort of *a priori* connection, between the second-order judgement and the objects of that judgement, has problems. Even if we are prepared to think of the awareness we have of our mental states as an intellectual operation, it seems that collapsing the distinction between our being aware of being in a given state and our judging that we are in that state, may leave us unable to give an adequate explanation of why our self-ascriptive judgements are authoritative.[5]

We have so far considered how plausible an account of self-knowledge results from the HOT approach to the awareness we have of our mental

---

[4] This is roughly Peacocke's criticism of Burge. (See Peacocke 1999, ch. 5.) Note, however, that the claim here is not that Burge is a proponent of the HOT approach, nor that he takes such 'top-down' warrant as the only, or indeed sufficient, warrant for self-ascription. His task is the narrower one of identifying such a warrant. The claim is rather that the proponent of the HOT approach to our awareness of our thoughts, would be able to appeal only to the kind of warrant that Burge introduces for our self-ascriptive judgements.

[5] There is a dispositionalist version of the HOT approach according to which the consciousness we have of our own mental states is constituted by our being *disposed*, rather than actually, to judge that we are in that state (see Carruthers 1998). Such an HOT approach does not I think fare significantly better than the version already discussed. The approach claim still seems to get things the wrong way around. Our being aware of a state is held to be constituted by our being disposed to judge we are in it, rather than as common sense would have it, being part of what makes us disposed to judge we are in it. The account faces similar problems to the standard HOT approach in explaining the authority that attaches to the judgements that we make about our mental states, and in acknowledging the awareness a relatively simple creature might have of its own states.

states. We have not yet considered what consequences the approach would have for the suggestion that such awareness is necessary for explaining first-person reference. We argued that we need to appeal to a subject's awareness that she is thinking or uttering in explaining first-person thought. However, if we accept the HOT approach, the suggestion that we appeal to our awareness that we are thinking or uttering in order to explain the self-consciousness inherent in first-person thought amounts to the suggestion that we appeal to first-person second-order thoughts in order to explain first-person thought. But this suggestion is transparently circular. So, whatever independent plausibility the HOT approach has, it cannot, if construed in this way, be accepted if we want to appeal to our awareness that we are thinking or uttering in order to explain first-person reference.

However, perhaps we need not construe the HOT approach as appealing to already understood first-person thought. Let us go back to the reductionist discussed in the last chapter. Let us suppose that the reductionist concedes that the kind of reflexive contents ungrounded in any self-conception or self-awareness that he offered as first-personal contents are not first-personal in the normal sense of the term. He might agree that in common usage we reserve the appellation 'first-person content' for those contents that are not only reflexive, but for those contents that the subject self-ascribes. However, he may argue, we can also explain the latter without appealing to any problematic capacity for self-awareness or first-person reference. What it is for a subject to be aware of being in such reflexive states can be explained in the same way that we explained what it was for the states to be reflexive in the first place. The suggestion will be that we can construe the awareness of a reflexive content in terms of a second-order reflexive content. We may not be happy to call first-order reflexive contents first-personal, but we should be happy to call such second-order reflexive contents first-personal. And, he will urge, our account of what makes the second-order content reflexive need draw as little on the capacities for self-awareness, or self-conception, as the account of what makes the first-order contents reflexive. The subject simply needs to show the relevant kinds of behavioural response, not only to features of its environment, but to representational states of itself.

The success of the strategy of appealing to second-order, merely reflexive, judgements of this kind to explain first-person thought would depend upon the plausibility of ungrounded reflexive self-ascription as an account of the awareness we have of our mental states. However, with the discussion of the HOT approach, we now have reason to be doubtful about whether such ungrounded self-ascriptions could provide an adequate account of our awareness of our mental states. We, therefore, have reason to doubt whether a reductionist account of first-person reference that appeals to higher-order reflexive states will be any more satisfactory than a reductionist account of first-person reference that appeals first-order states.

2. THE FIRST-ORDER INTENTIONALIST APPROACH TO AWARENESS

In recent years the standing alternative to a perceptual or HOT approach to awareness of our mental states has been the *first-order intentionalist approach*. This approach allows that a creature can be in a state of awareness where that state is independent of the creature judging that she is in a given state. To put it as Dretske does, we can distinguish between a creature's awareness *of* such-and-such a psychological state—which is a matter of her judging that she is in such-and-such a state—and her awareness *with* such-and-such a psychological state—which is a matter of her being aware of something by being in that state. However, on this approach the awareness that a creature has that is not dependent upon her judging that she is in a given state, gives her awareness only of whatever is the intentional or representational object of that state. So if we say that a subject is aware of seeing something blue then that can be taken to mean either that she judges herself to be seeing something blue or that she is aware of a blue thing. Exactly what account we give of the intentional relation required for her to be aware of a blue thing is a further issue. For some it is being in a state that represents a blue thing and that feeds immediately into the control and regulation of behaviour; for others it is having a blue thing as an intentional object where that notion is taken as primitive; for yet others it involves not only representing a blue thing but also attending to a blue thing.

Of course, accounts such as these seem, on the face of it, much better fitted to playing a role in the explanation of conscious perception, than in the explanation of conscious thoughts. However, let us suppose that conscious thoughts can also have their intentional objects. (Of course, if they do not then the first-order intentionalist option cannot even be applied here.) On such an account, a thought will be conscious in so far as the subject of the thought stands in a given intentional relation to the object of the thought.

Unlike the HOT approach, this account is able to draw on a form of awareness that pre-exists, and can be invoked as warrant for our self-ascriptions. However, it is not simple to explain how the first-order awareness stands to support our second-order judgements. It is not clear, for example, *how* my consciously thinking that *P*, where consciously thinking that *P* is understood as standing in a given relation to *P*, supports in *any* way my self-ascription, that is, my judgement that I am thinking that *P*. On the account envisaged, it is the proposition or state of affairs *P* that I am aware of in a given way. How can my awareness of the world, my awareness of *P*, where *P* is some fact about the world, entitle me to make any judgements about myself?

One idea we could adopt is Dretske's earlier suggestion that introspection is a kind of displaced perception.[6] Given appropriately connecting beliefs I am able to perceive that something is the case even though I am not able to perceive the objects that make it the case. I see that the tank in the car is full, to use Dretske's example, by looking at the gauge on the dashboard. The ability to perceive that *k* is *F*, by perceiving some object other than *k*, depends upon a belief that an appropriate connection exists between the properties of the object seen and *k*. In the example given, it is relatively easy to say what the connecting belief is to be. My belief that the tank is full when the dial points to '*F*', combined with my seeing the dial as pointing to '*F*' is what enables me to have the displaced perception that the tank is full.

The nature of the connecting belief in the case of introspection is less easy to specify. My knowing, via introspection, that I am seeing something blue will involve my seeing something blue, however this needs to combine with a belief that connects the property of the object seen, that is, blueness, with a property of me, that is, the property of seeing blue. It is however hard to see what this belief can be. The belief that 'I see a blue object whenever there is a blue object' is clearly not a belief we want to attribute to a rational subject. It is clear that there can be a blue object, and I can have information that there is a blue object, even though I cannot see one. On the other hand if the belief is supposed to be a belief to the effect that 'I see a blue object when I see a

---

[6] Dretske seems to no longer hold the view (see Dretske 1999). Dretske in a yet more recent paper (Dretske, forthcoming) denies that introspection tells a subject what she is thinking—as opposed to what she is thinking *about*. He, himself, will therefore not accept the assumption made here that introspection is a source of self-knowledge.

blue object', then while the belief is guaranteed to be true, it is trivial. That we are having difficulty in giving the content of the connecting belief is, of course, not a surprise. For what we are trying to do in giving the content of the connecting belief is answer the question: what makes my self-ascription of an experience one to which I am entitled given only the world directed content *P*? If there is a cognitive state that is to connect my seeing the blue object to the belief that I am seeing a blue object, it look it looks as though we will have to have already solved the problem of how my apprehension of something in the world can ground my attribution of it to myself. What we have identified here is that there is a *prima facie* problem about taking my access to one fact (that there is a blue object) as justifying or entitling me to a belief about a quite distinct topic, that I am seeing a blue object. We can call this the 'two topics problem'.[7]

It should be said that Dretske himself does not spell out what, if any, connecting belief is required in the case of introspection. He does make it clear that he takes introspection to be a somewhat special case. While my seeing that the tank as full depends upon my taking myself as having reason to believe that the position of the pointer is a reliable indicator of the state of the tank, Dretske claims that in self-ascribing an experience, subjects do not need to assure themselves that there is a reliable connection between them seeing something blue, and their attribution of seeing something blue to themselves. What Dretske says is that, in occupying the state of seeing something as blue, the subject already has all the information she needs about how she is seeing the world.

When I, an external observer, try to determine what state *P* means in system *S*, I do not, whereas *S* does, occupy the state whose representational content is under investigation. *S*, therefore, *has* information—whatever information is carried by state *P*—that I do not. . . . The system itself necessarily occupies a state that carries information about what the world would be like if the system was functioning properly. You and I do not. (Dretske 1995: 52)

In order to self-ascribe the experience all a subject needs is the ability to conceptualize it as an experience she is having of the world. All this seems absolutely right. However, what we wanted to know was what account we should give of the ability to take a mental state or action as ours when we were in it or doing it. In other words what we wanted to know was what grounds, for example, my ability to conceptualize my

---

[7] Thanks to Dick Moran for suggesting the name for the problem. He, of course, does much in Moran 2001 to illuminate how we might solve something like it.

seeing a blue object as *my seeing* a blue object—given that all that I am aware of is the blue object. Our 'two topics problem' was not concerned with what entitled me to self-ascribe *P*, rather than *Q*, given that I am seeing *P*, but rather with what justified me in *self-ascribing* at all, given that I am seeing *P*. I think we are now in a position to see that the appeal to displaced perception does not answer the 'two topic problem', but must assume it has been solved.

Before moving on, I should make it explicit that Dretske concentrates his discussion on perceptual introspection, and not on introspection with respect to belief or action. However, in so far as the first-order intentionalist approach to awareness is even applicable to belief or action, the same basic model must be extendable to introspection in those cases. If I am conscious of *P*, with my belief that *P*, then my capacity to know through introspection that I have such a belief will be the same as my capacity to believe that I believe that *P*. My belief that I believe that *P* is warranted by my being in an intentional state with respect to *P*, and having the capacity to conceptualize that state as a state of my believing that *P*. Similarly, if I am conscious of *P* through judging *P*, then my capacity to know through introspection that I am judging *P* will be my capacity to believe that I am judging *P*. My belief that I am judging *P* is warranted by my judging *P*, and being able to conceptualize that as an act of judging *P*. This all seems fine. However, without any more said about what grounds my conceptualization of the belief or judgement, as *my* belief or judgement we are not going to have answered the 'two topics problem'.

Dretske's approach falls into a group of accounts that we can call *content-based accounts* of our epistemic relations to our mental states. A content-based account of our awareness or consciousness with a mental state or action holds that such awareness is constituted by the state or action having a certain content. A content-based account of self-ascription has it that such ascriptions are justified or entitled by the content of other states that ground the self-ascription. Our problem with Dretske's account, in essence, was that it failed to solve the 'two topic problem' without circularity. However, we might now wonder whether the problem lies in the *structure* of the account, or only with the nature of the content it centred on.

I want briefly to consider the suggestion that while we are right to adopt a content-based account of both the awareness we have of our mental states and actions, and of our self-ascriptions of them, we are wrong to think that the relevant content is pure object-directed content. We can take it that our self-ascriptions are content-based, but take the contents on which they are based as being richer than those already supposed. There are two ways we can go here.

1. First-personal content-based accounts

Perhaps the contents on which our mental self-ascriptions are based are already first-personal? Suppose that the content of my perception, when I see a blue object, is not well represented by 'the object is blue' but rather by 'I am facing a blue object'. In that case the first-order intentionalist will hold that the awareness—my awareness *with* my mental states—that grounds my ascriptions of my mental states will be given by first-personal contents, such as the content 'I am facing a blue object'.

Now, to the extent that the grasp of such a content requires the subject to be able to have first-person thoughts the account can play no role of the kind I have suggested in our explanation of first-person thought. Rather than underlying a capacity for reflexive reference by means of 'I', it would assume it.

However, even setting aside that problem, a question remains about how my perception that I am facing a blue object supports my judgement that I am *seeing* a blue object. Although now both the content of the perception and the self-ascriptive judgement are assumed to have first-personal content (the former non-conceptual, the latter conceptual), the former content concerns my spatial relation to objects in the world and not any mental facts about me. So, we will again face a kind of two topics problem, where the two topics are my spatial position and my psychological states. If rather than appealing to the content 'I am facing a blue object' we appeal to the content 'I have an experience as of facing a blue object' in order to bring the topics together, we will have assumed what we were trying to explain.

Note that here we have again dealt only with our introspective knowledge of our perception. What of my knowledge that I am judging that *P*, for example? A parallel first-personal content-based account must claim that in judging that *P*, I am in some state that has the content 'I am judging that *P*' that grounds my judgement that 'I am judging *P*'. But again, that threatens to be precisely the kind of state we have been trying to characterize.

2. Egocentric content-based accounts

A further possibility would be to draw on a distinction between contents that are egocentric and contents that are first-personal. Egocentric contents are perspectival and, in the appropriate system, self-indicating. Egocentric contents are however given by monadic notions such as 'to the right' and 'up ahead' in contrast to first-personal contents that are given by relational notions such 'to the right of me', 'in front of me' (see Campbell 1994: 119). Further, the contents are linked in such a way that while one can grasp the egocentric contents without any capacity for first-personal thought, given such a capacity a subject who sees that something 'is up ahead' or 'to the right' is able immediately to infer that something 'is up ahead of me' or 'to the right of me'.

Could it be that what legitimizes the transitions here could legitimize my judgement that I am seeing P given that I am in fact seeing P? It seems we again face a version of the two topics problem, in that the former such contents concern my spatial relation to things in the world and not to mental facts about me. In order to draw upon an inference of the form 'A is up ahead', so 'A is up ahead of me', we would need to enrich the content of my awareness of my mental states, so that it has some form such as 'experience, around here, as of facing a blue object' that legitimates the inference 'I have an experience as of facing a blue object'. However, if the account of spatial self-ascription is going to function as a model for psychological self-ascription, it seems inevitable that we will operate with a quasi-perceptual account of our relation to our mental states. What sense can we make of a mental state being 'around here' unless our access to it requires a quasi-perceptual faculty? And we have already argued against given such an account of our normal relation to our mental lives on the grounds that it leaves open the possibility of a subject not taking the 'experience around here' to be hers.

If we take our awareness of our mental states to be constituted by us being in states with a given content, whether first-personal or egocentric we are going to have a problem explaining what legitimizes their self-ascriptions. Either the contents will be distinct from that of the self-ascription or they will be the same. If they are distinct then we face the two topics problem. If the contents are the same, then we presuppose that the subject can think contents of a kind that we have set it our task to explain. In the light of this we should consider whether we can provide an alternative to the content-based account of our awareness of our mental lives.

3. NON-CONTENT-BASED ACCOUNTS OF AWARENESS

Peacocke (1999) offers a non-content based account of psychological self-ascriptions. He argues that we can be entitled to self-ascribe a psychological state independently of taking some distinct representation to be true. In particular, we are entitled immediately to self-ascribe *conscious* psychological phenomena; such phenomena immediately warrant their own ascription. Moreover, for Peacocke a state's being conscious in a way that warrants its own self-ascription is not merely a matter of its having a certain *content*.

Peacocke asks consciousness to play the role played by agent's awareness in the agency account of self-reference. If we can get clearer about how Peacocke thinks we need to understand what it is for a state to be conscious, if it is to be apt for immediate self-ascription, we will have something to draw on in characterizing agent's awareness. Let us, therefore, turn to Peacocke's non-content based account of psychological self-ascription.

3.1 Peacocke on representational independence

In asking about the grounds of our first-personal beliefs Peacocke makes a distinction between what he calls 'representationally dependent' and 'representationally independent' uses of the first-person. As he puts it:

A use of the first-person, in a particular belief with the content "I am F", is *representationally dependent* if:

(i) "I am F" is the content of one of the thinker's current mental states, a state which represents that content as correct; and

(ii) the thinker forms the belief "I am F" by taking the mental state mentioned in (i) at face value, in respect of this content. (Peacocke 1999: 265).

The basic idea is that representationally dependent uses of 'I' are those derived from representations that are, roughly, representations of oneself. A representationally independent use of the first-person is a use that is not representationally dependent. So, a representationally independent use of the first-person is a use that does not rely upon the subject taking any such representation of themselves at face value, and so is a use that cannot be validated by any such representation. A representationally dependent use is, of course, an instance of what I have called a content-based self-ascription. On this distinction the self-ascription 'I am facing a blue object' based on a perceptual presentation with the non-conceptual content 'I am facing a blue object' involves a representationally dependent use of the first-person. The self-ascription 'I see that there is a blue object' involves a representationally independent use of the first-person. The notion of a representationally independent use of the first-person suggests the possibility of a non-content based account of self-ascription.

Although it will be something of a diversion from our central task, I want to spend a little time clarifying the significance and nature of Peacocke's distinction. The distinction given by Peacocke seems to me to reflect, and give us a useful way of articulating, Wittgenstein's famous distinction between uses of 'I' as subject and as uses of 'I' as object.[8] Those uses of 'I' that are representationally dependent are uses of 'I' as object, whereas those uses of 'I' that are representationally independent as uses of 'I' as subject. Wittgenstein himself, and others following him, have articulated the distinction by claiming that uses of 'I' as object rest on an identification of the subject referred to with something else, and so are open to a certain kind of error. Uses of 'I' as subject were supposed not to rest on any such identification, and so to be immune from error through misidentification.

However, there are reasons for thinking that this notion of immunity to error through misidentification is the wrong way to get at the intuitive distinction. First, there is an absence of identification, and so a corresponding kind of immunity, that holds of a large number of referring terms other than 'I'. For example, some perceptual demonstratives, 'that blue patch' say, are not plausibly construed as securing reference by means of the subject identifying one thing as another, and thus as being subject to the kind of error that can arise as a result of such identifications. Thus, the lack of an identification component does not in itself have a particular connection with self-consciousness.

Secondly, and more importantly, there are uses of 'I', that Wittgenstein seems right to think of as uses of 'I' as object, that do not rest on a identification by the subject of herself with something else and that are therefore immune to error through misidentification. Consider the claim that bodily awareness immediately grounds first-person self-ascriptions,

<hr />

[8] Wittgenstein (1958: 66–7).

without the need for an identification, because it delivers information only about ourselves, and delivers it as information about ourselves. If the claim is true, my judgement that 'my hair is blowing in the wind' will, if made on the basis of bodily awareness, be immune to error through misidentification. Consider also the claim that perception of our environments can immediately ground first-person self-ascriptions, without the need for an identification, because it delivers information only about the space we are in, and delivers it as information about the space we are in. If the claim is true, my judgement that 'I am in front of the door' will, if made on the basis of normal perception, be immune to error through misidentification. Both these cases do not involve any identification as part of the grounds of the subject's self-ascription. They do, however, both seem to involve a representation as the grounds of the subject's self-ascription. It now seems promising to suggest that we think of uses of 'I' as object, as uses that depend upon a subject accepting a representation of herself as thus and so, and uses of 'I' as subject, as uses that depend on no such representation.

However, Wittgenstein's construal of uses of 'I' as object in terms of an identification, rather than in terms of representational dependence, does enable us to see that in fact Peacocke's construal of representational dependence needs some extension. There must be representationally dependent uses of 'I' that do not depend merely upon the subject taking a single representation at 'face value'. The uses of 'I' as object, that Wittgenstein construes as identification dependent, also appear to be to be representationally dependent. Thus we need to distinguish between the following two types of representationally dependent uses of 'I'.

First, there are identification dependent uses of 'I'. There are cases in which the use of 'I' is based upon an identification of an object by the subject as themselves. Consider a case where I come to believe that I am wearing my shirt inside out on the basis of seeing myself in a mirror. In such a case our first-personal belief seems to be based on a representation whose content is 'that woman has her shirt on inside out', and a belief that 'I am that woman'.

Secondly, there are examples, of the kind Peacocke identifies, that are identification-free uses of 'I'. Such uses of 'I' do not require an identification such as 'I am that woman' as well as a representation of how things are. They are rather based directly on how things are represented to me as being. They are uses that are based on my taking some experience at 'face value'. The case where I see a door in front of me and conclude that 'I am in front of a door' is given by Peacocke as the paradigm of such a case. However, beliefs formed directly on the basis of bodily awareness can be thought to be representationally dependent in this way. (But note that we are going to have to gloss 'taking at face value' carefully if we are to get the phenomenology right.)

There are two further clarifications I want to make with respect to Peacocke's distinction. First, we can raise a question about the *content* of the experience upon which identification-free representationally dependent uses of the first-person are based. Peacocke seems to assume that when I make the representationally dependent judgement 'I am in front of a door', I take at face value a perceptual representation with the first-personal content 'I am in front of a door'. However, going back to the distinction between egocentric and first-personal contents we might want to allow that there will also be uses of 'I' that are based on taking egocentric perceptual contents at face value. Consider, the belief 'I am in front of a door' based on taking a perception with the content 'door up ahead' at face value. We would surely want to count such a use of 'I' as a representationally dependent one.[9]

Secondly, suppose I believe that I have no coat and suppose that I believe that I am wet. I may infer that I have no coat and am wet. Or suppose that I believe that I believe *P* and believe that I believe *Q*. If I came to believe that I believe that *P* and believe that *Q* it would normally be because I inferred it from *P* and from *Q*. However, although it is perhaps an abnormal way to reach the belief, I may infer that I believe *P* and believe *Q* from my beliefs about what I believe. In both cases what I infer will depend upon the contents of the beliefs which act as premises. Now, it seems natural to think that such uses are representationally dependent given that they are uses occasioned by representations. Such uses are, however, not quite captured by Peacocke's definition.

We can, I think, capture such representationally dependent uses of 'I' as those which involve an identification, those which are based on an appropriate egocentric content, and those which involve an inference of the kind just given, by a slight alteration to Peacocke's definition. First, let me assume that we can understand the notion of inference as a relation between contents such that 'I am in front of a door' can be inferred from the content 'A door is up ahead', 'I am F' can be inferred from the contents 'that woman is F' and 'I am that woman' and 'I am F and G' can be inferred from the contents 'I am F' and 'I

---

[9] This point is made in Bermúdez (2002).

am G'. Let us then take representational dependence to be understood as follows:

A use of the first-person, in a particular belief with the content 'I am F' is representationally dependent if:

(i) 'I am F' is the content of one of the thinker's current mental states, a state which represents that content as correct, or 'I am F' can be inferred from the content of the thinker's current mental states, states which represent the contents from which 'I am F' can be inferred as correct; and

(ii) the thinker forms the belief 'I am F' by taking the mental state (or states) mentioned in (i) at face value, in respect of this content (or these contents).[10]

With the notion of representational dependence clarified, I want now to consider how we should understand the phenomenon of self-ascriptions that are allegedly representationally independent. Self-ascriptions that are representationally independent are, of course, independent of supporting representations, but they are not therefore made without warrant. Such self-ascriptions can after all be knowledgeable. Peacocke's idea is that in the case of representationally independent self-ascriptions, the grounds of the self-ascription, say the self-ascription that I am seeing a table, lie not in some *representation* that such and such is the case, that I am seeing a table, for example. Rather the grounds lie in the *fact* that such-and-such *is* the case: that I am seeing the table. Thus, my seeing a table or believing that the table is brown can be my reason for taking myself to see the table or to be believing that the table is brown. However we again face the two topics problem: why does my seeing *the table* enable me to ascribe anything to *myself*?

Now, for Peacocke, my merely seeing something or believing something is not sufficient to warrant self-ascription. Peacocke also emphasises

---

[10] Note that we could opt for a less local way of classifying uses as representationally dependent or independent. Peacocke has suggested to me that we might take a use of 'I' to be representationally independent if the belief in which it occurs rests ultimately on first-person beliefs all of which involve uses of 'I' which are representationally independent in the original sense. On this understanding the status of a use of the first-person based on prior uses will be inherited from the status of those prior uses. However, as long as a subject forms her first-personal beliefs by taking certain representations, whether first-personal or not, at face value I think there will be a point in calling these uses representationally dependent, even though they will not be subject to quite the same kinds of falsity if they are based on uses of 'I' which are themselves representationally independent. In particular, the case where I base my belief about my beliefs on my earlier *self-ascriptions*, rather than my current commitments, captures an interesting case of where I seem to treat myself as an object.

that, in the central case, the seeing or believing must be conscious.[11] The view is that a conscious state or activity can stand as the reason for its own ascription, merely in virtue of its occurrence rather than in virtue of some representation of its occurrence, in a way that essentially non-conscious states or activities cannot—and this is surely right.

Why is it that a conscious state is the paradigm case of a state functioning as the reason for its own ascription? The obvious thought here is that the *consciousness* of the state is playing the role that a representation of it would otherwise. The idea would be that while we need a representation of a state in order to ascribe it, where the state does not figure as part of the ascribing subject, we do not need such a representation as long as the state figures as a conscious state of the ascribing subject. Given this, we need to elucidate the nature of *consciousness* in a way that will explain what allows a conscious state to play this epistemic role, in the absence of a representation of it.

It is clear that Peacocke operates with neither of the accounts of consciousness identified above. He does not construe consciousness as exhausted by the content grasped. Nor does he adopt an HOT approach to consciousness. However, it is hard to be sure exactly how he does construe consciousness and why he holds that a mental state needs to be *conscious,* rather than non-conscious, if it is to function as a reason for its self-ascription. Of course the obvious thought here is that the belief must be in some way accessible to the ascribing subject if it is to function as a reason at all, and that a conscious state is accessible to its subject. But now we need to explain how a state can be accessible to a subject, and accessible in a way that warrants her taking it to be *her* state—if she has the concepts—in the absence of any representation of it. We need some explanation of how a conscious state or activity can play the same normative role with respect to our self-ascriptions as a representation that we are in such a state or engaged in such an activity.

---

[11] Peacocke in fact allows for knowledgeable self-ascriptions of belief which are not based on any underlying conscious state. Such ascriptions are knowledgeable only if made in circumstances in which the speaker would also be willing to make the first-order judgement with the content of the belief self-ascribed. I am not sure what Peacocke would say about the possibility of self-ascriptions of perceptions that are not based on any underlying conscious perceiving. If we are capable of non-inferentially judging ourselves to have, for example, seen things even when we are not conscious of having seen them, then we may similarly want to say that our so judging is only knowledgeable if we would have been conscious of seeing them, had we not been so preoccupied etc. Of course spelling out the conditions of the 'would' here will be a complex task, but I will set it aside at this point.

In essence, what we are asking the appeal to consciousness to do is to solve the two-topic problem. That is, we need to explain, in a way that does not invoke a representation of the state as hers, how perceiving some object in the world, or judging some proposition *P*, can entitle the subject to a belief about herself, and her mental states. If Peacocke's account is not to fall prey to the two-topic problem, it needs to provide an explanation of how a state's being conscious allows it to play the normative role he claims.

It may help us to see what is going on here if we step back a little to distinguish between two possible accounts. On the one hand suppose we claim that the mere occurrence of a state or activity with a given *content* is sufficient for the state or activity to act as the reason for its own ascriptions. On the other hand suppose we claim that the occurrence of the state or activity with a given content is not sufficient to entitle the subject to self-ascribe it. Rather, it is something about the *mode*—in contrast to content—of the state or activity that allows it to play the normative role that it does.

On the first option, any explanation of our entitlement to the self-ascription would have to appeal to the content of the state or activity. If the content were first-personal (or egocentric) we would not have a representation independent use of 'I'. If it were not first-personal we would face the two topic problem. Perhaps we could argue that the mere occurrence of a content that feeds into the psychological economy of a subject can function as the basis for its self-ascription simply because the self-ascription is truth preserving in that context. To use an analogy of Campbell's, if we have a close circuit TV system feeding information from within a single room all we would need for the implication from 'dog' to 'dog in room' to be secure is that the cameras all be in fact placed in a single room. The presence of a dog is sufficient to justify 'dog in room' just because that is how the system is wired. (See Campbell 1999: 99.) However, this is not a model we can attribute to Peacocke. To hold that it is simply a combination of content with background wiring that secures the justification for the self-ascription is to accept a kind of pure externalism with respect to self-knowledge that Peacocke (I think rightly) rejects.

So, we need to ask what sense we can make of the second option. The claim is primarily that the warrant for our self-ascriptions comes, not from the occurrence of a state with certain content, nor from some fortuitous piece of wiring, but rather from the mode in which the content occurs.[12] Note that the idea that the normative relations of a state or activity depend on more than just the content of that state or activity is an already widely accepted one. We accept, for example, that we do not rationally judge that P on the basis of our doubt that $P > Q$ and belief that P but do on the basis of our beliefs that $P > Q$ and P. We accept that the force (or quality) of our attitudes is an essential dimension of their normative relations to each other. The second option presented here suggests that there is a dimension to conscious states or activities that enables them to augment the content of such states and activities in such a way that we can solve the two topics problem. There are, however, at least two stages to the task of making good this second option. First, we need to *characterize* the mode of occurrence of the thoughts or judgements that enables them to function as the reason for their own ascription. Secondly we need to *explain* what it is about such a mode of occurrence that enables it to play the normative role it does in relation to our self-ascriptions. We need in other words to explain why it is that my self-ascription is justified given that it is based on a thought or judgement occurring in that mode. Of course we can expect a decent attempt at the first task to provide us with the means of accomplishing the second.

4. SELF-AWARENESS AND CONTROL

For Peacocke, self-ascriptions made on the basis of conscious states or activities are representationally free uses of 'I'. They are warranted self-ascriptions in virtue of both the *fact* of occurrence, and the *mode* of occurrence, of the states or activities self-ascribed. What is required at this stage is a characterisation of this mode of occurrence—consciousness—that does not appeal to a representation of the state or activity in question.

Peacocke does provide us with some further detail about how to characterize what is involved in the consciousness of a conscious attitude. His main suggestion is that a state or activity is conscious in a way that provides for non-representationally dependent uses of 'I' if it *occupies* our attention without being the *object* of it. Peacocke identifies a number of distinct mental phenomena that can be said to occupy without

---

[12] See Thomassen (2000) for an articulation of the two options. (See also ch. V of Husserl 1973 for the distinction between the content and the quality of an act.)

being objects of attention—perceptions, conscious attitudes, tryings and actions. Some further elucidation of what is meant by the claim that one's attention is occupied in the case of conscious thought is given by the suggestion that when a thinker is engaged in conscious thought he is engaged in a task of selection. The subject engaged in conscious thought is 'in effect selecting a certain kind of path through the space of possible thoughts—thoughts contents—available to him' (Peacocke 1999: 213).

Given that Peacocke's is a general thesis I am not clear how this clarification helps to provide a general account of consciousness that enables it to play this role. However, the task we face here is in fact a more manageable one. We need not aim to give a *general* account of what allows conscious mental phenomenon—whether conscious judgements, conscious perceptions, conscious emotions and sensations—to be self-ascribed immediately. Indeed I am sceptical of there being a common underlying property that can be appealed to in giving an informative general account. It may be that the best general account will be one that offers something like the following minimalist definition of consciousness:

(*Def*) A state or activity is in conscious mode *iff* it can serve (in a creature with sufficiently complex conceptual abilities) directly as the reason for its own ascription.

Our aim, then, is to look only at those thoughts and utterances understood as actions, and ask in virtue of what mode of occurrence *they* might have the property of standing as the reasons for their own ascription. Given that aim, Peacocke's remark is helpful. I will suggest that in the case of thoughts and utterances the relevant mode of occurrence, which warrants the immediate self-ascription of the thought in question, should be understood in terms of agent's awareness. I will further suggest that agent's awareness is the result of acting on the basis of an assessment of possibilities for acting.

We can start by noting the phenomenological appeal of the suggestion that we have agent's awareness and that it may play the role we have identified. We do seem to have distinctive awareness of what we are doing both in the case of physical and mental actions. We know what it is like to reach out and pick up something, or to come to a decision with respect to some question. Further we seem to have such awareness without any perceptual or quasi-perceptual feedback from the action we carry out. It seems to us that we know what we are doing not from being presented with our actions, and taking such presentations at face value. That we have a non-perceptual awareness of our actions is supported by more than phenomenology. In the case of physical actions there is an increasingly impressive set of experimental data that suggests that our awareness of our physical actions precedes the receipt of any feedback information from the action carried out.[13] If our awareness of our physical actions does not come from informational feedback from the action, then we can expect the same to be true for our mental actions. Given that we seem to be aware of what we are doing not in virtue of being passive receivers of information about the action done, we can suppose that we have such awareness in virtue of our being the producer, or agent, of the action.

The features that set apart active phenomena, from passive phenomena, seem to be the features of origin and control. We think of active phenomena as originating in the subject and as being under her control. I have noted that this does not mean that we need take all our actions to be voluntary or subject to our will. Consider the case of mental actions. There will be many mental actions that are voluntary: many of our suppositions, assumptions, imaginings. And there will be many that are not: our judgements, doubts, denials. Nevertheless such acts of mind are subject to our rational control in a variety of ways. They are, of course, constrained by our rationality and by the content and nature of the attitudes we already have. Nevertheless, we assume that our own rational assessments direct the course of our thoughts: our thoughts are the immediate products of such assessments.

Consider, for example, what happens when we judge that something is true. We do something like accept or endorse a given thought in the light of our awareness of the possible judgements we could make, and the reasons in favour of one over another. While judging is not something we can merely will to do, it is something that we do and could prescind from doing. If our assessments as to the truth of *P* find *P* to be true we will judge *P*, and if they find *P* to be false, we will deny *P*. Also in play will be the subject's weighting of her reasons, the practical consequences of moving to judgement or not, the subject's cognitive tendencies—on whether she tends to judge rashly with scant reason or is cautious about judging, requiring a surfeit of evidential reassurance.

---

[13] See James (1890); Della Sala *et al.* (1991, 1994); Cole (1993); Cole and Paillard (1995); Marcel and Tegner (1995); Haggard and Magno (1999); Haggard and Eimer (1999) and Haggard (2003). Marcel and Nimmo-Smith (forthcoming).

I want to suggest that having this kind of control over one's mental life provides a primitive, representationally independent kind of awareness of what one is doing, and that this awareness is agent's awareness. For a subject to have rational control over her mental life she must have the capacity to assess possibilities available to her, and be able immediately to act on such assessments. For the activity of assessing possibilities available to make sense, as the basis of determining her thoughts, the possibilities must be possibilities for her to think in one way rather than another. The core suggestion is that the very idea of an action produced by an active assessment by an agent, carries with it the idea of an assessment by an agent of actions *for her*. For a subject to engage in an assessment of what to do is for a subject to determine what *she* should do. The suggestion then is that any action produced directly on the basis of an active assessment by an agent will be an action of which the agent is aware of as hers. Suppose it is right to say that when a subject judges, doubts or questions one thing rather than another, as a direct result of assessing what to think, she thereby has an awareness of what she is thinking. It is then plausible to suppose that, were the subject to have the appropriate concepts, this would be sufficient to entitle her immediately to self-ascribe her thoughts.

There are two objections, coming from opposite directions, the discussion of which will help bring out the nature of the suggestion being mooted. First, it might be denied that rational control involves any form of awareness. Rational transitions can take place at an unconscious level for a subject without requiring any conscious participation on the subject's part.

Secondly, it might be objected that although rational control pre-supposes self-awareness on the part of the subject, it is a kind of self-awareness that already invokes a capacity for first-personal self-ascription. Thus, far from helping us characterize a notion of agent's awareness on which self-ascription and self-reference could rest, instead such awareness requires a capacity for self-reference.

Suppose that a subject has the beliefs P, $P > Q$, $\sim Q$ and is rationally guided to drop her belief that $\sim Q$ and accept Q. This transition, that maintains rational order, could seem to take place in a number of ways.

1. The subject has the beliefs P, $P > Q$, $\sim Q$. We can suppose that there is a sub-personal rational mechanism that it automatically brings about that she drop her belief that $\sim Q$ and accept Q in such a way that no self-awareness is required for belief formation and for rational

order to be maintained. In this case attitudes (and perhaps desires) operate with various forces, and according to various sub-personal constraints, to bring about revisions.

2. The subject has the beliefs P, $P > Q$, $\sim Q$. We can suppose that the subject comes to revise her beliefs on the basis of having self-ascribed her beliefs and the options available to her. Suppose the subject has the beliefs 'I believe P', 'I believe $P > Q$', and 'I believe $\sim Q$ and on that basis comes to self-ascribe the options 'I can give up P', 'I can give up $P > Q$' or 'I can drop my belief that $\sim Q$ and judge that Q'. An assessment of her options may lead her to drop her belief that $\sim Q$ and accept Q. In this case the subject deploys first-person self-ascriptions in making her judgement and in maintaining rational order.[14]

However, these two cases do not seem to exhaust the possibilities. We may indeed have rational control in the ways described. However, intermediate between these cases is the case where we have deliberation without self-ascription.

3. The subject has the beliefs P, $P > Q$, $\sim Q$. Suppose she then concludes that either P is true, or $P > Q$ is not true, or $\sim Q$ is false and Q is true, and drops her belief that $\sim Q$ and judges that Q as a result of a consideration of the possibilities she is aware of as possibilities. In this case the subject considers the possibilities and immediately judges accordingly.

The active consideration operating in the third case seems possible without the subject either self-ascribing, or indeed having the capacity to self-ascribe, her beliefs. The question now is whether the active consideration over the possibilities the agent is conscious of puts the subject in a different relation to her concluding judgement than in the case in which rational order is maintained only via various sub-personal constraints. In this case, when she acts immediately on the basis of a consideration of possibilities, her act *is* her decision as to which one of the possibilities to go for.

It seems highly intuitive to say that the subject's relationship to that action is such that, *were* she to have the concept of the first-person and the concepts of belief and judgement, we *would* take her to be entitled immediately to self-ascribe her concluding judgement. The story about *why* that is the case, in my view, involves two elements.

---

[14] For these possibilities see Shoemaker 1996, Chapter 2.

1. *Agent's awareness*

The act produced by a process of considering what to do is a conscious act—one of which the subject is agent aware—and there is a general entitlement immediately to self-ascribe those states and activities of hers which are conscious.

2. *Rational connections between actions and self-ascriptions*

A subject is rationally entitled to self-ascribe an act carried out on the basis of a consideration of how to act because of rational connections between the nature and pre-suppositions of her act and her self-ascription.

I have suggested that the process of determining how to act already pre-supposes first-person elements in way that makes the subject entitled to self-ascribe any act she performs as the result of such a process. What are the relevant pre-suppositions?

(i) It is a pre-supposition of agency that the subject has possibilities available to her, such that *she* is able *immediately* to exercise them.

(ii) It is a pre-supposition of agency in thought that the subject is led by rational or practical considerations in exercising one of these possibilities rather than another.

(iii) We can assume that in considering her options a subject has knowledge of the possibilities in order to be able to realize one, rather than another, on the basis of her considerations.

Elements of these three points can be seen as expressed in the following from Moran:

> One must see one's deliberation as the expression and development of one's belief and will, not an activity one pursues in the hope that it will have some influence on one's eventual belief and will . . . Were it generally the case that the conclusion of his deliberation about what to think about something left it still open for him what he does in fact think about it, it would be quite unclear what he takes himself to be doing in deliberating. It would be unclear what reason was left to call it deliberating if its conclusion did not count as making up his mind. (Moran, 2001: 94)

Moran talks about deliberation, which may call for more than I have in mind. However, setting that aside, we can see the quotation as suggesting the view that a subject who self-ascribes an action she carries out guided by her consideration of what is true is entitled to take the action to be *hers,* because hers are the only actions that can be carried out immediately on the basis of such a consideration. Further, a subject who self-ascribes an action, guided by her consideration of what to do, is entitled to take the attitude as being an action of φ-ing, because φ-ing is the action that she has practical knowledge of as a possibility, and which her consideration of what to do immediately led her to do. If we take the mode of occurrence of the mental action or activity to be given by its being the product of a process of assessment by the subject we have reason to think that an action that occurs in that mode can stand as the reason for its own self-ascription.

The puzzle we faced is why the transition from thought (or utterance) with the content 'P' to the self-ascription 'I think (or utter) that P' is acceptable given that from the subject's perspective the transition seems to cross a gap between radically different and unrelated topics. The appeal to agency seems to step in at this point to show that the supposed gap between the content 'P' of the thought or utterance and the content 'I think (or utter) that P' can be closed when the thought or utterance is an action. The gap is closed for the subject when we think of the occurrence of the thought or utterance as a product of rational agency because thoughts and utterances that arise out of a process of agency, arise as possibilities that the subject has realized on the background of determining what she will do given a grasp of what she could do. Thus, in being determined by her, in this way, an act of a subject arises as hers.

Suppose we accept the two elements of the story. We accept that there is agent's awareness that is independent of a capacity for first-personal self-ascription and that accompanies rational control. And we accept that the fact that our actions are the products of rational control means that there are rational connections which secure a rational entitlement to self-ascribe one's actions. A question remains about relation between these two claims and about nature of agent's awareness.

We could both bring together these two claims and characterize agent's awareness in what we can call *The Constitution Thesis for Agent's Awareness: A subject being agent aware of her action is constituted by the action being the product of the subject's consideration of possibilities, grasped as possibilities.*

According to the constitution thesis, we are agent-aware of our actions *in virtue of* carrying them out as a direct result of an active consideration of ways we might act. The mode of acting in virtue of which ones action is conscious is, on the constitution thesis, acting as the result of an active assessment of ways one might act. Thus it is the process by means of which an action is produced that determines whether it is conscious in a way that makes it liable to stand as the reason for its own self-ascription.

I accept the constitution thesis. That is, I hold that agent's awareness of an action is a product of its being brought about by a certain process of rational assessment which results immediately in action. It seems plausible that the point at which a creature actively evaluates at a personal level the possibilities for action is the point at which she gains a primitive self-consciousness of what she is doing. As long as a creature's actions are lead by non-deliberative or sub-personal systems there is no reason to suppose it is weighing up possibilities, and so no reason to suppose that it need bear any special relation to its own actions. However, once the creature starts, at a personal level, to determine what she should do or think, it is plausible that she must become aware of the possibilities as possibilities for her, and aware of the resulting action as hers.

Further, if we were right to hold that active rational control not only implies, but itself secures or constitutes agent's awareness, we would have made progress in giving a non-representational account of agent's awareness, which would in turn will allow for non-representational uses of 'I' based on such awareness. There are thus significant explanatory advantages to accepting the constitution thesis. One might worry that the thesis is reductive. Our agent's awareness of our actions is no more than acting on the basis of an assessment of known possibilities for action. However, given the logic of the arguments, if we are to give an account of self-consciousness, we must give way to explanations in terms of simpler processes and forms of consciousness at some point. Perhaps this is the point to succumb, if we are not to take the phenomenon as primitive.[15]

Unfortunately, constitution theses are notoriously difficult to make out. Suppose that we can establish that active rational control coincides with awareness of the relevant kind. Suppose also that we can provide evidence that the development of an awareness of our thoughts and actions coincides with the development of an ability for deliberation and active assessment. Suppose, furthermore, that we take ourselves to have established that there are tight rational and conceptual connections between the notion of somethings 'being a possibility that an agent realizes on the basis of an active assessment' and the notion of it 'being a possibility that the agent is aware of as hers'. Even so, we would be some distance from establishing that rational control implies agent's awareness *because* a subject being agent aware of her action is *constituted* by the action being the product of the subject's active assessment of

---

[15] Hamilton (forthcoming) argues that taking self-consciousness as primitive is our only option.

possibilities. There is always room to suppose that the kind of self-awareness involved in the agent being aware of her action is distinct from, but conceptually related to, the agent's capacity for control.

It should be noted also that, even if we accept the constitution thesis, there is still considerable work to be done. Suppose that there is a basic kind of agent's awareness that is constituted by an agent's acting on an active evaluation of possibilities available to her. Our account of how such awareness comes to be constituted by the agent's activity is going to have to draw on yet more primitive notions of awareness, in particular the subject's awareness of the possibilities available, and the awareness of them *as* possibilities. If rational assessment brings about a form of self-awareness when we are aware of ways we might act, we are still going to have to explain that prior awareness of such templates for action.

If we cannot make out the constitution thesis it may be that we can make no stronger claim than what we can call the *Conditional Thesis for Agent's Awareness*: *If a subject acts directly on the basis of a consideration of possibilities, grasped as possibilities, then she will be agent aware of her action.*

The conditional thesis will be true if rational control is sufficient for awareness of a kind that is more primitive than our capacity to self-ascribe our attitudes, and that entitles us immediately to self-ascribe our judgements. However, even with only this much before us, we have made some progress. If it is right to say that there is a capacity for agent's awareness more primitive than our capacity for first-person reference; and if it is right to say that such awareness is involved in our conscious thoughts and utterances, even where there are no first-personal or egocentric representations that we take at face value, we are then able to draw on such awareness to explain what makes a user of a term or concept governed by SRR a self-conscious self-referrer. Such a user refers to herself first-personally in virtue of using 'I' in a thought or utterance she is agent-aware of carrying out. That will be the paradigm case the features of which constitute the fundamental elements of first-person reference. As we said earlier, there will be cases in which a subject may be said to be using a term or concept governed by SRR without her being agent-aware that she is using it. She will nevertheless count, on the account offered, as referring to herself first-personally. However, she will only do so in virtue of her capacity to be agent-aware and in virtue of the relation of such a case to the paradigm case.

5. CONCLUSION

In the preceding discussion I have tried to characterize the nature of agent's awareness as follows:

1. Agent's awareness is a familiar feature of active psychological phenomena rather than passive ones, and is therefore a feature of paradigm thoughts and utterances.

2. Agent's awareness is an awareness we can have without conceptualizing or self-ascribing it. It is a non-conceptual, non-first-personal feature of thoughts and utterances.

3. Agent's awareness is a feature of thoughts and utterances that the thought or utterance has by virtue of its mode of occurrence.

4. Agent's awareness is a feature of thoughts and utterances that the thought or utterance has if they fall under the rational control of the agent.

5. Agent's awareness is an awareness I have of my thoughts or utterances neither by my judging that I am thinking or uttering, nor by my having any perceptual or quasi-perceptual awareness of the action. Rather, my self-ascriptions based on such awareness are representationally independent.

6. Agent's awareness must be capable of *immediately grounding* first-personal knowledge of our actions, for a subject with the relevant conceptual capacities.

It was further suggested that:

7. Agent's awareness is a feature of thoughts and utterances that the thought or utterance has *in virtue of* being the product of an exercise of active rational control by the agent.

If we are unable to secure this final constitutive claim we can at least be satisfied with the claim that the kind of primitive self-awareness that is necessary for, and conceptually implied by rational agency, is distinct from first-person reference and can play a role in its explication. It was further noted that, whether the constitutive claim can be made good or not, there will be a notion of consciousness that precedes and enables the form of self-awareness occasioned by rational agency.

The claim then is that there is a primitive from of agent's awareness that is not first-personal, but is a form of self-awareness, and that is present when we think and utter. Furthermore, it was argued that, working in concert with SRR, such awareness is able to secure the kind of self-conscious self-reference that is properly called first-person reference.

PART II

Actions and Self-Knowledge

7

Introduction to Part II

As a physical and psychological being with a history and a context there is of course lots for me to know about myself. However, in giving a philosophical account of self-knowledge we are concerned not so much with what is in fact true of me, but with certain sources I utilize *as a subject* to gain knowledge of myself. When we talk about self-knowledge, rather than knowledge of what is in fact oneself, we are concerned with ways we have knowledge of ourselves as ourselves. So, which sources of knowledge should we concentrate on if we are to give a philosophical account of self-knowledge? The sources of knowledge that we concentrate on are those that exhibit a first-person third-person asymmetry: they are such that, while seeming to give us knowledge of ourselves, could not give us knowledge of another. They are sources of knowledge that are dedicated to providing the users of such a source with knowledge only of themselves.

There is of course a long tradition in philosophy that has it that self-knowledge, understood in this way as knowledge of ourselves *as ourselves* will deliver up knowledge only of our psychological properties, with introspection as the source of such knowledge. There is a contemporary trend, starting perhaps with Strawson, that has it that we *can* also have knowledge of our physical properties that is nevertheless knowledge of ourselves as ourselves. On this way of thinking, perception, both of our local environment and of our own bodies through bodily awareness, are sources of knowledge of our own physical properties that are capable of providing self-knowledge.

However, it seems to me that the traditional view was right in thinking that we have self-knowledge only of our own psychological states and activities, but wrong to think that that means that such knowledge delivers knowledge only of our psychological properties—it can, also deliver knowledge of our physical properties. Borrowing O'Shaughnessy's distinction between that which is 'purely mental' and that which is 'psychological', I would want to say that while we do indeed need to get away from idea that the problem of self-knowledge should be equated with the problem of explaining our knowledge of purely mental phenomena, we equally need to distance ourselves from the idea that we can have self-knowledge that is not dependent on psychological self-knowledge. I hold, *pace* the contemporary trend mentioned above, that self-knowledge will always involve knowledge of psychological phenomena, but hold physical actions to be psychological phenomena.

It is an implication of the discussion that follows that on some ways of knowing them, our knowledge of our actions, in particular, gives us self-knowledge, and this is knowledge of phenomena that are both psychological and physical. The attempt to give an account of our knowledge of our actions poses many of the same problems posed by the attempts to give an account of our knowledge of beliefs, desires and perceptions. Like our knowledge of our beliefs, desires and perceptions, our knowledge of our actions appears to combine first-person authority with no obvious way of explaining the grounds for such authority. Standard models of epistemic warrant appear to be inadequate when we turn to consider the authority the subject has over certain of her own states and activities.

I have, in the first part of this book, made some suggestions as to how we should understand the knowledge we have of our mental actions. In this part I shall turn to consider what account should be given of the knowledge we have of physical actions. In particular, I shall be concerned to introduce and explore a problem we have in explaining our knowledge of our own physical actions. It is the purpose of this part of the book to try to give an account of such knowledge, making good the idea that our knowledge of our physical actions constitutes an important source for self-knowledge. This task will take up the bulk of the next two chapters. As an implausible view of actions has, in my view, bedevilled our thought on what a plausible account of our knowledge of actions is likely to consist in, the first of these chapters is concerned with the question of what actions are. I argue in favour of an account of actions that takes them to be primitive psychological phenomena, rather than composite constructions out of purely mental states and movements of the body. It would take very much more discussion than is even attempted here to set out fully, and defend the account of actions offered. Instead, Chapter 8 aims to offer the essential elements of an account that needs to be in place for the consequent discussion of self-knowledge to be intelligible. In Chapter 9, I turn to give the account of our knowledge of actions so understood. The final two chapters will be concerned to consider the role of bodily awareness, understood as a perceptual faculty, in our account of self-knowledge.

8

What are Actions?

It has been common to attempt to provide an account of action by providing necessary and sufficient conditions in terms of supposed more basic phenomena for what it is for someone to act. Standard attempts to provide such necessary and sufficient conditions have, however, come to seem as likely to fail as attempts to provide non-circular necessary and sufficient conditions for the concept of knowledge. The accounts offered, typically founder on the possibility of deviant causal chains of one kind or another. Pessimism about the possibility of providing an analysis of actions of this sort is, I want to argue, to be recommended. It is to be recommended because asking the question of why the concept of action may not amenable to such an analysis, naturally leads us to an account of action that is more plausible than the ones being tacitly assumed. Standard analyses of the concept of action fit naturally with a view of actions themselves as complex combinations of bodily movements with other more basic psychological phenomena. The thought that we can give an analysis of actions, in terms of, say, reasons, intentions, tryings along with movements of the body, combined with the idea of a causal connection, is justified if actions themselves are complex constructs, constituted out of these basic building blocks as components. A view of actions as constituted by the right kind of causal relations obtaining between certain more primitive mental events and processes—typically thought to be in some way internal to the acting subject—and certain physical events or processes: movements of the body, is arguably the standard one. Part of the reason that this view seemed natural is that despite the dominance of externalism as a thesis about belief content, there is an abiding assumption that that which is mental is in some way internal to the subject and that which is physical, as bodily movements are, is external. Actions, which in some way seem to cross the division of mental and physical, are thus assumed to be, properly speaking, some sort of 'metaphysical hybrid' of internal and external elements.[1] Once this picture is rejected, there is scope for thinking of actions as unities, not composed out of distinct merelogically proper parts. Actions can be taken as basic elements of the psychological repertoire, much as beliefs are, despite their dependence on movements of our physical bodies.[2]

The suggestion that the concept of action does not admit of a reductive analysis in terms of more basic mental phenomena does not of course mean that there is nothing to be said about the nature of actions. There may be necessary conditions for something being an action that needs to be explored. Actions have distinctive causal histories and purposes and these stand to be mapped. Actions are known in certain ways by ourselves, and by others, and these ways have to be described and explained.

1. PESSIMISM FOR THE PROSPECTS OF A CONJUNCTIVE ANALYSIS

Let it be proposed that necessary and sufficient for a subject to carry out an intentional action of φ-ing is that she has a reason to φ, tries to φ, and that her trying to φ causes a movement of the body that is a φ-ing.

So, A intentionally φs *iff*

---

[1] The phrase 'metaphysical hybrid' is taken from Williamson (1995). It will be clear that I owe a lot to that paper: the thesis being put forward here about actions has its crucial elements in common with Williamson's thesis about knowledge, and I have drawn heavily on Williamson's presentation for help on how to present it. The introduction of Williamson (2000) asks whether similar moves he makes in relation to knowledge might be made for action. Central elements of the thesis itself are to be found in O'Shaughnessy (1980). A clear statement of the thesis presented here is however hard to extract from that work. This is both because of all the *other* things that are going on, and more importantly because O'Shaughnessy seems unable to quite let go of the view that actions (and so for him successful tryings) must be constructs of mental strivings and non-psychological physical events (pp. 207–13). A similar line as that proposed here is also taken in Wilson (1989) which argues against a causalist reduction of intention in action.

[2] I will try, as far as is aesthetically bearable, and I fear beyond, to reserve the phrase 'bodily movement' to refer to an agent's actions of moving her body—raising her arm, bowing her head etc—and use the phrase 'movement of the body' to refer to arm risings, and head bowings which may not be an agent's actions. This seems marginally easier to live with than the subscripting and use of symbolism favoured by others (e.g Hornsby 1980 and O'Shaughnessy 1980).

(i) A has reason to φ

(ii) A tries to φ

(iii) A's trying to φ causes a movement of her body that is a φ-ing.[3]

I take it that the proposal is familiar from standard analyses of action. The proposal is faced with at least three sorts of counterexample.

First we can consider cases where the subject has a reason, and so tries, to φ, and this causes her to ϕ, that as a matter of luck results in her φ-ing. My desire to kill the deer causes me to fire the gun. I miss the deer but the sound of the gun shot causes the rock fall, which kills the deer. We do not want to say in these cases that I succeeded in intentionally killing the deer. How serious such cases are for the attempt to give an analysis of actions in terms of necessary and sufficient conditions rests on whether we have a workable notion of basic actions. In so far as deviancy enters the picture after an action identified as basic has been completed,[4] the attempt to give necessary and sufficient conditions can be restricted to the more modest project of providing an analysis of basic actions. We can say that as long as my act of φ-ing, caused by my having a reason and so trying to φ, is identified as basic then the consequent vicissitudes of fate cannot undermine the account. I will assume that we do have a workable notion of an action as basic. What notion of basic action we should operate with is something I will return to in Chapter 9.

The second type of counterexample is more serious. Here we consider cases in which the subject has a reason to φ, tries to φ, and her trying to φ causes a movement of her body which is a φ-ing, but is a φ-ing only by luck or chance. My desire to kill the deer causes me to try to fire the gun, I am so shocked at what I am doing that my hands clench, and the gun goes off.[5] Here the movement of my body is caused by my trying to φ, because of a reason to φ, but not in the right way. Suppose we have a substantive—not circular or trivial—condition, call it C, that

---

[3] There may of course be analyses that do not demand specifically a causal link. And there are analyses which include only reasons, movements of the body and a causal connection, excluding tryings or willings. The standard causal model starts with Davidson.

[4] Of course, in so far as my moving my finger, which let us say is a basic action, is the action of my turning on the light, talk of the action having been completed should not be construed as talk of the temporal span in which the effects in terms of which the action is described take place. The act of turning on the light can be over before the light comes on.

[5] This is case is modelled on Davidson's climber who has reason to drop his friend and on realizing that that is so, drops his friend (Davidson, 1973: 79).

is offered as a candidate for determining what constitutes causation in the right kind of way. I think that we are likely to view any such a candidate as leaving it open for us to construct a case in which a trying to φ results, in a way that meets C, in a movement of the body which is a φ-ing, but in which due to some twist of fate we would not count as an intentional action. We would feel confident that that possibility had been closed only if we had independent reason to think either that there was an *a priori* connection between there being an intentional action and there being a movement of the body caused in a way that meets C, or reason to think that there was a metaphysical necessity connecting movements of the body caused in a way that meets C and intentional actions. However, as things stand we have no non-circular candidates for C that give us any reason to think either is true. Any candidates for C we can think of—that C ensures that the bodily movement is a direct result of the trying, or that there is nothing about the occurrence of the bodily movement that is accidental given the trying—seem to turn out to be, depending on how they are interpreted, either inadequate or to already presuppose the concept of an action.

Take for example the directness claim. If the claim is that the causal route from the trying to the bodily movement must not be causally mediated then it seems much too strong. After all my trying to raise my arm is surely mediated at least by my muscles contracting. And further, we can imagine unusual looping causal pathways that, due to some prosthetic device for example, effectively support intentional actions. It looks very much as if 'direct' in this context is going to mean something like: a movement of the body is caused directly by my trying *iff* the movement of the body that occurred as a result of the trying was the very movement that I tried to bring about. But that is tantamount to claiming that we have actions just when we have successful tryings. While this is true, it does not seem to me that we any longer have an account that does not already invoke the idea of an action, since my trying to act is successful only in so far as it results in my acting. It is not successful merely in virtue of bringing about a movement of my body of the same type that would have been brought about were it to result in the intended action. I think we are going to face the same kind of problem if we appeal to the idea that the movement of my body must be caused non-accidentally by my trying. What is going to determine whether or not the causal link is accidental is whether the trying was successful or whether it failed.

Of course it is not possible to prove that an analysis of actions along the standard lines will not be forthcoming. There may be some as yet unknown, but metaphysically necessary, causal condition that would make good the account. No such proof is being attempted here. All I am attempting is to raise sufficient pessimism about the possibility of such an analysis in order to motivate the formulation of a non-reductive account, and to stop the fact that standard analyses of action are incompatible with a non-reductive account from militating too strongly against the latter.

There is another, rather different, kind of counterexample to the claim that sufficient for action is a trying to φ (because of a reason to φ) causing a movement of the body that is a φ-ing. Here the concern is that the described causal chain can take place within an agent, so to speak, without the participation or engagement of the agent. So the smoker lights her cigarette despite her hatred and disapproval of what she is doing—she does it in a sense against her own will. The claim is that we do not in such case have intentional actions, properly so called, because we do not have full agency. Frankfurt is most notable for raising cases of this kind.[6] The questions raised by such challenges are first, whether it is necessary for action that there be a certain kind of participation by the agent, and secondly, what condition would satisfy such participation. For my part I think it is clear that we can have action in the absence of participation of the kind identified. The unwilling smoker does act. I do not, however, mean to address these questions here. Rather, I want to note that it is an advantage of the suggestion that actions are such as to admit of no analysis by necessary and sufficient conditions that, on it, there is scope to leave these questions open. In so far as we are attempting to give an analysis of a concept by providing necessary and sufficient conditions we are committed to settling what can be properly called an action. We are also committed to settling what the condition is that is met in those cases where we want to say the agent fully participates in their action. Now of course it is open to such an analyst to offer a catholic account to the extent that she can allow a disjunction of conditions that something must meet in order to be an action. It can be said that the action of the reluctant smoker in lighting her cigarette counts as one variety of action meeting fewer conditions than the action of the untroubled or brazen smoker. But to offer such an account is to take it that the different varieties of action

---

6 See also Velleman (1992).

will be clearly determined and distinguished from one another by the conditions used to individuate them. Of course, even when we are not attempting any such analysis we still need to be able to answer the question as to whether we have an action in a given case, but the answer does not have to be given via reference to a set of pre-given conditions. It is open to us to deal with such questions on a case by case basis.

2. ACTION AS A UNITY

If it is the case that standard analyses of the concept of action fail, how does such failure effect what we think actions are? I have said that behind the standard analyses of action is a picture of actions as complex constructs, built out of components referred to in each condition. However, the connection between the project of giving an analysis of a concept and the project of giving the metaphysics of that referred to by the concept is not simple. As has been said, we cannot prove that independent necessary and sufficient conditions along standard lines cannot be given for the occurrence of an action. There is nothing in principle to rule out the possibility of there being articulable conditions, in terms of reasons, tryings, and movements of the body that are extensionally coincident with the concept of bodily action. In so far as the analyst is concerned with a search for such conditions, I may be perplexed at her decision to spend her time in that way, but I have no argument with her. However, standard analyses of the sort I have referred to can be taken to be doing more than identifying conditions that happen to coincide with the occurrence of actions. Rather, it is supposed that they *explicate* the concept. It is supposed that anyone who understands the conditions, statable without use of the concept, which are offered as necessary and sufficient will understand what is meant by the concept itself.[7] If it is right that actions should be taken as unities and considered as metaphysically basic as tryings or beliefs, then it not clear what motivates an analysis of the concept of action in terms of an inner reason or trying, and some movement of the body appropriately connected. In the absence of obvious reasons to accept

---

[7] There is, as has been brought out by Peacocke in recent years, the distinct project of identifying what he calls the possession conditions for a concept: necessary and sufficient conditions for the possession of a concept. However since the project of giving possession conditions does not involve giving conditions independent of the concept it must not be seen as an attempt to decompose the concept in the way standard analyses are.

the analysis its main motivation would seem to come from a view of actions as metaphysical hybrids: events or occurrences constituted out of metaphysically more basic parts.

Theorists about actions have not been insensitive to the fact that actions, despite having physical, and so external, success conditions, like other psychological aspects of a person seem to have a unitary nature. Danto's denial that actions be thought of as compound events, and his discussion of how we come to know our actions, clearly reflects an understanding of actions as somehow basic unities, not constructions of other elements. The account that follows here owes much to and is in close agreement with his account.[8] But very often even those who can be taken to be offering an analysis of the kind we have discussed want to secure the unity of the action as constituted out of distinct component parts. Consider the following from O'Shaughnessy:

> When a man intentionally raises his arm, the following happens. His arm rises; he tries to raise his arm; and the latter event causes, along acceptable bodily paths, the physical event of his arm rising. These are logically necessary and sufficient conditions of an intentional action.[9]

He goes on to ask what analysis we are to give of the action. Is the action the arm rising, suitably caused, or is it the causing of arm rising, by the trying, or is it identical with the trying to raise the arm: the trying that caused the arm-rising?[10]

O'Shaughnessy's favoured answer is that 'the act of raising the arm is a complex event, constituted out of a causally linked pair of events, the trying and the arm rising, that are "made for each other"'(1973: 383). He is keen to stress that the two events out of which an action is constituted have particular close connections 'there exist unique binding forces between these events that should make of their union something more than a mere conventionally concocted parcel of events.' (386)

O'Shaughnessy's remarks illustrate very well two opposing demands. On the one hand, to give an account of a single, unified phenomenon that seems to be both mental and physical, and on the other to construe action as built on a mental event that has ontological independence from its physical manifestation. O'Shaughnessy identifies as necessary

---

[8] See Danto (1973).   [9] O'Shaughnessy (1973: 383).

[10] This seems to be Hornsby's answer in her *Actions* (1980). And the way she draws the analogy with causal theories of perception suggests that it is. However, there are signs both in that early book, and in her later work, that a view more like that being recommended here might be in play.

for action, a trying-act that results in a movement of the body, where the trying-act is construed as an 'inner' mental event. It is an event distinguishable from the actions carried out, and independent of any subsequent movement of the body. A trying-act is the same in cases where it is successful and where it fails. Indeed for O'Shaughnessy it is the factor common to actions and mere tryings. This analysis combined with the assumption that the answer to what an action is needs to be constructed from the elements identified as necessary for action is what forces O'Shaughnessy to think he has to make his choice between the four options he cites. Given this picture, the theorist does indeed have to choose whether the action is properly thought of as identical with the trying-act that happens on this occasion to be successful, or identical with the bodily movement, or some combination of the above.

Given the choices that he has set himself O'Shaughnessy is surely right to opt for the latter. But better still not to have to make the choice. If we are right, that the conditions identified are, at most, only necessary conditions then the action itself need not be identified with any one or parcel of the events being identified here. So, in offering an account of what an action is in terms a parcel of events at all, albeit not a 'conventionally concocted' one, O'Shaughnessy can be judged to have gone further than justified. The claim being made here is that we need not join him in attending to the task of tying tightly together the different component events identified as necessary for action, the internal and the external, because actions do not factorize into such events in the first place.

So far, most of what has been said has been negative. The main thrust of the discussion has been to urge that we should not aim to produce a reductive account, along standard lines, of what an action is. We should not have such an aim as it seems unlikely to be successful and would in any case contradict the natural thought that (bodily) actions are primitive unified psychological occurrences with external existence conditions.

Before moving to try to pull together the admittedly modest claims that can be made once we have given up the ambition to produce a reductive account, I want to explore some positive considerations for taking actions, rather than combinations of intentions, tryings and movements of the body as basic. The positive argument centres around the role that actions play in explanations and justifications of our own and others' responses to them. Consider a case where I am angry with someone for what they have done, and they are ashamed in turn. In many such cases, at the centre of any explanation or justification of my anger or their shame will be the action itself.

Suppose I am angry with Elmore for making a V-sign at me, in the presence of those I respect. Suppose that I am angry with him because he acted in a way that humiliated me and showed a failure to respect me. I am not angry with him merely for trying to act in such a way. Although I might be angry for someone for trying to do this, in this case I am angry with him in part for the humiliation he has caused. Nor am I angry with him for moving his body in a certain way. If he had moved his body inadvertently, I would not have been angry. I might have been embarrassed, but I would not have been angry, having accepted that he merely moved his body without acting. Nor it seems need my anger be explained by the fact that he tried to produce a V-sign at me *and* that his body moved in a certain way. Nor by the fact that he tried to produce a V-sign at me *and* that his body moved in a certain way *and* that there was causal connection between the two. Rather we can reasonably suppose that in this case my anger is explained and justified by what he has done, for the way he has acted to humiliate me, and not by these conjunctions of more basic facts.

Suppose Elmore is ashamed of the way he acted to humiliate me. Again we can suppose that the explanation of Elmore's shame lies not in what he tried to do, although there may be cases like that, nor in the mere movements his body made, nor in some combination of the two but rather in the way he acted against another.[11]

The example given involves the role actions play in the explanation and justification of certain kinds of emotional response. But in fact, at the centre of any explanation of our responses to each other as persons—our understanding each other's utterances, our predicting each other's future behaviour and so on—will be actions committed. Of course none of the above shows that there cannot be a set of independent conditions such that if they are met they will be sufficient to explain and justify the relevant responses. However, it is hard to avoid the suspicion that for any reductive combination of conditions

---

[11] The same kinds of considerations come in to cases of punishment. Suppose that we punish someone for murder only if they acted to kill. Even if someone tried to kill another, and as a result of her trying, her body moved involuntarily and in such a way that it caused a death, she is not thereby punishable for murder. She may deserve punishment for an attempted murder, and for manslaughter, and indeed we might think she deserves special punishment because the killing was caused by her attempt at killing, but she cannot be punished for murder. Without the action there is no murder to be punished for.

in terms of tryings, bodily movements and causal connections, we will be able to show that they are met without there being the response we set out to explain and justify. This, and the obvious complexity that is going to be required for any such conditions, set against the naturalness of explanation and justification in terms of actions gives us positive reasons to take actions as basic.

Let me now return to consider what more modest account of actions we might give if we give up the ambition to produce a reductive account in terms of other more basic phenomena. The most general way of stating the central external condition for something to be an action is to point out that an agent cannot be said to have acted unless something has been done. 'Acting' is a success verb. Just as you cannot be said to have seen an object unless the object exists, or know something unless it is true, you cannot be said to have acted unless there is something that has been done.

Moreover what has been done must match the description of what the agent is doing. Although it is hard to put it nicely, the point is a simple one: an agent cannot be said to have put the kettle on unless a kettle has been put on, an agent has not raised her arm unless her arm has risen and so on. Perhaps we can put the general condition in the following way:

P: If φ-ing is an action, then Aφs only if an event φ takes place.

When we are concerned with *bodily* action as we are here, we can further add that from a subject carrying out a bodily action it follows that there are movements of the subject's body. We can, however, say a little more than this. It seems that all bodily actions imply movements of the body because they imply bodily movements, which are themselves actions, and have movements of our bodies in their success conditions (from P). So, an agent has not carried out an intentional bodily action unless she has moved her body and her body has moved. How we identify the relevant class of bodily movements, and so the corresponding class of movements of the body, will depend upon our view of the ways in which we identify the possible bodily movements a subject can carry out. I think that this is fixed, in the normal case, by the subject's own practical grasp, via her body image, of what bodily movements are possible ones for her. They are presented to the subject as a range of ways she might act, without doing anything else.[12]

---

[12] Note that there are bodily actions such as holding my body still, or refraining from reaching out, that may seem not to have *movements* of the body in their success conditions. I however want to use 'movements of the body' in a broad enough way for a

When we put all these thoughts together, we get the suggestion that we take bodily actions to be unified psychological phenomena with external existence conditions of which the following three principles hold.[13]

(P1)   If φ-ing is an action, then Aφs only if an event φ takes place. (*Success condition*)

(P2)   If φ-ing is a bodily action, then Aφs only if A moves her body in some way w. (*Bodily actions imply bodily movements.*)

(P3)   Moving one's body in way w is an action. (*Bodily movements are also bodily actions.*)

The principles encode the two basic claims about bodily actions mentioned above. First, that actions are dependent upon success. If someone tries to act and does not succeed there is no action. Of course, if trying is a mental action then in so far as we try we do act, but there is no bodily action. Secondly, that all bodily actions—whether raising my arm or writing my name, presuppose that the agent moves her body. These two claims, given the assumption that bodily movements are also bodily actions, give us the claim that all bodily action implies the existence of movements of the agent's body. The derivation of this latter claim from the three principles is as follows:

(P4)   A moves her body in way w only if a movement of A's body in way w takes place.

(From (P1) and (P3)) (*Bodily movements imply movements of the body.*)

(P5)   If φ-ing is (any) bodily action, then A φs only if a movement of A's body in way w takes place.

(From (P2) and (P4)) (*All bodily actions imply movements of the body.*)

It is worth asking at this point how well such principles characterize bodily action as opposed to other psychological phenomena. Of course, given that the principles are stated in such a way that being a bodily

body held still or an arm kept back at the side to count as a movement of the body. (For a discussion of those bodily actions I take as basic, see the discussion in ch. 9, s. 2.1.2.) There are yet further putative actions, sometimes called negative actions, such as my not going to my friend's party because I am too tired, which do not seem to involve even restraining or holding my body. However, it seems to me that if such putative actions are indeed actions they are not bodily or physical actions.

[13]   I think we can also claim that someone cannot be said to have the concept of bodily action unless they accept these principles.

action figures explicitly as a condition they, trivially, stand to characterize only bodily actions. The more substantial question at issue is whether there are unified psychological occurrences the existence of which imply a movement of the agent's body in the way specified by these principles, but which are not actions. To get to an answer to this, let us start by asking whether (P5), which was derived from our three principles, does not by itself give us the characterizing feature of bodily action. That is, we might ask whether the following principle is true if applied to psychological phenomena other than actions:

(P5')   If φ-ing is a psychological phenomenon, then Aφs only if a movement of A's body in way w takes place.[14]

It might be said that such a principle is inadequate to identify actions because someone's being in a state of pain, which is not an action, is such as to imply a movement of the body in response. But it is clear that bodily movement is not part of the conditions for the existence of a pain, even if it is part of the conditions stating what would happen if the pain was functioning as it was supposed to. Perhaps unfortunately, paralysis does not always remove from one the ability to feel pain, even though it removes the ability to move in certain ways.

A more revealing objection to the suggestion that (P5') gives us the identifying feature of actions comes from cases of a subject who perceives or remembers that her body is moving. In such a case there seems to be a psychological occurrence that is not an action, but that implies a movement of the agent's body. From 'A perceives that her arm is rising' we can infer that A's arm is rising. For factive mental states, if they are attitudes towards a content that implies a movement of the subject's body then, the subject being in that state will imply that her body moved.

Now it is open to us to try to dispatch such cases immediately by claiming that our principles are concerned only with psychological phenomena at the level of types. If we take φ to range only over attitude or process types (believing, perceiving, seeing, hearing, remembering, moving, lifting, throwing etc) then since perceiving *per se* does not

---

[14] A word on the use of psychological phenomena is needed: by psychological phenomena I mean only that it is a phenomena of subjects, rather than mere objects. I do not mean that it is internal, or non-physical. Further, I reserve the phrase psychological occurrence or phenomenon for occurrences or phenomena that are personal and so ascribed to a whole subject, rather than to any part of her. So something legitimately studied in psychology may not be a psychological phenomenon in this sense.

imply movements of the body we may not have a problem. In so far as the cases offered are problematic only because of a certain peculiarity of content in certain token perceptions, we are justified in ignoring them. I am, however, not going to ignore them. Allowing the principles to be sensitive to differences in content despite sameness of process and attitude type, enables us to come to a clearer understanding of why implied bodily movement is a mark only of bodily action, and not other psychological attitudes and processes.

We cannot of course undermine such cases by saying that perceiving and remembering are not properly mental states because they involve some external conditions, but rather are hybrids of 'seemings to see' and the objects seen. To insist on such a construal would be to undermine the account of actions being suggested here. Nor can we undermine such cases by saying that perceiving and remembering involve the subject standing in a relation to a certain propositional content whereas acting does not. For, acting ascriptions can be put in terms of a relation between the subject and a propositional content, although in such cases the state of affairs expressed by the proposition is taken to be *made* true, or *brought about* by the subject rather than registered or recalled. Let P be the proposition 'The kettle is lifted on to the cooker'. The subject can be said to bring it about that P, in lifting the kettle onto the cooker, as she can be said to perceive that P, in perceiving that the kettle is lifted onto the cooker and to remember that P, in remembering that the kettle was lifted onto the cooker. Furthermore, perception and memory ascriptions, like action ascriptions, can seem to put the subject in a relation to an object rather than a proposition. A subject can be said to see or remember the kettle just as she can be said to lift it.

One suggestion might be that (P5') would be adequate if it captured the distinction between those psychological phenomena that are static, which are states of a person, and those that are dynamic, which we can think of as processes or events in which a subject participates. The suggestion is that we might exclude the above cases by saying that only those psychological phenomena that are *events or processes* and that imply movements of the subject's body, are bodily actions. But it can be replied that while 'perceiving that p' or 'remembering that p' are in central cases used to refer to mental *states* they can also be used to refer to events or processes. They can, for example, be used to refer to the process of looking at the kettle on the cooker and to the process of recalling the kettle being on the cooker, and so, of course, they can be used to refer to the process of looking at, or recalling, the movements of one's own body. Given that we can identify even dynamic psychological occurrences that imply movements of the body, modifying (P5') in the way suggested will not give us a principle sufficient to characterize actions.

Some will think that it is obvious what is missing here. It will be said that bodily actions do not simply imply movements of the subject's body, they cause those movements. If that were so, then we would have solved our problem. Since seeing my body move cannot precede my body moving, there is no question of the seeing causing the movements being seen. However, we can doubt whether the right way to characterize the relation between bodily actions and movements of the body, is as causal. The claim being made above, that A's body moving is being taken to be an *a priori* condition of A's carrying out a bodily action, does not sit altogether easily with the claim that A's bodily action caused A's body to move. It might be that a sufficiently broad notion of causation will allow both claims to be true. What perhaps we ought to say is not that bodily actions cause the movements of the body implied, but rather that where we have bodily actions we have an agent causing her body to move. It is not the case that where we have a subject seeing or recalling a bodily movement, we have an agent causing her body to move.

However, it is better to avoid these sources of controversy, and focus on a less metaphysically committed difference between bodily actions and those processes by means of which we record or recall our bodily movements. While it may be problematic to say that bodily actions cause the movements of the body, that they imply, it is less problematic to claim that bodily actions determine the movements of the body that they imply. It is less controversial because the explanation of such determination may or may not be causal. It allows us to leave the precise metaphysical relation between the bodily actions and the implied movements of the body open.[15] While, it is necessary, for there to be a recording or recalling of the movements of my body, that there be such movements, the fact that I record or recall them need be no part of the explanation of why there are such movements. In contrast, in the case of bodily action, such action both implies that there are movements of the body and plays a part in explaining why there are such movements.

[15] I favour a view on which movements of my body are thought of as part of the non-personal realizing, or supervenience, base of my bodily actions, so that the relation between bodily action and bodily movements are thought to be vertical rather than horizontal. We then have a picture on which the bodily action can be used in a 'top-down' explanation of the movements of my body, without causing it.

So if we modify (P5') in the light of these considerations we can now ask whether it is the case that that the following principle is true only of bodily actions.

(P5") If φ-ing is a dynamic psychological occurrence, then Aφs implies that, and determines why, A's body moves in way w.

It may be said that this does not get us our result because there are cases in which we can appeal to A's seeing her body move in our explanation of A's body moving. Cases where A sees her body move and the movement is explained by her moving it in order to see it, may be thought to provide such a possibility. However, the crucial difference between such cases and the case of bodily action lies in the fact that we know immediately from the fact that Aφs, where φ-ing is a bodily action, both that A's body moves and that Aφs will partly explain why and how A's body moves. From knowing merely that A sees her body move, we know that A's body moved but we have no reason to think that A's seeing will enter into an explanation of why A's body moves.

The most interesting objection to the attempt to use (P5') to circumscribe those dynamic psychological occurrences which are actions comes, perhaps unsurprisingly, from such phenomena as instinctive responses. Consider, for example, the startle response. Being startled, let us suppose, is a particular kind of basic emotional state manifested, and arguably constituted by, a bodily response. It is perhaps plausible to suggest that someone who does not exhibit bodily movements characteristic of the startle response cannot be said to be in the emotional state of being startled. It is true that there is not much determinacy in *which* movements are characteristic of being startled. The movements seem to be characteristic in the sense of being sudden and jerky rather than in the sense we have been using, as movements of this or that limb. Perhaps, however, distinct stimuli will give rise to distinct kinds of startle response characterized by ways of moving the body, in the relevant sense. We then have a candidate dynamic psychological occurrence: starting, which implies that the subject who starts moves her body in a characteristic way. However, it is far from clear that we should take such a startle response to be an action. While starting is perhaps not a mere reflex response, in the way that a movement of my leg is a response to being hit just below the knee, it seems odd to count it as a fully fledged action. Some might be tempted to answer the challenge posed by saying that such responses are not obviously *psychological* phenomena in the relevant sense—but rather sub-personal occurrences we can rule out by fixing the limits of the psychological in the appropriate way. Others might argue for a category of primitive, emotion-based actions, such as fleeing through fear and squealing through joy, and count the startle response as one of such a kind. Obviously, the decision as to how to classify such responses would require more of a theory of action than is going to be offered here.[16]

However, one thing that seems to be emerging here is that where there is a question about whether a 'bodily-movement-implying' dynamic psychological phenomenon is an action is also where there is a corresponding question about whether it is genuinely psychological and satisfies (P5"). Thus while there may be ways of further refining, or clarifying, (P5") so that it is true only for straightforward cases of action, for my purposes P5" is enough. It can stand as a principle to identify candidate actions and I do not rule out or in further refinements. One possible, amendment to, or clarification of, P5" might be to require that, for there to be determination and explanation in the relevant sense, there needs to be a content match between the content of the psychological phenomenon ascribed and the structure of the movement of the body it stands to explain. In the case of bodily action the content of the action of my moving my arm determines and explains the way my body moves. The fact that I am startled might explain why my body moved. But the content of the startle response itself does not seem to explain why, say, my hands fly up—some kind of more external explanation is needed. I am not, however, going to go further in to that here. Let us take it that in so far as P5" is true of a given psychological phenomenon, that phenomeon is at least a borderline action. And given the flexibility introduced by the notion of determination, this should be enough to allow us to say (P5") seems to be acceptable for identifying bodily action, but allows for borderline cases.

---

[16] Briefly, on the story, I would be inclined to say that something would not be an action unless, as a necessary condition, there was some sense in which it was selected by the subject relative to the subject's body image. Thus the startle response would not count as an action. Since my body image would be used to fix the relevant class of the ways my body moves, ways which are utilized in the statement of (P5"), it may be that the startle response does not imply a movement of the body in any way which falls within the class of the relevant ways *w*. However, and more likely, if it is the case that my startle movements feed into fixing my body image, then my being startled would imply a bodily movement in the relevant class. What seems clear though is that the startle response could, say, in a newborn subject, be a psychological state which implied a bodily movement, which for that subject, at that point, was not one of the ways *w* falling within the class of possible movements fixed by the body image.

Now that we have modified (P5) in an attempt to mark the distinctive features of bodily actions, we should go back to (P1), (P2) and (P3), from which (P5) was derived. Our discussion of (P5) has left us with the suggestion that what is distinctive of bodily actions is that they are dynamic psychological occurrences that imply and determine movements of the body. With this in mind let us re-state our principles in a way that does not involve essential reference to the notion of bodily action, by referring only to dynamic psychological occurrences that imply and determine movements of the body, rather than bodily actions.

(P1*) If φ-ing is a dynamic psychological occurrence, then Aφs implies that, and determines why, an event φ takes place.

(P2*) If φ-ing is a bodily dynamic psychological occurrence, then Aφs only if A moves her body in some way w.

(P3*) Moving one's body in way w is a bodily dynamic psychological occurrence.

therefore:

(P4*) A moves her body in way w implies that, and determines why, a movement of A's body in way w takes place.

(From (P1*) and (P3*))

and

(P5*) If φ-ing is a bodily dynamic psychological occurrence, then Aφs implies, that and determines why, A's body moves in way w.

(From (P2*) and (P4*)).

The above principles suggest that actions of moving one's body are basic to physical action. In particular, all other bodily dynamic psychological occurrences, whatever else they are, are actions of moving one's body. And given that actions of moving one's body imply movements of the body, this implies that from any bodily dynamic psychological occurrence we can infer a movement of the body. The account takes the action of moving one's body as basic. However, it also gives us a means of identifying such actions. Any bodily dynamic psychological occurrence that plays the role that the action of moving one's body plays in these principles will be equivalent to a subject's movement of her body. Suppose we take any bodily dynamic psychological occurrence—a χ-ing, say. If we substituted A's χ-ing for A's movement of her body in (P2*) then, given (P3*), from the fact that A moves her body it follows that Aχs. (From 'If φ-ing is a bodily dynamic psychological occurrence, then Aφs only if Aχs' and 'Moving one's body in way w is a bodily dynamic psychological occurrence' it follows that A moves her body in way w only if Aχs.) Also, from substituting χ-ing in (P3*), given (P2*), from the fact that Aχs it follows that A moves her body. (From 'χ-ing is a bodily dynamic psychological occurrence' and 'If φ-ing is a bodily dynamic psychological occurrence, then Aφs only if A moves her body in some way w' it follows that Aχs only if A moves her body in some way w.) Thus, if A moves her body then Aχs, and if Aχs then A moves her body. To put it as Williamson might, bodily movements are the most general bodily actions. Whenever we engage in bodily action we carry out the action of moving our bodies.

I have suggested that we should take bodily actions as primitive psychological phenomena, and not as metaphysical hybrids of more basic components. I have also made the minimalist suggestion that we should take all bodily actions to be bodily movements, with movements of the body as success conditions. Whatever is made of the latter suggestion, the claim that we should understand actions as basic unities is taken as a constraint on the task of accounting for our knowing of our actions. This task is the concern of the next chapter. Before moving to that task, however, I want consider the relation between actions and tryings. This constitutes something of a digression; the reader not particularly interested in tryings may want to skip ahead to the next chapter.

3. ACTIONS AND TRYINGS

Even if actions are not amenable to a conjunctive analysis along standard lines, because they are not to be properly thought of as metaphysical psychological hybrids constructed from inner mental tryings, and external movements of bodies, there is obviously work to be done in clarifying the relations between actions, tryings and movements of bodies. To do this properly would require an investigation in the metaphysics of action beyond anything I mean to embark on here. Let me however, with the hope of at least sketching the view I have in mind look at what the options are and indicate which I think we should go for.

A number philosophers claim that whenever someone acts they try or will to do something. They hold that a necessary condition of a subject φ-ing is that the subject is trying to φ. Many accounts of action consider the necessity of trying in action as evidence in favour of the view that there are tryings, or willings which are psychological events distinct from actions, and further that such tryings or willings are psychological events which are constituent parts of actions. They are taken to be constituent parts of actions in virtue of being constituent events of a complex event that is an action. However, these further commitments do not follow directly from the claim that trying is necessary for action. First, to claim that in acting a subject also tries, does not in itself commit one to a substantial psychological category of 'tryings'. Of course, we might allow that in so far as an action has the property of being something that the subject tries to do, then there is a trivial sense in which the action is also a trying. However, we certainly cannot assume that just because a subject tries when she acts that she carries out a trying, distinct from the action. Second, even if we were to allow that in acting a subject also carries out a distinct trying, it does not follow that such tryings are parts of the action. The former claim can be true, without the latter being true. Being a part of an action is only one way in which trying may be necessary for action. Trying maybe distinct from, but necessary for, acting if trying was, say, a distinct but necessary precedent of action.

There are usually two arguments in play with respect to tryings, which together aim to establish the thesis there are tryings that are psychological events that cause bodily movements. In reaction to this, theorists tend either to take actions to be constructs of such tryings and the bodily movements caused, or to offer a view of actions as merely tryings that cause bodily movements.

The first argument aims to establish the claim that whenever we act we try to do something. The claim is made that actions, as opposed to mere movements of the body, involve the subject being directed towards a goal. In some cases that goal will be specified in terms of a distinct prior intention a subject forms about what to do, in some cases the goal will be specified in terms of what Searle (1983, ch. 3) calls the intention in action. Either way, it seems we can say that in acting the subject has a goal, and thus can be described as attempting to, aiming to, or trying to do something. What the subject is trying to do will give us the description of the action that she carrying out, if she is successful.

The second argument aims to establish that such tryings need to be understood as mental events that cause movements of the body in successful action and fail to cause bodily movements in failed actions.

The argument stems from a consideration of failed action. When we fail to act, because of motor failure, say, we say that although we failed to act, we at least tried. The fact that, in cases of failure to act, we nevertheless manage to try to act is taken to suggest that we try to act also in those cases in which we succeed in acting. Now, this is not a particularly good argument.[17] From the fact that I tried to act when I failed it does not follow that I would have tried had I succeeded. Tryings may be just what you get when you have failed action. But let us for the moment go along with the assumption that we retain a feature of successful action in failed action, and agree that the case of failed action may give us a reason to think that even when we succeed in acting we also try to act. It is the next step of the argument that is problematic. The further suggestion is that it follows from a consideration of failed action, not just that all actions involve the subject in trying to do something, but that trying is a personal level psychological event that is a component in both failed and successful action. The only difference between a successful action and a failed one is taken to lie in whatever is left over when you take the trying away from a successful action: both actions and failed actions have the trying as a common component. Some theorists, *the minimizers*, argue further that the subject's action, as opposed to its consequences, is in fact complete once the subject has tried to act and is therefore identical with their trying.[18] On this account the difference between an action (which is a trying) and a *mere* trying lies in the consequences of each. Others will take actions to be complex events involving the supposed trying and whatever movements of the body are supposed to follow from it.

However, the discussion above allows us to see that we may agree that trying is necessary for action, and that failed bodily actions involve trying, without agreeing that tryings are common between actions and such failed actions. It will help us see the options available, to someone who rejects the view of tryings as component parts of actions, if we consider the argument below:

1. Successful actions are tryings.[19] (Assumption)
2. Failed actions are tryings. (Assumption)

---

[17] See Wilson (1989, pp. 157–9) for a good discussion of such an argument.

[18] I am using Ginet's term for such a position (see Ginet 1990: 47). Hornsby (1980) and (1997) *seems* to be a minimiser.

[19] By actions here I mean physical actions.

3. Successful actions imply movements of the body.[20] (Assumption)

4. Failed actions do not imply movements of the body. (Assumption)

5. Tryings are uniform. (Assumption)

therefore:

6. Tryings do not imply movements of the body. (from 2, 4, 5)

therefore:

7. Successful actions are not tryings. (from 1, 3, 6)

therefore:

8. Successful actions are tryings and successful actions are not tryings. (from 1, 7)

We have a number of options if we are to avoid the conclusion. Claim 4 seems almost undeniable. And it is likely that a denial of claim 2, the claim that failed actions are tryings, will be accompanied by a denial of claim 1, that successful actions are tryings. I will therefore consider only the options of denying 1, 3, and 5.

Option 1
We might deny claim 3, that successful actions (metaphysically) imply movements of the body. If we deny claim 3, but hold on to the claim that successful and failed actions are tryings, and that tryings are uniform, the option we have is that we identified as the minimizer option. Hornsby raises a similar point as follows:

> If the thesis that the movement *is the same as* the action were correct, then the three sorts of events we began from [the attempt, the action and the movement of the body] would prove to be such that a single event is of all these three sorts: the action is itself movement and attempt. If we favour a certain uniform account of trying, however, we have a reason to think the movement is distinct from the attempt. (Hornsby 1997: 96)

If we take the movement to be independent of the attempt we must take the action to be independent of either the attempt, or the movement, or both. The minimizer chooses to take the action to be independent of the movement but not the attempt.

[20] The claims of what successful actions imply or failed actions do not imply are intended as claims about what the event itself—that is the successful action—implies or does not imply. It is the essential properties of the relevant action that is at issue, and not trivial implications true in virtue of descriptions.

Option 2
We might deny claim 4, that tryings are uniform. This would enable us to take actions to be kinds of events that imply movements of the body if successful, and not if not, and take both successful and failed actions to be tryings, but of distinct sorts. Some tryings may imply movements of the body and some not. We can call this the *disjunctivist view* of trying.[21] When a trying is a case of action, that is, a successful trying, it might be conceived of as a bodily action that is a movement of the body, whereas a trying, in the case of failed action, may be only a truncated action, with no movement of the body.

Option 3
We might deny claim 1, that successful actions are tryings. On this option, if we retain the assumption that trying is necessary for acting, that there are tryings in both successful and failed cases, and that tryings are uniform, we are likely to think of tryings as psychological events that are pre-cursors, perhaps causal, of action.

There are, of course, also the options of denying more than one claim. We might deny 1, 2 and 3; deny 1 and 2; deny 2 and 3 or deny 1 and 3. But let me consider the advantages and disadvantages of denying one of 1, 3, and 5 singly. There are more or less plausible aspects to all three options.

The Option 1 view, denying that our actions imply movements of the body, but holding that they *are* psychological events *of the same kind* as take place when we fail to act, seems discordant with our common sense of things. Let me confine myself to noting that to take things as so is to take our contact with another's action to be via something distinct from and consequent to the action itself. The action is over before the movements of the body commence otherwise the action could not be a trying of the same kind as in the case of failed action. When we see, feel, hear someone's dancing what we are in fact seeing, feeling and hearing are effects of a completed action.[22] There are of course many things that a defender of the view that actions cause movements of the body can say in response to the objection. They can point out that cases of 'direct' perception are the exception and that perception of something via its effects

---

[21] Such disjunctivism about trying is obviously modelled on disjunctivist views in perception and elsewhere. (See, e.g., McDowell 1986, 1994; Snowdon 1980/81, 1990; Martin 1997b, 2004.)

[22] See O'Shaughnessy (1980: 130–2) for this criticism. See Hornsby (1997) for a response to it.

is a commonplace. We see the bomb exploding in seeing the shrapnel scatter and the flame burst, even though it's exploding might be taken to be the cause of the scattering of shrapnel and flame. So too, it might be said, we see the subject moving her arm by seeing her arm moving.

However, I do not intend to argue decisively against any such possible account here. My claim will only be that we have a *prima facie* reason to reject the view that our bodily actions are tryings in just the same way as our failed actions are. We *seem* to be able to say that if an agent moves her body, and is witnessed, then it is her action that is perceived, and not merely an effect of it. Further, it seems that a central reason for us taking ourselves to perceive the agent herself and not merely her body is that we perceive her actions themselves.

Option 2 is the view that we try both when we succeed in acting and when we fail, but that in so trying we carry out different acts. In the former case we do the thing that we are trying to do. In the latter case we carry out a truncated action that we know only as a trying to do the thing we were trying to do.

An advantage of this view seems to be that it allows us to combine the thought that we act by trying, that in acting that is *all* that we have to do, with the thought that actions are not merely mental actions. On this view when our tryings are successful they just are the actions the agent produces. When the trying fails however the trying is only a truncated action, it is precisely only a trying.

It may be said, this picture does not sit well with how we see things when we take ourselves to be agents faced with the situation of not knowing whether we succeeded in acting or not. In such cases we tend to comfort ourselves with the knowledge that 'at least we know that we tried to act', and in doing so we seem to be doing something more than merely articulating to ourselves our predicament: that we do not know whether we acted or merely tried. We seem rather to have fixed on something *positive* we know in either the case that we acted or that we did not, that is, our knowledge that we tried. If the disjunctivist holds that for us to know that we tried in a case of ignorance, is for us to know nothing more than that we either acted or merely tried, the claim that at least we know we tried cannot act as an *advance* on knowing that we either acted or merely tried.

The disjunctivist may respond that she need not deny that the *knowledge* that we are trying to do something might be a common component across the case of successful and unsuccessful action. The disjunctivist might acknowledge that both when we act and when we fail to act we try to do something, and that in a case of ignorance about whether she succeeded in acting, an agent can at least know that she satisfies the property of trying to do something. What she will deny is that the explanation of this knowledge, that we are trying, need appeal to any *act* of trying of the same kind, and with the same dimensions, as we commit in the case that we fail. In short, the fact that the disjunctivist denies that distinct acts of trying are common components of actions and mere tryings, may not commit her to denying that satisfying the property of trying to do something is common to acting and merely trying.[23]

A further objection might be that in having only one concept of trying, our common understanding conflicts with the disjunctive view. If this were so, it would mean that the disjunctivist account was reformative of normal usage. However, the evidence from normal usage seems to be far from decisive. Moreover it is not clear that our disjunctivist need deny that we operate with a univocal concept of trying. She may acknowledge that there is a single concept of what it is to try to do something—perhaps, to be a psychological occurrence that is the immediate product of practical reasoning—but also deny that only one *kind* of psychological event may bear that property. It would only be a non-derivative nominative concept of 'tryings' that she would need to hold to be equivocal.

What of the plausibility of Option 3, denying claim 1, and endorsing the view either that there are no tryings involved at all in the positive case, or that actions are not tryings but rather that tryings are pre-cursors to action?

Consider the first possibility, that there are no tryings in the positive case. We might think that the disjunctivist has not, as advertised, shown that tryings are not uniform because there are two kinds of tryings—actions and mere tryings. Rather in arguing that there are actions and mere tryings with no psychological event in common, she has in effect argued that there are tryings in the case of failed action alone. If we want to insist that there are tryings in both the successful and unsuccessful case we might think that they are distinct from but necessary precursors of the action.

Such a view of tryings as distinct from, and no part of an action, may seem to have to an advantage over the disjunctivist in being able

---

[23] Although it may commit her if we assume that knowing that she tried is a singular item of knowledge that requires knowing what constitutes the trying in each case.

to apply the concept in the successful and unsuccessful case while retaining a uniform notion of trying, which our ordinary usage might seem to recommend. We only have one word for trying, it might be said, because we have one basic notion of what a trying is. However, this combination of views leaves us with a concern. There is a worry that the account leaves tryings as too detached from the actions they initiate. Both the suggestion that tryings are parts of actions, and the disjunctivist suggestion that successful tryings are identical with the action, and as such quite different from a mere trying, effect a very tight metaphysical connection between actions and tryings. This may seem to be an advantage when we bear in mind the intuition, expressed earlier as an advantage of the disjunctivist view, namely, that we act by trying, that to act, to try is *all* that we have to do. And indeed the intuition that, in the relevant sense of trying, to try to φ all we have to do is carry out the action of φ-ing. What sense can we make of this connection between actions and tryings, if tryings, while being necessary for actions, are quite distinct from them?

Perhaps the intuition that we act by trying can be read in two ways, and that on its weaker reading it can be met. On a stronger reading the claim that we act by trying implies that there is just one thing we do: try, and that thing is therefore identical to our action. On a weaker reading the claim that we act by trying may be taken merely as a causal claim about tryings with respect to actions. If we were to say, for example, that tryings are necessary for actions because they are the *causes* of them, then there is clear sense in which to act all one has to do is to try. If ones trying is causally sufficient, in the circumstances, for acting, then all one needs to do to bring about the action is to try to act. On this reading, to say that all one has to do in order to act is to try, is on par with saying that all that is needed for the bomb to explode is for the fuse to be lit. It is true that this account will have it that the agent does more than just try when she acts. She will, if the trying is successful, also do what she tried to do—an action which will be distinct from the trying. Her doing φ will be caused by her trying to φ. The suggestion will be that the claim that 'in acting all we have to *do* is try' should be read as 'trying is sufficient for acting' and not that there is only one thing done.

The theorist who holds that a successful action itself is the trying, whether she holds that such a trying is also a movement of the body or not, will continue to object to the view. Note there are further reasons to retain the thesis that if there are indeed tryings in the case of a successful action, then the action is the trying. Let us assume that we take actions to be personal level psychological events. Then on the view that actions are tryings, in contrast to the pre-cursor view, we have to ascribe only a single personal level psychological event to an acting subject, the action itself, rather than two connected actions, the trying and the action. Further, the view enables us to construe the action itself, and not some intermediary trying, as both the direct product and aim of our practical reasoning, intentions, decisions and so on. Finally, our phenomenology of our actions seems to suggest that when I act and raise my arm, say, there is just one single unified event of which I am aware.

I have said that it not my concern to give a full account of the ontological relations between actions and tryings, but only to indicate the options and state my own view of them. I am, therefore, not going to seek to further adjudicate between the options presented. I will rather state my own inclinations in the matter.

It is obviously my view that we cannot deny claim 3—that physical actions imply movements of the body. No event of the same primitive metaphysical kind as a physical action can occur without a matching bodily movement occurring. On this view, when one fails to act, the failure lies not in the fact that some event that was 'really' ones action, or part of ones action, failed to have the consequences intended. Rather the failure lies in there being no event of the primitive kind ones action is. In my view matters with respect to claims 1 and 5 are less straightforward.

They are not straightforward, I think, due to some equivocation inherent in our use of the concept trying. We tend to use the concept of trying to indicate a descriptive property of a psychological event—say, that it is purposive. On such a use we have reason to think that a number of distinct kinds of psychological event, including successful actions, will be tryings. Thus we can accept claim 1, that actions are tryings and give up on claim 5, the uniformity assumption.

If, however, we take tryings to constitute a psychological natural kind, and take actions to be primitive unities, then we must deny claim 1—that successful actions are tryings, but may be able hold on to claim 5, the uniformity claim. Our attitude with respect to claim 5 should rest on the results of an enquiry about what falls under the extension of such a concept. Are tryings a uniform kind of distinct psychological precursor to action?[24] Or perhaps failed actions constitute a uniform class of trying events? Or perhaps tryings are both distinct psychological precursors

---

[24] It may be that in some cases of successful action there are tryings that are distinct precursors to actions but I am not convinced of the reasons to generalise.

to action or are failed actions—either because failed actions just *are* such distinct psychological pre-cursors to action or because tryings are a disjoint class after all? I do not intend to answer these questions. I am somewhat sceptical of discovering a metaphysically significant class of tryings at all but have not ruled it out. The important point in my view is that if such tryings exist they are not actions or parts of actions.

In summary, I take claim 3 to be true, and on a certain descriptive understanding of the concept of trying take claim 1 to be true and claim 5 to be false. However, I do not rule out a proper use of the concept on which claim 1 is false and 5 is true. Now, to our knowledge of our actions.

9

On Knowing One's Own Actions

1. INTRODUCTION

Given the recent debates about self-knowledge and first-person authority it is surprising that there has not been more discussion about our knowledge of our actions.[1] It is surprising because our knowledge of our own actions seems, *prima facie,* to share many of the features of our knowledge of beliefs and perceptions, that have given rise to these debates.[2] At least this is what I want to suggest in this chapter. Indeed, a significant motivation for this chapter is to place discussion of our knowledge of our own physical actions firmly alongside our knowledge of other psychological phenomena. I will outline what seem to be intuitively plausible features of our knowledge of our actions, and consider what account we might give of such knowledge that respects those features. A suggestion as to what form an account of our knowledge of our actions should take will be offered. The account offered follows the lead of Anscombe, and others, in eschewing an observational or perceptual model of our knowledge of our own actions. Our knowledge of our actions seems, like much of our knowledge of our other psychological states, events and processes, to be immediate and non-observational and to be gained independently of a perception of what is known. However, unlike other psychological phenomenon, it is not the case that what is known is not the sort of thing that can be observed. We often observe each other's actions, and also our own.

---

[1] There was a flurry of papers on the subject in the early 1960s. (See O'Shaughnessy 1963; Anscombe 1963; Donnellan 1963; Broadie 1967; Olsen 1969; Danto 1963.) Since then there has been Anscombe's classic *Intention,* and an important discussion in Velleman (1989). The situation has changed somewhat with the recent appearance of Roessler and Eilan (eds) (2003).

[2] See Cassam (ed.) 1994; C. MacDonald, B. Smith and C. Wright (1998); and Shoemaker (1996) as key sources for the work that constitutes these debates.

The claim that knowledge of what we are doing is not typically acquired on the basis of perception or observation is not, of course, as uncontroversial as the claim that we do not typically know our beliefs or judgements on the basis of observation. Whereas only the most radical behaviourist would claim that for a subject to have knowledge of what she believes she must perceive the behaviour her belief produces, it is much more plausible to claim that in order for a subject to know what she is doing she needs to perceive the action that she produces. I consider it to be more than likely that our capacity to know our own actions depends, in various ways, on our capacity to perceive our past actions and our world. Nevertheless, in what follows, I will be concerned to develop an account of our knowledge of our actions that allows that the epistemic basis of our knowledge of the particular action we are carrying out is, typically, not perceptual.

This task constitutes the explicit content of the chapter. However it is also, my hope that the discussion of the knowledge we have of our own actions will serve to illuminate and extend the range of possible sources for self-knowledge. By 'self-knowledge' I mean not just knowledge of that thing which is in fact the knower, but knowledge of ourselves *as* subjects. The account sketched here aims to give us a way of knowing of our own actions that is available to us in virtue of being the acting subject. Chapter 11 will then be devoted to contrasting the status of bodily awareness and our awareness of ourselves as agents as sources of self-knowledge in this sense.

2. FEATURES OF OUR KNOWLEDGE OF OUR OWN ACTIONS

Let us consider a simple case of action. I want to catch my friend's attention and I raise my arm in order to do so. Now consider my knowledge of my action of raising my arm. Intuitively, such knowledge is puzzlingly easy to come by. I seem to know directly and authoritatively that I am voluntarily raising my arm in a way that I do not know other's actions directly and authoritatively. Further, when I know that I am raising my arm, I seem to know it no later than when I have started to raise it. In particular, I do not seem to have to await perceptual information, for example, that muscles are contracting and that my arm is rising in order to know it. Also, wanting to know what I am doing seems to be all that is required in order for me, in normal cases, to know what I am doing. If I wonder what I am doing when I am raising my arm, I seem to be immediately supplied with an answer. My knowledge of what I am doing seems, normally, to be immediately available given that I am acting. Let us separate these features of our knowledge of our action under three headings and say that intuitively our knowledge of our actions appears to be:

1. *First-person authoritative*
An agent seems to be in a better position to know her own actions than others are.

2. *Independent of perception or investigation*
Our knowledge of our actions appears to be spontaneous and to be given immediately upon acting. It does not seem to require any investigation or to be based on perception.

3. *Relatively transparent or self-intimating*
Our actions, like other psychological phenomena seem to have a certain conditional epistemic availability to us. It does not seem to be the case that our all actions could as a matter of brute fact be beyond our ken.

Let us go through these features in a bit more detail:

2.1 Authoritative

I am going to take first-person authority with respect to a given subject area to imply that there is the possibility of an epistemic first-person third-person asymmetry with respect to that area. Here the asymmetry must be taken to lie not simply in the fact that the subject can in central cases know more or better than others, with respect to that area, because they are around a lot or are more interested. Rather, the subject can know more, or better, because they know in a way which is in principle unavailable to others. So let us say:

X is first-person *authoritative* with respect to a fact, *P*, that concerns *X*, iff in central cases of *X*'s judgements concerning the fact, *P*, that concerns *X*, we can say that *X* is in a better position than others to know *P*, because *X* knows *P* in way in principle unavailable to others.

Given this understanding of first-person authority it is, I think, plausible to claim that we are authoritative with respect to our actions. This authority is exemplified by the fact that when a subject acts, and so moves her body, we take the subject to be authoritative relative to others, about whether she *acted* in so moving or not. Consider the case where I intentionally raise my arm. Given that there is an action of me raising my arm, it will almost always be the case that I am able to know that I raised it, and know in a way that others do not. Others will look to me to know whether I raised my arm voluntarily. If I tell them that it was a voluntary act on my part, and not an involuntary, unwilled, movement they will presume me to be right. Of course it is possible that I am deluding myself. It is also possible that I fail to be sincere and have reasons for wanting the person to think that, contrary to the facts, I acted voluntarily. However, for the main, and in the normal case, it will be presumed that I am in a better position to say when I am acting, and when I am not, than they are. That is, I shall claim, because I have a way of knowing whether I acted that others don't that makes me first-person authoritative with respect to my actions. We might not take a subject as authoritative about her action described merely as a movement of her body. However, as long as we keep clear the distinction between authority with respect to movements of the body (arm risings), and authority with respect to *actions* (arm raisings), then it is clear that there is a first-person third-person asymmetry with respect to the latter.[3]

Let me emphasize that on this understanding, first-person authority with respect to our own actions *does not mean* that it is not possible for us to be wrong about whether we acted, nor that another cannot be better position than me to know whether I acted.

We are not infallible with regard to our actions and can clearly think that we acted while having failed—due to some motor failure, say—to do so. On an occasion where such a thing occurs another may be in a position to put me right. But note that we have here a parallel with perception, and belief. We claim a first-person authority with respect to our own perceptions, and beliefs, even though we can think that we are perceiving something or having a belief when we are not.

Further, given the possibility of self-deception and unconscious action, we might fail to know that we are acting when we are. In such cases, another subject who sees us moving may be better able than us to know that we are acting. My deep desire to catch someone's attention may result in my voluntarily dropping my handkerchief, but the desire

---

[3] It should be noted that given bodily awareness—kinaesthesia in particular—it might be thought that we in fact also have first-person authority about whether our bodies moved. It seems to me that the nature of the authority attached to such cases is complex, and is weaker than the phenomenon identified, but I will not discuss it further here.

may be a sufficiently uncomfortable one for me entirely to disavow the action, and for me to think that it was involuntary.

Nevertheless, it seems clear that given certain background conditions which we are entitled to take as met (such as that the subject's body is functioning normally or that there are no special repressive mechanisms in place) we can assume a first-person third-person asymmetry over the question of whether the subject acted.

2.1.1 Authority with respect to knowing that I acted vs. authority with respect to knowing what I did

Let us suppose that it is agreed that we do *seem* typically to know *that* we have acted in a way that is in principle unavailable others, and agreed that this seems to give us a certain kind of epistemic authority over our actions. It may nevertheless be said that this cannot give me authority over *what* I have done. To know *that*, it may be said, I have to have recourse to my perceptual faculties. And if my knowledge of what I have done is grounded in perception, then any first-person third-person asymmetry in my knowledge of what I have done will be due to the fact that only I have perceptual access through bodily awareness to the activities of my own body. It will not be special to action, but rather will be a feature of my knowledge of bodily movement more generally.

Well, we can clearly be ignorant, relative to others, about many of the things we have done. The tendency to describe our actions in terms of their effects—effects that may well be unknown to us—means that we very often can be said not to know what we have done. Given that actions can be described in terms of their consequences, and given that I can be ignorant of the consequences of my actions, I can be ignorant of my actions under such descriptions. It is perhaps mainly for this reason that we overlook the authority that we have over own actions.[4] So, it is important to acknowledge that I do not seem to have

---

[4] Physical actions are not the only psychological phenomena we describe in terms of their consequences. We ascribe mental actions in terms of their consequences—we say things like 'Your decision not to go to the party was a decision not to meet NN' even when the subject being addressed does not know NN or that NN was to be at the party. Note that in a not dissimilar, but much more restricted way, we ascribe people beliefs in terms of their implications or presuppositions. ('Your belief that women are foolish is a belief that your own daughter is foolish', 'Your belief that water is wet is a belief that H_2O is wet', for example.) Perhaps, the way we very often re-describe the objects of perception, beyond any capacity the viewer has to recognize the objects as falling under those descriptions, comes closest to the action case. ('He was looking at a genuine Goya, priced at ten pounds and did not buy it'.)

any special authority about *what* I am doing when what I am doing comes under the description of unintended consequences. With respect to such actions I seem to be at no significant advantage. However, it does not follow from this that I do not typically have authority about what I am doing relative to descriptions which are more basic. If there are descriptions of actions that are somehow basic, we *can* make our claim a claim about our authority over our basic actions.

One suggestion might be that if we take intentions or tryings as necessary for action, then there will always be a description of my actions in terms of what I intended or tried to do, and that description may be thought basic, relative to other descriptions. It may be said, I do seem to be authoritative about what I have done when what I have done is described under the description drawn from what I intended or tried to do. Certainly, actions described in terms of unintended consequences will be excluded as relevant to the authority thesis on this suggestion. However, I do not think that the suggestion that construing authority in terms of what the subject is intending, or trying, takes us very far.

First, our intentions or tryings can themselves appear to fall under competing descriptions. So we can say: 'You think you are intending (or trying) to ring the door bell of No 6, but you are not, that's No 4's bell you are intending (or trying) to ring.'[5] Such *de re* ascriptions are common place. The claim would therefore have to be that we are authoritative about our actions under descriptions taken from what we are *de dicto* intending or trying to do? We will come back to this.

A second concern is that it is far from obvious that intentions or tryings, *understood as distinct precursors to action*, are necessary for actions. Consider the case for intentions. It is possible, and in indeed plausible, to hold that that there can be deliberate actions which are not preceded by any intention to act. One might think that intentions should be understood as effective ways of storing conclusions of practical reasoning for the future, which are not needed in cases where an action itself is the conclusion of an exercise of practical reason. I can raise my arm on seeing my friend without having formed any prior intention to do so. Perhaps it will be replied that the intentions that give us the descriptions under which we are authoritative over our actions are not prior intentions, but rather intentions in action.[6] There is always, it may be said an intention in action, even if there is no prior intention.

---

[5] The example comes from O'Shaughnessy (1980) vol. 2, p. 85.
[6] See Searle (1983) ch. 3.

Of course, the nature of the objection depends somewhat on how the distinction between prior intentions and intentions in action are construed. But if intentions in actions are supposed to specify the purpose of the action then a problem remains. If a subject always acts with an intention (an intention in action, perhaps), and the subject can be construed as being authoritative with respect to her intention, it is still implausible to claim that she is in general authoritative with respect to her actions when those actions are described in terms of what she intended to do. Consider a subject intending to get a ball in the corner pocket in a game of snooker. Suppose that the subject acknowledges that this is the right way to describe what she is intending or trying to do. Imagine she strikes the ball and the ball rolls into the corner pocket. While we do want to say that the subject is authoritative about whether she acted, and indeed about her purpose in acting, it seems implausible to claim that the subject is authoritative, in contrast to others, about whether she is getting the ball in the corner pocket. Thus, drawing a description of an action from an intention is not sufficient to give one authority over the action.[7] The trouble with descriptions in terms of what a subject is intending to do is that they seem to avert to the subject's main purpose or motive in doing what she is doing. It seems, however, that while the subject will also be authoritative about what her purpose in acting is, and authoritative about the fact that she is acting for the purpose of doing one thing rather than another, she may not be authoritative about whether her purpose came off. Indeed the subject may act intending to do something that she knows full well she may not succeed in doing. If intentions, whether they are prior intentions or are intentions in action, are to be used to identify which actions we know authoritatively, then we are going to have to have a way of dividing those intentions, knowledge of which seems to be sufficient to secure for the subject knowledge of her action, from those intentions knowledge of which will not.

Consider the case for tryings. As we saw in the previous chapter, if tryings are understood to be personal-level psychological events that

---

[7] It is not in fact clear how Searle himself intends to specify the content of intentions in action. He talks of intentions in action as being given by the content of the agent's experience in acting, a content which is not satisfied if the agent does not do what she experiences herself as doing. It is not clear what relation holds between the content of such an experience and the agent's primary purpose in acting. It may be that by intentions in action Searle does not mean some mental state distinct from the action, but rather simply the content of a basic action being carried out, in a sense I am about to specify. In which case, I am in agreement with him.

precede, but are not themselves the action, then it is possible to deny that we try to act whenever we succeed in acting. We might very plausibly hold that, even if in some cases of successful action, cases where the subject seems to expend particular effort, or cases where there is a good chance of the subject failing to act successfully, the subject can be said to have tried prior to her acting, in other cases a subject can simply act without trying. Or, we might hold the stronger thesis that tryings are always kinds of degenerate or failed actions, such that a subject can only properly be said to have tried to do something if she has not done it. The claim would be that trying should be identified relative to the subject's purposes in acting, and that she will be taken to have acted when securing her purpose and merely tried when not. However, as was made plain in the previous chapter, it is not my concern to settle these issues here. Nevertheless, the fact that there is a question over the necessity of trying stands as a concern for the suggestion mooted. However, the real problem, as in the case of intentions, is that descriptions of our actions in terms of tryings do not seem to identify a narrow enough class of actions to be those over which we are authoritative. Even if we try to act, and are authoritative about our trying, we need not be authoritative about whether we succeeded in trying. Suppose I tried to pot the pink, and know that I tried to pot the pink. It does not follow that I know that I potted the pink.

2.1.2 Basic actions

I think we are likely to do better in identifying which actions we have authority over if we consider the class of actions we can call basic actions. Basic actions are those actions a subject can carry out directly, without having to do anything else; and they are the actions that a subject needs to do in order to do anything else. Thus, whatever a subject does in acting she does it by carrying out one, or more, basic actions directly.

Although I shall make some suggestions, I do not aim to settle here the question of what kinds of action description are rightly used to identify basic actions. I do, however, want to consider how to *approach* the task of settling which kinds of action description pick out basic actions. And I do want to suggest that we have reason to suppose that those actions identified as basic actions will be actions which we can know authoritatively.

To answer the question of which actions are basic actions, we need to consider what it means to say that an action is one that the agent can carry out directly, without doing anything else.

On one reading of what it is to be an action carried out directly, it is unlikely to do much to help us identify the descriptions under which our actions are known authoritatively. Suppose that we take my action of moving my arm to be the same action as my action of potting the pink ball. If it is claimed that the former action is something I do directly, then it seems that the latter, being the same action, will also be something I do directly. But we were hoping to explain my authority over one, in the absence of authority over the other. Thus, it seems that if the notion of doing something directly is to help us draw the line in the right place, we must either take actions to be individuated more finely, understanding the notion of doing something directly as being relative to a description of, or content ascription to, the action.

Let us assume that we take the classification of basic and non-basic actions as relative to a description of the action. The obvious construal of the notion of an action's being one I can do directly is that the action, under a given description, is reflected in a certain way in practical planning. Let us suppose that I am in a situation of determining what to do, governed by some overall aim or purpose. Suppose, for example, that I want to win a game of snooker. I reason that to win the game I need to pot the pink, and know that to pot the pink I need to move the cue, and in order to move the queue I need to move my arm. There are a hierarchy of ways of identifying the action I aim to carry out. The claim is that at the base of that hierarchy will be the identification that gives us the basic action. The hierarchy will stop with those actions that I can just do, without any need to determine or know the *means* by which they should be done. It will stop with those actions that are part of the repertoire of things that I know how to do, without needing to know how I do it. The claim is that for any agent, in a given situation, there will be a class of actions, members of which, the agent is entitled to take as actions that she knows how to execute successfully, and any process of determining what she is to do will result in a command to execute one of those actions that she is entitled to take as knowing how to execute just like that.[8]

If we understand the notion of a basic action as basic with respect to action determination by the agent in this way, then whichever actions

---

[8] The notion of a basic action that is being invoked here is, in essence, the notion of a telelogically basic action articulated in Hornsby (1980). Searle (1983) also identifies a basic action, similarly, as an action an agent is able to intend and perform without intending to perform any other action as a means to perform it.

we think are basic actions, it seems that we are justified in supposing that an agent will have some grasp of, or access to, the possible ways she is able to act directly. For, if an agent had no such grasp of the possible ways that she could act directly, we could make no sense of the agent determining to act in one way, rather than another, in order to realize her overall aim. Given that the ability to carry out a basic action is pre-supposed by the ability to carry out any action, we then are justified in supposing that it is a pre-condition of any action that an agent has practical knowledge in virtue of which she has a grasp of the possible ways she can act, that are in this way basic. If the above is right, we now have a way of seeing how it could be that an agent can be first-person authoritative not only about the fact that she has acted but also about what she has done. The suggestion is that knowledge of *what* one is doing, and not just knowledge *that* one is acting, comes from one acting against a grasp of possible things one could have done as basic actions. It is one's opting to carry out this basic action rather than that which, assuming one has the requisite concepts, will give one the description under which one is authoritative with respect to the action.

We can further see why this results in limits to my authority. Although I may be authoritative with respect to a basic action φ, and I may intend or try to do ϕ by doing φ, it will not follow that I am authoritative with respect to my actions ϕ. It will not follow, because I may not be authoritative about whether by doing φ I succeeded in doing ϕ. So, while I might intend to pot the snooker ball by moving my arm forward, I can be authoritative about whether I moved my arm, without being authoritative about whether I potted the ball.[9]

There are two features of this way of identifying the class of basic actions that are worth emphasising. Given that basic actions are identified as those actions that a subject elects to do in order to fulfil her other aims, and as actions which the subject is entitled to take as those she can just do, which actions are basic for a subject will be both a subject relative, and context relative, matter. That is, different individuals will have different sets of actions which are basic for them, and a given individual will have different sets of actions which are basic in different

[9] Note that we have here a close parallel with our authority over our perceptions. I know authoritatively that I am seeing, and I know what I am seeing, but my authority over the latter seems only to extend to descriptions in terms of basic observational concepts. Further, what counts as a basic observational concept seems to vary with subject and context.

contexts. The matter will be dependent upon the subject's practical knowledge.[10]

A traditional way of drawing the boundary around the class of basic actions is in terms of bodily movements. The implicit assumption has been that the same class of actions, bodily movements, would be basic across individuals and across situations. It is clear that a large number of those actions identified in terms of certain core bodily movements are likely to constitute a stable class of those actions we take as basic. Raising my arm, lifting my foot will usually be basic for most people at most times. However, on the construal given above, some actions identified in terms of certain kinds of description of bodily movements may turn out not to be basic. Consider the often discussed example of a task that has become automatic: tying one's shoelaces. It is plausible to think that the individual movements of one's fingers may not, in a given case, be basic. The description of the action in terms of a description of individual movements of individual fingers in a particular way will not be the description that comes at the bottom of the hierarchy when the subject determines what to do. Given that the subject knows how to tie her shoelaces, just like that, we can suppose that the action that comes under the description of 'move in such a way as to tie my shoelaces' may be basic for her. We can perhaps think of the subject's selection of a basic action (in order to fulfil her main intention or aim) as functioning in such a way that once initiated the minute execution of the action will be taken over by processes that are sub-personal.[11]

So, on this understanding of a basic action, there are descriptions of actions in terms of bodily movements that may not be basic for a subject at a given time, although they may be for another subject or for the same subject at another time. The question now is whether the above also shows that there could be actions that are *not* described as bodily movements that *are* basic. Tying our shoelaces, uttering 'I', writing one's name, and, plausibly, such actions such a picking up a cup that is in easy reach and in full view, might seem to be actions that are basic for most adult subjects but which might not be thought to be described in terms of bodily movements. However, whether one wants to say this, depends on how narrowly we circumscribe what counts as describing an action as

---

[10] Note that Searle also makes the point that basic actions will be relative to the agent and her skills. (See Searle 1983, p. 100.)

[11] In fact there is good evidence for the claim that, with most actions, the precise movements of the body of the subject acting will be determined by sub-personal processes. (See Campbell 2003 and Marcel 2003.)

a bodily movement. If we take descriptions such as 'move my body in the way required for tying my shoelaces' or 'move by body in the way required for writing my name' as descriptions of movements of the body then basic actions are bodily movements. If we were to think of bodily movement descriptions more narrowly then we would take basic actions to extend beyond those actions we identify as bodily movements. Note, however, that we have good reason to adopt to the broader usage. In tying my shoelaces, writing my name or picking up my mug what I do is directly move my body in some way. I do not bring about the result that my shoelaces are tied, my name is written and my mug raised at a distance. Rather there is a set of bodily movements that I can carry out as a single act, without doing anything else: the movement of my body required for tying my shoelaces, writing my name and so forth.

The suggestion that we understand basic actions as actions that are operationally basic, I think, provides us with a principled reason for taking our basic actions to be actions over which we are authoritative. Suppose we act, governed by our overall aims, by selecting a basic action. If basic actions are those actions we are entitled to take as actions we know how to carry out, without knowing how to do anything else, then in acting on the basis of that selection I will act immediately able to know what I am doing. The suggestion also draws the boundaries between those actions over which we are authoritative and those which we are not, in the intuitively right place. Those actions which we take ourselves to *know* how to carry out 'just like that', moving our arms, picking up the cup just before us, writing familiar words, playing familiar tunes, do seem to be those actions we can know that we are doing immediately, without any needing to know that we have done anything else, or needing to check by monitoring feedback from bodily awareness or other perceptual faculties.

In summary, it seems hard to deny that we are authoritative relative to others about the fact that we have acted when we have. But, it seems, we also have reason to think that there is an important asymmetry relative to others in our way of knowing *what we have done* in central cases. It has been claimed that, in order to act, a subject must select an action that is operationally basic for her. An action will be operationally basic for her if it is one she knows how to do 'just like that'. That is, it is an action she can do by doing no more than electing to do it. Now, in order to be able to select a basic action to serve her aims, we can assume that the subject must have a practical grasp of the possible basic ways that she might act. Given that only the agent *herself* can chose to act in one way rather than another, relative to that grasp, we seem to have the materials to account for a way she has of knowing what she has done that could not be available to anyone other than the agent. When an agent's action is the choice she makes as a result of an assessment of things she *can* do just like that, and that she grasps as things she *can* do just like that, the agent is entitled, in the absence of any contrary reason, to claim knowledge of what she has done. It is knowledge that does not call on the subject's perceptual faculties to provide immediate grounds (even if perceptual faculties are called in in the execution of the action). We will come back to this picture of the subject's knowledge, but if it is right, the suggestion that a subject who acts is authoritative relative to others about her actions—both in terms of what she has done and of whether she acted—becomes compelling. Further, on this way of seeing the circumstances of action, we have some explanation for the second feature identified above of our knowledge of our actions.

2.2 Independent of perception or investigation

Perhaps the most notable and problematic feature of our knowledge of our own actions is that it appears to be immediately available to the subject who is engaged in acting, and who is aiming to answer the question as to whether she is acting. Such knowledge does not seem to have to await the testimony of our perceptual faculties.[12] We do not seem to need to feel our muscles clenching and our arm rising, or to see the trajectory of our hand, in order to know what we are doing. Perceptual knowledge is, without doubt, required as part of the background that makes action possible. However, it seems that in order to know what we are doing in the case of an individual action, we do not need to perceive simultaneously, either via bodily awareness or our other five senses, what we are doing.[13] In this way our knowledge of our action

---

[12] Of course, the thesis that knowledge of our actions is non-perceptual owes much to Anscombe. However, *pace* Anscombe I do not think we need to think of knowledge of our bodies through bodily awareness as non-perceptual. I therefore mean to include bodily awareness among those sources not directly necessary for knowledge of what we are doing.

[13] Experimental psychological data confirms that action awareness is not grounded in, and does not depend on, perception of the action, either via bodily awareness or via our other five senses. First, it finds that subjects are typically aware of acting before their bodies move. (See Haggard and Magno 1999, Haggard and Eimer 1999, and Haggard 2003). Secondly, it finds that subjects who lack bodily awareness can be aware of acting with observation. (See Cole 1993, and Cole and Paillard 1995.) Thirdly, subjects who are

is relatively *a priori*: that is, it is not acquired, or justified, via perceptual evidence in a given case, although it does rest on the obtaining of background conditions which we are entitled to take as met, and which themselves may garner support from perceptual information.

2.3 Relatively transparent

It is not just that I do not seem to have to perceive that I am acting in order to know that I am acting, nor just that I am authoritative when I do judge that I am acting. Also, the subject's actions, like other psychological phenomena seem to have a certain conditional epistemic availability to the judging subject. We can obviously fail to know that we are acting, as when we are acting absentmindedly or are repressing what we are doing. But, it does not seem to be the case that our actions can, as a matter of brute fact, be beyond our ken. It is, I think, very hard for us to imagine an agent who is capable of asking herself the question 'What am I doing?' not being able normally to answer the question correctly. This would be to imagine the agent capable of reflexive thought, voluntarily carrying out one action, rather than another, and yet not knowing that she is acting. It seems to me, however, that we cannot, in Shoemaker's phrase, envisage a creature who is simply self-blind with respect to her actions in this way. There seems rather to be a necessary and conceptual connection between a subject acting and her knowing what she is doing.[14]

There are two different kinds of action, which ought to be separated here. Many have argued that we need to distinguish non-intentional actions—actions, such as finger tappings, chair shiftings and tongue

---

paralysed or lack body parts can take themselves to be acting, in the normal way, even although they are obviously not receiving perceptual feedback from a moving limb. (See James 1890, Marcel and Tegner 1995 and Marcel and Nimmo-Smith (forthcoming).) Fourthly, subjects suffering from the phenomenon of Anarchic Hand, and who are not aware of seemingly purposive movements of their bodies as their actions, typically have reliable perceptual (including proprioceptive) feedback with respect to the movements of their bodies, but *are* damaged in that area of the brain taken to be responsible for motor specifications. (See Della Sala *et al.* 1991, 1994.)

14 This connection is noted by Olsen (1969) and Broadie (1967). Note that someone who denied that our knowledge of our actions was *independent of perception or investigation* might still accept that it must be *relatively transparent*. They might hold that it is a condition of something being an action that it be generally known to the agent, but hold that our actions are known to us on the basis of perceptual information. They would then have to say that when the subject is blind to their movements, their movements cannot be actions.

movings, done for no reason—from intentional actions. If there is such a distinction, then we might imagine that while our intentional actions are likely to prove accessible to us in the way characterised, our non-intentional ones may not.[15] I think that the issue that this raises is whether we are right to think of such putative non-intentional actions as genuine actions at all, rather than bodily movements brought about by a purposive sub-personal system that we are not responsible for. It is perhaps plausible to claim that we could be entirely epistemologically disassociated, that we could be 'self-blind' with respect to them. But notice, that to the extent that an action is taken to exhibit genuine *agency*, by which I mean that that the action is taken to fall under *the agent's* control, such disassociation does not seem possible. Consider a case where a subject is acting—counting using the fingers of her right hand, say—and then acts in a way incompatible with carrying on doing the former—picking up her cup of tea with her right hand, say. If we want to say that the subject herself is *genuinely* controlling both actions, rather than that some sub-personal system is, we want to explain how the second action relates to the former, in the case where the subject is supposed to have no possible access to the former. If there were a general disassociation for the subject between the perspective from which the question 'what am I doing?' gets answered, and the perspective from which she carries out her actions, we would have the possibility of a subject deciding to pick up her cup of tea, wondering if her action could bring to an end or disrupt, or indeed be disrupted by, other actions she was unaware of carrying out. But in turning the subject's actions into possible external impositions in this way seems to get things quite wrong. If what I am doing can be said to be controlled by me, I must at least have the power to initiate it or to will it to cease when I have reason to do so. The control and regulation of my actions as the actions of a unified agent seem to require this. And surely if *I* have the power to initiate or to stop what I am doing, then what I am doing must normally be in some way accessible to me. Thus for an action to be within a subject's control and responsibility the subject must be capable of knowing what she is doing. Given the ability to ask the question 'What am I doing?' the subject's awareness of what she is doing must normally feed into an answer.

---

[15] See, for example, O'Shaughnessy (1980, vol. 2, ch. 10) and Ginet (1990: 3). By a non-intentional or sub-intentional action is meant not just an action which is not intended under one description but an action that is intentional under no description.

With these features of our knowledge of our action identified, I want now to explore some possible accounts we might give of our knowledge of actions and to sketch out the approach I think most promising. Some of the accounts explored do not sit well with the intuitively plausible features identified, and some have other shortcomings. However, nothing I say here about the accounts I set aside, in favour of the one I think most promising, will be sufficient to show that they could not be made good, or could not explain, or explain away, the features identified above. My hope, nevertheless, is that enough critical work will be done to motivate a consideration of the account I think we should go for.

3. POSSIBLE SOLUTIONS

3.1 The Dual Component model

Certain theorists about belief have attempted to solve the problem of how it is that we have relatively *a priori* knowledge of our beliefs despite their relational character, by claiming that what we took to be a unified phenomenon is in fact a dual component one.[16] Thus our knowledge of our beliefs on this account divides in to two parts: (a) knowledge of a narrow component, of which, as subjects, we have a distinctive kind of knowledge—knowledge by introspection, and (b) knowledge of an external component not knowable by the subject in any distinctive way. The dual component theorist tries to explain how it is that our knowledge of our beliefs has the features it has, despite being relational, by adopting a dual component theory of belief and an account of our knowledge of each element. If this is a natural move to make in dealing with our knowledge of our beliefs, it is an even more natural move to make in dealing with our knowledge of bodily action. It has been common to think of actions as the combination of at least two separate components: a psychological component—an intention, or trying, and a non-psychological one—a movement of the body. If this were to be our view of actions, then we could say that the features that we have taken to be features of our knowledge of our actions are in fact only features of our knowledge of our tryings or intentions. Our knowledge of our intentions is authoritative, *a priori* and transparent, but our knowledge of our bodily movements is not. As Donnellan puts it:

---

[16] Putnam's original paper, Putnam (1975), suggested this move. It is also developed in McGinn (1982).

What this suggests is that our knowledge of our own intentional actions is complex, that it divides up, so to speak, into an element of 'direct awareness' . . . and other elements to which observation is relevant.[17]

To try to explain the knowledge we have of our actions by claiming that it is in fact knowledge of two more primitive components is not, I think, the right direction to move in.

First, such an account makes a critical part of my knowing what I am doing a matter of perception. Given that we have perceptual access to other's bodily movements we might think that it fails properly to capture the first-person/third-person asymmetry involved in the first-person authority claimed be a feature of our knowledge of our actions. Also, such a dual component account clashes with the independence of perception feature of our knowledge of our actions. The account has it that my knowledge that, for example, I am raising my arm depends not only upon my knowing immediately that I intended or am trying to raise my arm, but depends also upon perceptual information that my arm is rising. In so doing it fails to explain a feature of our knowledge of our actions we found plausible. Moreover, it threatens to conflict with the feature of relative transparency. If my knowledge of my actions depends directly upon a perceptual component in this way, then given the possibility for widespread brute error that perceptual capacities leave room for, we should expect to find such a possibility in the case of action. It maybe that the dual component theorist can explain why we must normally be able to know what we are doing, despite adopting a partially perceptual model. She may argue that since our normal conditions for initiating action require information about the nature of our bodies, via perceptual feedback, perceptual breakdown would in fact rob me of my capacity to act, by robbing me of a grasp of what possible things I could do. If this were the case, there would not be the possibility of actions to which I was self-blind in the case of perceptual breakdown. However, even given perceptual breakdown, we may think that a subject would in fact be able to continue acting for a short time, relying on past information for a grasp of the possible actions she could carry out. And it is not plausible that she would be unknowing about such actions simply in virtue of that breakdown. The theorist might also have some other reason for saying that there is a conceptual dependence between our acting and our knowing that we are acting, so that there

17 Donnellan (1963: 407).

would be no actions in the case of perceptual breakdown. *Prima facie,* however, it is hard to see what her reason might be. But the reason cannot be the attractive one that there is something about the conditions under which we act which is already apt to provide us with knowledge of the action. This cannot be her reason because, on her account, to know what I am doing I have to wait to receive perceptual information, that is not available at the onset of the action, about what my body is doing.

Second, the dual component model seems to be partly motivated by the assumption that an account of the knowledge we have of our intentions or tryings, an account that was supposed to explain the distinctive features of action self-ascription, can non-problematically be provided. The assumption seems to be that our intentions or tryings will involve no external component and will be capable of being the objects of direct awareness. However, first of all, we would need to make sense of such direct awareness of any supposed internal components of our actions, and, secondly, we have no good reason to think that the contents of our intentions or tryings will be any more independent of their relations to external elements of the environment than the contents of our beliefs and perceptions. It is highly plausible to think that a creature inhabiting an arm free world cannot even intend or try to raise an arm.

Thirdly, the model can seem unsatisfactory for much the same reason that a dual component theory of belief, and of the knowledge we have of our beliefs, has struck theorists who think of belief as a unified psychological state as unsatisfactory. If we think of actions as unified psychological phenomena, along the lines sketched in the previous chapter, rather than as aggregative constructions of psychological and non-psychological components, then we are not likely to adopt the view outlined above.

Considering how a dual component theorist will respond to the problems raised brings out the fact that there are in fact many different forms of dual component account. There are as many different forms of dual component account as there are combinations of the different accounts of the nature and knowledge of a person's knowledge of her intentions or tryings, on the one hand, and of nature and knowledge of the movements of her body, on the other. The dual component model envisaged above is only one version of a dual component account.

In dealing with the first problem raised above, it is important to stress that a contemporary dual component account is likely to hold that our knowledge of our actions depends not just on our five senses, but also centrally on bodily awareness.[18] And given a view on which bodily awareness is necessarily awareness only of my body, there is room to say that, even in the perceptual component, there is a first-person third-person asymmetry. So, there is room to say that first-person authority can be reflected in both components of the dual component account. However, on the account it will still be the case that I need to await the deliverance of my perceptual capacities in order to know whether I have raised my arm.

This has seemed to be phenomenologically counterintuitive, and to conflict with empirical research. It rather seems that my raising my arm, say, gives me, *ceteris paribus,* knowledge that I moved my arm without my having to monitor feedback from bodily awareness. It has not been doubted that this knowledge is set against a background that makes it unnecessary for me to check to see whether my motor system is in working order. Or that having reason to think that our motor system is playing up is very likely to result in an appeal to the testimony of our senses to check whether we acted. Nor is it doubted that keeping up an accurate schema of what basic actions are possible, and so being able to continue acting at all, will require perceptual feedback on the position of my limbs and so on. But none of this gives us reason to think that any such feedback is part of my immediate grounds for my knowledge that I am raising my arm, when I am.

We can imagine our dual component theorist, in response to the second problem raised above, rejecting the assumption that our knowledge of our intentions or tryings will involve direct awareness of some component, narrowly construed. What account the dual component theorist comes to offer of our knowledge of our intentions or tryings will depend on what account she thinks right for mental phenomena in general. So, instead of taking our knowledge of our mental states and actions to be due to some kind of internal perception, she might think it due to some reliable mechanism. Or she might think that our intentions or tryings can function as reasons for their own ascription. Whatever account is adopted (and it may be an account that embraces an externalist individuation of intentions and tryings) will then be combined with an account of our knowledge of our bodily

---

[18] Of course we can also come to have knowledge of the movements of our bodies from observing and listening to others—someone starting can tell me that I have touched them, or someone can verbally inform me that I have moved—but such sources are clearly not operative in the basic case.

movements, and perhaps our knowledge of the relation between our bodily movements and our intentions or tryings, to give an account of our actions. However, it needs to be noted that once the theorist has embraced the idea that intentions or tryings depend upon external elements, much of the motivation for giving an account of our knowledge of our actions by thinking of actions as divided into two components falls away.

However, recalling the third problem, even given adaptations of the kind discussed, if one operates with an understanding of actions as unified phenomena, then however compelling in themselves the component parts of the account offered are—the account of our knowledge of our intentions and of our bodily movements—the resulting account of action is unlikely to be accepted.

So far, we have supposed that our dual component theorist is committed to a dual component theory of action and, thus, of a dual component account of our knowledge of our actions. Might it not be possible for a theorist to meet the third problem by agreeing that our actions are unified psychological phenomena, but holding that our knowledge of them nevertheless comes in two parts? Here the suggestion would be that I have knowledge of my intentions or tryings, however such knowledge is construed, and also knowledge of my bodily movements, through bodily awareness and/or ordinary perception, and that these two kinds of knowledge are what enable me to know what I am doing. On this account, my knowledge of what I am doing will be essentially indirect. According to this version of the dual component account, intending or trying is at most a necessary condition of, but not a component part of, an action. So, on this account, my knowledge of my intending or trying is knowledge only of a necessary condition—perhaps a causal antecedent of my action—not of my acting. And any observation of my body moving will not in itself give me knowledge of what is in fact my action. If we held a unified account of the nature of bodily action, but adopted a dual component account of our knowledge of such actions, we would in effect adopt an account on which our knowledge was always inferred from the knowledge that necessary conditions for my acting where satisfied. Given the continued presence of a perceptual condition, such an account would again conflict with the non-perceptual nature of our knowledge of our actions claimed above, and threaten to conflict with the transparency claim. However, identifying this possibility does raise the question of whether our knowledge of our actions is based on some kind of inference from knowledge of necessary conditions, combined with background conditions.

3.2 The Inference Model

The suggestion that we appeal to an inference to explain our knowledge of our actions can only be the suggestion that we make inferences about our actions from, either our observations of our bodies, or from our knowledge of the precursors of actions: intentions or tryings.

The idea, in the former case, would have to be that I come to know what I am doing from making an inference on the basis of perceptual information, through bodily awareness and the other senses, about the movements of my body. It seems clear that, if the remarks made above against the dual component theorist's idea that part of our knowledge of our own actions flows from our sensory access to our bodily movements were well taken, then this account will also be held in doubt. It will sit well with neither the non-perceptual nature of our knowledge of our actions, nor with their relative transparency.

What of the suggestion that we infer that we are acting from our knowledge that we are intending to act, or trying to act, together with an assumption that our motor systems and so on are all in working order? Well, first, it is very important to stress that trying, in this context, has to be understood, much like an intention, as an independent precursor of my actually acting. If the picture is that my trying is a proper *part* of my action, then it would conflict with our unity thesis for actions. If the supposition is that my trying *is* my acting then, while there may be objections to the identification, the attempt to give an account of the trying would be to give an account of the action. Given this clarification, on this version of the inference model I have knowledge of my actions via direct knowledge only of my intentions or tryings and the assumption, say, that my motor system is in working order. Consider the account as told for intentions. (And given the idea of my trying as an independent precursor of my acting, I think that what will be true for intentions will be true for tryings.)[19] On this account, I

---

[19] If my trying to do something is not supposed identical with, or part of, my acting when successful, then in order to preserve the assumption that my acting is my doing something we would have to assume that trying is not all I have to do to act. But if we assume this, then it seems that the gap between tryings and actions will be much the same as that between intentions and actions.

know that I am doing φ indirectly as an inference from knowing that I intend to φ, and that my motor system is in working order. The first thing that strikes us about such an account is that it does not fit our naïve understanding of what is going on when we know we are acting. It does not *seem* to me that I know I am raising my arm as a result of inferring that I am from my knowing that I intend to raise my arm; it rather seems that I know that as a result of my raising my arm. On this account no further epistemic support is given by my doing anything. But, even putting aside these considerations, without more being said the grounds given in the account do not seem to be sufficient to ground knowledge that I am φ-ing. Maybe I usually do what I intend to do, but all too often, even if I could do what I intend to do, I do not. It would seem that my intention to φ, plus assumptions about my motor system working properly, may plausibly ground a justified hypothesis that I will φ, but it does not seem able to ground my *knowledge*. The above inference models do not seem easy to accept. There are more sophisticated variants of the latter form of the inference model. These, however, fall under what I call the Anticipation Model which will be discussed later on.

3.3 The No-Reasons Model

In reviewing accounts of self-knowledge with respect to belief, Peacocke identifies what he terms 'no-reasons accounts'.[20] According to no-reasons accounts, our beliefs about our beliefs count as knowledge although they are held on the basis of no reasons. In particular the first order belief does not constitute, on such an account, my reason for my self-ascribing my belief.

As we saw earlier, the simplest of such accounts has it that as a matter of fact agents like us, due to some internal mechanism, only self-ascribe beliefs that they actually have. Given that a self-ascription of the belief that P is a reliable indicator of a belief that P, if we accept reliablism about knowledge, it can be said that by such self-ascriptions agents like us express knowledge of their beliefs. The equivalent account for the self-ascriptions of actions would have it that as matter of fact we tend be reliable about what we are doing, due to some non-epistemic feedback mechanism, and in virtue of that we are capable of knowing what we are doing.

---

[20] I take this description from Peacocke (1998) and (1999).

Such simple reliablist accounts make the connection between the psychological phenomenon, and the knowing of it, seem entirely brute. They, therefore, tend to be embellished in such a way that the relation between the phenomenon and the knowing of it is a rational relation, either because it is partly constitutive of the relata, or because it is taken to have some wider rational significance.

Similar embellishments could clearly be proposed for our account of our knowledge of our actions. We might take actions to be self-intimating as a matter of conceptual fact. So movements of our bodies that we were normally unable to self-ascribe would not count as actions. We might also claim, with Burge, that an ability to be authoritative about her own actions is a pre-requisite for a critical agent, and take this to be sufficient to confer the status of knowledge on to the agent's self-ascriptions.

Both suggestions have considerable plausibility about our natures as agents. However, if the suggestions are taken to constitute an account of what makes a subject knowledgeable with respect to her actions, the no-reasons theorist will face the same question: how do these truths secure *knowledge* for the subject when they might seem to suppose it?[21]

With respect to the first suggestion, while it may be true that certain processes or activities count as actions only if they are epistemically accessible the subject in a certain way, this does not mitigate the need for an independent account of the way in which they are epistemically so accessible.[22] With respect to the second, while the essential role played by self-ascription for the critical agent may confer some warrant on it, it is hard to suppose that the only warrant for such self-ascriptions accrue from their rational roles. We would expect some more local epistemic relation to hold between the action and its self-ascription distinct from that role, and expect it to explain, at least in part, why the self-ascription counts as knowledgeable. That explanatory task seems pressing.[23]

---

[21] Peacocke attributes such epistemic accounts to Shoemaker and Burge and makes this point in criticism of them (see Peacocke 1999, ch. 5).

[22] Note that Shoemaker, himself, suggests that we may take his claims to be claims about the metaphysical nature of belief, rather than constituting an account of how we know our beliefs (see Shoemaker 2003: 400–1).

[23] Note that Burge himself may not disagree. He claims that the rational role of self-ascriptions confers warrant on them, and denies that a source of a perceptual nature could confer the right kind of warrant. He does not deny that there may be other sources of warrant. Despite the claimed incompleteness of Burge's account, it will be obvious that much else that is said in this paper is influenced by the discussion in his 1996, and 1998 papers.

3.4 The Anticipation Model

One obvious way to make true our beliefs about an area in which we have control, is to bring about what we believe rather than have our beliefs conform to the facts as they are independently are. Our actions are, paradigmatically, an area over which we have control. One suggestion for why we seem to be authoritative about what we are doing, and why we are able to know what we are doing without any process of evidence gathering, is that we do what we believe we are going to do. Velleman, in his *Practical Reflection*, advances a sophisticated development of this suggestion. Velleman advances the basic thesis that our knowledge of our own actions has the features it has because we normally do what we believe we are going to do. However, his account also aims to meet the question as to why we should be motivated to do such a thing—why do we not just wait and see what we do and form our beliefs about what we are doing accordingly? The answer is taken to lie in a deeply rooted desire for self-knowledge, in particular a desire to know what we are doing. Given a desire to keep up with what we are doing, we will be motivated to bring it about that we accurately foresee what we are going to do, and that motivates us actually to do what we foresee doing. Furthermore, Velleman identifies intentions with self-fulfilling expectations: to form an intention is to form a belief about what I will do, that I am poised to make true on account of my desire to know what I am doing. Given a framework in which I do what I expect to do, a most effective way for me to get myself to do something—which is after all what an intention is—is to expect that I will do it.

Velleman's account has the attractive feature that it explains the transparency of our actions and the spontaneous, relatively *a priori*, nature of the knowledge we seem to have of them, while also allowing that the authority we have over our self-ascriptions is not groundless. He distinguishes between having knowledge that is adduced from evidence, and knowledge that is supported by, though not adduced from, evidence. We are, on his account, justified in claiming to know what we are doing, not because we form the belief about what we are doing on the basis of evidence, but because we form the belief within a framework that we know makes the belief true. Self-knowledge is a kind of justified invention.

Before considering this account further, it is worth noting that it too has a parallel account in the literature on the self-ascription of belief. Accounts of belief self-ascription that have it that the reason our self-ascriptions tend to be authoritative, while appearing spontaneous or groundless, is that what in part determines the beliefs we have is what we are inclined to self-ascribe. If our beliefs are in this way ascription-dependent—we believe what we take ourselves to believe—then there is no epistemic gap between our belief that *P* and our taking ourselves to believe *P* that needs to be bridged by reasons or evidence.[24] We need to be careful, however, to distinguish three distinct claims that may be conflated. First, few would doubt that our self-ascriptions are determinative of our beliefs merely in the sense that answering the question: 'Do I believe *P*?' will tell me, almost always, whether I indeed do believe *P*. This is just transparency. Secondly, few would doubt that settling an answer to the question: 'Do I believe *P*?' will not only tell me whether I do indeed believe *P* already, but will also settle any questions I may have of whether to believe *P*. As Evans has made clear, our procedures for determining whether we believe *P* are the same as the procedures for determining whether *P*.[25] However, neither this claim, nor the former one, commit us to the view that my second order beliefs, my beliefs about what I believe, are in any way epistemically or ontologically prior to my first-order beliefs. Rather, what they make clear is that our beliefs, and our beliefs about our beliefs, are in a kind of concord. Thirdly, and more contentiously, in claiming that our belief ascriptions are determinative of our beliefs we might be saying, not just that the same procedures can be used to answer both questions, but rather that the process of determining what I believe is, in the normal case, what brings my beliefs about. This makes my self-ascriptions ontologically and epistemologically prior to my beliefs, and introduces a kind of psychological idealism in being committed to there being no fact of the matter about what I believe prior to my reflections explicitly about what I believe.[26]

Velleman's idea that our knowledge of our actions is somehow invented has most in common with the third claim identified: in both cases our self-ascriptions have the features they do because the

[24] See Wright (1989) and (1998).

[25] Evans (1982: 220): 'I get myself in a position to answer the question whether I believe that *p* by putting into operation whatever procedures I have for answering the question whether *p*.'

[26] An account such as this can easily give way to a kind of psychological instrumentalism—rather than taking it that there really are beliefs constituted by the practices of self-ascription, we might think that there are only the practices of self-ascription themselves, and that the beliefs ascribed are useful interpretational fictions.

self-ascriptions make the facts fit them. However, there are of course differences between actions and beliefs which make a significant difference to the acceptability of the accounts being offered. While actions are single occurrences that can be willed, beliefs are states that cannot. Thus, while we can make sense of a system that brings it about that it does φ, because it anticipates doing φ and desires self-knowledge, it is very much harder to make sense of a system that brings it about that it believes P somehow *because* it self-ascribes the belief P. The latter suggestion makes our self-ascriptions appear ungrounded and our beliefs, therefore, either arbitrary or a matter of will.

However, even if not problematically idealist, the trouble with accounts, of the sort Velleman proposes, is that they are—as he fully realizes—bound to seem to have things backwards. We seem to have reasons to do things that are not grounded in beliefs about what we take our selves to be about to do. Indeed, we could have reasons to do things without any capacity for first-person higher-order beliefs. Further, as we noted before, looked at naively our beliefs about what we are doing are given epistemic support by what we are in fact doing. Velleman, as we have seen, is keen to emphasise that an account of the kind he offers does not need to hold that our self-ascriptions are epistemically groundless and lacking in justification. Nevertheless, the justification a subject has for her belief that she is doing φ cannot lie in the fact of her doing φ. Rather, it must lie in the fact that the belief is held in circumstances in which, given the subject's desires for self-knowledge, the belief will ensure that she is motivated to do φ. While it seems right to say that such nesting of a belief can provide evidential support for the belief, it is hard to accept that this is the way epistemic support figures in the standard case.

Another important cause for concern is that this account works only by assuming that intentions, understood as beliefs about what we are going to do, are necessary for action. That makes the account unusable to someone who thinks we need form no such belief about our future action as a result of practical reason. If we hold the position mooted before, that we can generally just act as the conclusion of a process of deciding how to act, then we are not going to want to hold that a belief about what we are going to do is necessary for our knowledge of that action.

What an account such as that offered by Velleman does seem to get right, however, is that on it, our knowledge of our actions is not occasioned by some access to the action that is subsequent upon acting.

If we cannot reconcile this fact with the naive thought that we know what we are doing partly because we are doing it, then we may have to adopt such an account.

3.5 Knowledge through participation

Let us go back to the naive thought that our beliefs about what we are doing are given epistemic support by what we are in fact doing: we know what we are doing *because* we are doing it. Now let us suppose given the arguments presented above, that our action cannot function in our justification for its self-ascription in virtue of some perception of it, or inference from its effects or causal antecedents. What of the possibility that the action can function unmediated as the reason for its own ascription? Let us then consider a view according to which we know we are acting when we are, because, and for the reason that we are.[27]

Presented merely as such, the account faces a version of the two topics problem. It provides us with no explanation of how an action, in so far as it need only be world directed, can bear any normative relation to our judgements about ourselves to the effect that *we* are acting. To put it simply, what is it about Smith's raising her arm that can support Smith's knowledge that *she* is raising her arm? We need an account of the nature of Smith's raising her arm that makes it clear what thereby entitles Smith to self-ascribe her action.

Again, we may at this point say with Peacocke that it is not simply Smith's raising her arm that can function as the reason for Smith's self-ascription of the fact that she is raising her arm. Rather it is Smith's consciously raising her arm that stands to function as the reason for its own ascription.

The crucial question then becomes: how should we understand what it is for the action to be conscious? Let me again consider two familiar models.

(i) When we engage in an action in such a way that the action is one of which we are conscious, what we have is a kind of complex action involving two more basic actions. First, we have the action of doing φ and second, we have the action of representing the doing of φ. So our doing φ in a way that makes it an action of which we are

---

[27] The suggestion is, of course, drawn from Peacocke's 1999 account of our knowledge of our beliefs.

conscious is a matter of its bearing a relation to a complex action that involves not just a doing of φ but also an action of representing a doing of φ. Here, doing something consciously is a matter of its standing in a certain relation to something else I do. To adopt this as an account of what is involved leaves us, of course, requiring an account of what is involved in the subject representing her doing of φ.

(ii) When we do something consciously what we have is a single action done in a certain way. Rather than there being two actions, the doing of φ and the representation of the doing of φ there is rather just the one action; the doing of φ in a certain way or mode.

We might assume that for an action to be conscious in a way that makes it accessible to its subject—for it to be conscious in a way that makes it poised to stand as the reason for its own ascription—is for it to have a certain relational property, for it to bear a relation to some further act on the part of the subject. In particular, we might assume that it can have such a property only in virtue of the subject representing the action she has carried out. But this natural assumption is I think false. Instead, we should use (ii) as our model. Actions carried out in a certain way are conscious and able to stand without further representation as the reasons for their own ascription.

However, with only this much in place we are again left with two questions:

(i) What *way or mode* of acting makes an action conscious?
(ii) Why should an action that occurs in that way or mode qualify for knowledgeable *self*-ascription?

What seems clear is that an adequate answer to the first question should deliver an answer to the second question. If an action's being conscious makes it fit to stand as the reason for its own self-ascription, then what it is for the action to be conscious should make it clear why it does ground such self-ascriptions.

My suggestion again will be that I act consciously when I am agent aware of my action, and that I am agent aware of my action when it is something I actively control. Our actions are those things we know, not by observing them, or by reflecting about them, or accepting some presentation of them, but rather by actively engaging in them. Further, engaging in an action as something I control is engaging with the action as *my* action, and involves a primitive form of self-awareness. Because of this, the suggestion is, my conscious actions are apt *immediately* to warrant self-ascriptions, without mediating acts or representations.

A natural suggestion as to what characterizes an action carried out in a way that makes the subject agent aware, from an action carried out in a way that does not, is that that the former is carried out with a sense of control. We, of course, carry out many actions as a matter of habit, or as relatively automatically and inattentively, but when we are conscious of what we are doing—when we are agent aware—we seem to act with a sense of guiding our action, with a sense of control.

What is it for an agent to act with a sense of control? It must, at least, be for her to be aware of guiding her actions, to experience her actions as those she initiates and those she has the power to stop. In essence, we control our actions by acting on the basis of an evaluation of the possibilities open to us. I suggest that we have agent's awareness of our actions—and act with a sense of control—when we act on the basis of our evaluation of possible actions, grasped as possible.

On the suggestion being made to experience an action as controlled is for the action to be the result of a process of evaluation of the possibilities available, grasped as possibilities. Agent's awareness of bodily action would then involve the agent having a grasp of the possible ways that she could move her body as a basic action, and carrying out one action rather than another on the basis of an assessment of the possibilities available to her. The agent's grasp of which actions are available as basic actions will be based on a general grasp of the ways in which she can move her body without doing any thing else. This grasp will itself will be based on ways that she has moved her body in the past. It will also be based on a particular grasp of the position of her body at the time of action, which itself will be based on the ways she has most recently moved it.

Let us take a case of an agent with only two options: suppose that an agent has just one barely functioning arm that she can move in just one way. If the agent grasps the two options of 'moving arm up' and 'keeping arm down' as things that could be done as basic actions, and acts directly on the basis of an assessment of these options as 'to be done' or 'not to be done' the subject seems to have all that is needed to act with a sense of control. However, if this is what is involved with acting with a sense of control, then we have reason to think that acting with a sense of control gives the subject some awareness of the resulting action *as her action*. It is certainly the case that only the agent of an action can be engaged in her own actions in this way. Only the agent of action can act immediately on the basis of an assessment of options. This means that if the subject were to self-ascribe the resulting action she could not go wrong. But we also have reason to attribute to the agent awareness that it is *her* action. Acting directly on the basis of an assessment of the possibilities, grasped as possibilities, means she has grasped that action as a possibility for *her*. Her active evaluation only makes sense on the assumption that she is determining what *she* should do and in actively evaluating her two choices the agent manifests awareness that these are two ways *she* can act.

When the agent directly realizes one action or another, in such a context, I suggest that the presence of the action with a given content is sufficient to make the agent aware of what she is doing. Suppose our agent determines to keep her arm down and acts directly as a result of an evaluation of what to do. On the suggestion being made, the presence of her action with the content 'keep arm down' will be sufficient in the context to make her agent aware that she is keeping her arm down. The agent may not be able to *self-ascribe* her action, because she may not have the requisite first-person concept. However, acting directly on the basis of an assessment of how to act, given a grasp of the action as a possibility for *her*, will give her agent's awareness of what she is doing of a kind that would entitle her to self-ascribe the action had she the concepts.

We can summarize the line of thought as follows:

1. An agent acts with a sense of control when she carries out her action on the basis of an assessment of the possibilities, grasped as possibilities, of acting one way rather than another.

2. If an agent acts *directly* on an assessment of the possibilities, grasped as possibilities, of acting one way rather than another, she secures awareness of the possibility realized as an option *for her*.

3. Therefore, acting with a sense of control is acting with self-awareness.

4. Acting with such self-awareness is acting with agent's awareness.

There is of course more to be said about how to understand these various claims. In particular, there are different ways in which a subject can grasp the possibilities available to her, and there are different forms of assessment. We can expect there will be correlated notions of self-awareness. There might be agents who can fully conceptualize those actions which are possible as basic actions, and whose assessment of those possibilities is fully conceptual. The assessment leading to action will involve running through practical arguments in favour of one course of action over another. When their deliberations lead immediately to action they will be agent aware of the resulting action in a way that may be already conceptualized.

However, for the most part, and for most agents, this will be an overly intellectualist account of the grasp she has of her basic actions and of the nature of the assessment that leads to action. Usually an agent will have a practical, rather than conceptually articulated, knowledge of the basic ways she can move her body and will have ways of assessing how to act, given her aims, that does not involve running through a practical syllogism. She will rather have a correlate practical ability to select the action fit for purpose. Such an agent will have agent's awareness of her action that is correlatively non-conceptual. Such awareness may then constitute the grounds of any conceptual self-ascription of the action.

There may be agents who do not have the concepts to self-ascribe the action and who have *only* a non-conceptual grasp of the possibilities available and who can only evaluate them non-conceptually. There may be creatures that do not have the capacity to conceptualize the possibilities available to them, but who manifestly experiment and revise their strategies for getting what they want. Such creatures might nevertheless be thought to be agent aware of what they are doing.

Further, there will be creatures who function in some sense as rational systems in that it will seem right to say that they in some sense act on the basis of an assessment of possible actions, but for whom we do not want to say that they grasp the possibilities for action *as possibilities*, and so who do not act with self-awareness.

We now face the question, also raised in Chapter 6, of whether agent's awareness of an action is *constituted* by the action being the product of this kind of active assessment, or of whether it is only that agent's awareness is *conditional* on such active assessment, but standing in need of further explication. We again face a choice between accepting only:

1. *The Conditional Thesis for Agent's Awareness*
If a subject acts directly on the basis of a consideration of possibilities, grasped as possibilities, then she will be agent aware of her action.

Or accepting also:

2. *The Constitution Thesis for Agent's Awareness*
A subject being agent aware of her action is constituted by the action being the product of the subject's consideration of possibilities, grasped as possibilities.

I think we should accept the constitution thesis for physical actions also. On the account being offered an agent, whose action is the direct and immediate product of an active assessment by the agent of how to act, will *thereby* be made agent aware of what she is doing.

Suppose we take a subject who assesses whether to carry out one of three basic actions: ϕ, χ or ψ. And suppose that when a subject acts a content determined by her grasp of the ways she can move her body as a basic action is realized. Suppose that the subject assesses whether to do ϕ, χ or ψ and as a direct result of her assessment ψ-s. She thereby realises the action with the content ψ. According to the constitution thesis the presence of the content ψ, in the context of an evaluation of whether to ϕ, χ or ψ, gives the subject agent awareness that *she* is ψ-ing.

Although I am inclined to the constitution thesis, I am again not confident of being able to provide a direct argument for it. There are clear explanatory advantages to accepting it. If agent's awareness is constituted by our acting as a result of an assessment of possibilities for action, grasped as possibilities, then we require no further explanation of agent's awareness and are able to utilize it in our account of our knowledge of our actions. However, it is not easy to block the possibility that there is a form of self-awareness that is more basic than agent's awareness but that accompanies it.

Let me take the following as an outline of an account of our knowledge of our actions. We are able to act with agent's awareness understood as acting with a sense of control. Acting with a sense of control is acting *directly* on the basis of an evaluation of the possible ways of acting, grasped as possible actions. Acting directly on the basis of an evaluation of the possible ways of acting, grasped as possible ways of acting, is acting with self-awareness of a primitive form. Such self-awareness is constituted by acting on an evaluation of the possible ways of acting, grasped as possible actions. So, when my acting consciously acts as the reason for my self-ascription of the action, my self-ascription is knowledgeable because it rests on an awareness of what I am doing. Furthermore, this is not an awareness that is occasioned by or distinct from my acting, but is rather part of my acting in the way I have.

I have said that acting with agent's awareness, which is acting in a certain way which grounds our self-ascriptions, involves a form of self-awareness. This may give rise to objections. It might be said that properly speaking such consciousness cannot be a form of *self* -awareness as it does not involve a capacity for first-person reference.[28] Of course, if being self-aware is defined so that it implies a capacity for first-person reference, then this cannot be a form of self-awareness. However, it has been my concern to establish that we need appeal to a form of self-awareness more primitive than any capacity for self-reference. And however we label it, it is form of awareness which is such that a suitably cognitively equipped subject—a subject with grasp of the first person and the concept of an action—will immediately be able to *self*-ascribe the action they are conscious of in this way. A form of awareness that is self-indicating in this way clearly needs to be distinguished both from our awareness of the world and things around us, an awareness that may in many cases be quite independent of our ability to ascribe anything to our selves, and from our self-ascriptions themselves. I do not mind whether we call this primitive self-awareness, or something else. The point is the need to identify the need for, and nature of, the phenomenon.

By way of conclusion, let us see how the account sketched fits with the features of authority, independence of perception and investigation, and transparency introduced at the beginning of the chapter as intuitive marks of our knowledge of our actions.

Given the claim that, in central cases, it is the acting in a certain way that grounds ones knowledge of one's actions, we have an explanation of first-person authority. The agent who has agent awareness of her action will be first-person authoritative over her actions. The agent of an action will know in a way unavailable to others whether she is acting, because only the agent acts directly as a result of her assessment of the possibilities available, understood as possibilities. Furthermore, the agent will not only in general know that she is acting when she knows in this way that she is acting, she will also know what she is doing. As long as she has no evidence to the contrary, the agent is entitled to the assumption that her motor systems are working properly and that she has, on the basis of past action, a veridical grasp of both the general and particular possible basic actions open to her. In realising a movement of her body with a given content, as the *direct* result of an evaluation of the ways she might have moved it, grasped as ways she might move it, the agent can be said to know what she is doing. She can know what she has done in way not dissimilar to the way she could know which object she has picked out if she had a grasp of the possible objects available and

---

[28] This is what for example Casteñeda would say (see Casteñeda 1999: 251–92).

picked one, rather than another. However, it is important to emphasise a couple points made earlier. When it is claimed that our actions can act as the grounds for our knowledge of them, it is not being claimed that there is knowledge of them under any description. So, while the moving of my hand may be the potting of the pink ball, my knowledge that I am so moving it, does not by itself give me knowledge that I am potting the pink. The claim of first-person authority with respect to our actions is to be understood as relative to certain descriptions that can be regarded as basic. Authority is also compatible with the possibility of mistaken basic action ascriptions, of raising my arm, for example. My motor system could malfunction in such a way that my arm does not move, or that it lowers rather than rises, or I could for one reason or another have a non-veridical grasp of the possible actions open to me as basic.[29] It should by now be clear how our knowledge of our actions is not grounded on perception or investigation. There is obviously a considerable role played by proprioception and the other perceptual faculties in maintaining and updating a subject's grasp of the possible ways she can act. However, when an agent with a grasp of the

[29] Marcel (2003), presents fascinating data on action self-ascriptions in cases of proprioceptive illusion. Such cases seem to show that a subject who has the proprioceptive illusion that her (occluded) arm is to the left of a (non-occluded) light point, when the arm is in fact to the right of the light point, will (for a period after the onset of the illusion about the position of her arm) correctly move her arm left to the light point but will report that she moved it right. Thus, she will correctly report that she pointed at the light, but incorrectly report that she pointed at the light by moving her arm to the right. After a period, the data shows, the subject stops moving her arm to the correct position. How does the explanation provided above fit with Marcel's data? The view claims that an action is selected via an assessment of certain basic actions relative to the agent, and which action is selected will ground the subject's knowledge of what she is doing. Marcel's data seems to show that, in this case, the subject has authority relative to the description 'moving my hand to the light', but does not have authority relative to the description 'moving my hand to the left'. This suggests that, in this particular case, the basic description of the action for the subject is 'moving my hand to the light'. It seems that, despite the illusion, she knew how to move her arm to the light, just like that, without her knowing how to move it to the light depending on her knowing how to move it to the right. It also suggests that when the subject is required to judge on whether she is moving it to the left or the right, her verdict is a result of her proprioception of the initial state of her arm as to the left of the light, combined with her selection of the action 'move my hand to the light'. The fact that the subject is not inclined to judge that she moved her arm to the left, even though she did, further suggests that neither judgement about what she is doing rests on the subject receiving proprioceptive feedback from her arm which is clearly a result that is congenial to the claims made in this chapter. It is very likely, I think, that in a simpler case in which a subject is suffering from a proprioceptive illusion with respect to the position of her arm, and sets about deliberately to move her arm 'to the right' her final position will be consonant with her false impression of where her arm started off.

possible actions available carries out a single basic action, she need not turn to the testimony of her senses to know what she is doing. While my perceptual faculties are clearly required to give me knowledge of the things I might do, they are not required to give me knowledge of which out of the things I might do, I am doing. All that is required to give me knowledge of that, given the appropriate background, is to do it.

What of relative transparency? Given that acting consciously has been understood to be acting on the basis of an evaluation of possibilities available, grasped as possibilities, we have reason to think that any agent who acts while asking herself what she is doing will act consciously. An agent who acts on the basis of an assessment of possibilities while considering what she is doing, will be an agent who is asking what possibilities for action are being taken while assessing those possibilities. That must mean that the agent acts on the basis of an assessment of her possibilities, understood as possibilities. Given that acting consciously will, in the absence of any repressive mechanisms, be sufficient to ground a knowledgeable self-ascription, an agent who acts, and who asks herself what she is doing, will know what she is doing.

Having presented a suggestion as to how we might set about giving a non-perceptual, representationally independent, account of our knowledge of our actions, I want now to turn to ask the question of what role bodily awareness does play in giving us self-knowledge. I have argued that our knowledge of our actions is critical source of self-knowledge and that the source of our knowledge of our actions is not bodily awareness. In the following chapter, I want to bring out how I understand bodily awareness. In the final chapter I want to look more closely at the differences between bodily awareness and knowledge of our actions considered as sources for self-knowledge. I aim to clarify the respects in which bodily awareness does not provide a source of self-knowledge in a way comparable to agent's awareness.

10

Bodily Awareness

In recent years philosophers have began to take more notice of the fact that we have a sense, or group of senses—bodily awareness—other than the traditional five with which to gain information about our own bodies. It has, further, become widely accepted that we should give a perceptual account of bodily awareness.[1] This seems to be right, but what precisely is involved in such a claim is not always clear. Accordingly, before considering the role that bodily awareness plays in self-knowledge I want to set out how I understand the claim that bodily awareness is a perceptual faculty or, more realistically, set of faculties. Two claims can be made about at least some of our perceptual faculties. We can explain how we should construe bodily awareness as a perceptual faculty by showing the way in which the claims are true of bodily awareness also.

A. Sensory modalities give us information about the properties of objects, stuffs, features and places as located in a spatio-temporal domain.

The different senses, of course, provide us with information in very different ways. *A* is true most obviously of sight. Sight presents us with the properties of spatio-temporally located objects, stuffs, features and places in presenting us, in the normal case, with a spatio-temporal array. Touch also, although not typically presenting us with an array clearly presents us with objects and so on, as located. While less obvious it seems to me that an adequate treatment of the senses of smell, taste and hearing will have it that they too provide us with information about the properties of located objects, stuffs, features and places as spatio-temporally located. This claim may seem doubtful especially for taste and smell—it might be said that we can just have the sensation of

---

[1] Armstrong (1968) is perhaps the first to suggest such an approach. (See also Martin 1995 and 1997; Tye 1995: 94–6; Dretske 1997: 102–3; Bermúdez 1998, ch. 6; Crane 2003.)

tasting coffee or of smelling coffee without having an ability to ascribe the property of being coffee-smelling or coffee-tasting to anything we take to be spatial located. This seems to me to be wrong; in as far as we are unable at least to connect the property of being coffee-tasting to my mouth or the property of being coffee-smelling to the space around me, we will be inclined to think that we are vividly remembering or imagining rather than tasting or smelling. Once we distinguish between having a diffuse location with having no location at all, then I think we will take *A* to apply in these cases also. However, this dispute need not be settled here. All that is needed is that *A* is distinctive of at least some faculties which are indisputably perceptual. The second claim to be identified is:

B. Sensory modalities are capable of giving us information about properties specific to the sense in question (mono-modal properties) *as well as properties discernible from more than one sensory modality* (cross-modal properties)

It is a notable fact that our senses present us with a world in which there are properties specific to our modes of sensing it. We see colours, hear sounds, smell smells, touch textures, and taste tastes. And the only way we have of perceiving these properties is by using the dedicated sensory modality. In identifying a faculty as a sensory faculty we should therefore be concerned to identify what sensory properties it is licensed to present.

Bodily awareness is a faculty for which both claims *A* and *B* seem to hold. Let us take *A* first. When considering the other five senses already discussed, it is easy to adopt a view of the relevant egocentric perceptual space as somewhat poncho shaped—as the space centred around the body of the subject with a hole in the middle. The volume of space occupied by the body itself is taken to be perceptually out of view. Now of course some of the volume of space occupied by our bodies is perceptually out of view, but my no means all of it. Bodily awareness is the set of faculties responsible for providing information about that space internal to the limits of my body. It provides information both about the shape and orientation of that space and about the properties of places within it. Take for example my being able to tell that my arm is pointing upwards. Awareness of my arm and its orientation to the rest of the body are given to me by bodily awareness. I have a more or less stable body image, the changes and movements of which I am able to track. When my arm rises, my kinaesthetic and proprioceptive senses will tell me that it is on the move and will plot for me the path it takes and its resting point. Thus we seem to receive spatial information about the location of my arm of two kinds relative to the two spaces—the inner space mapped by my body image and the outer space.[2]

However its spatial properties are not the only properties that our capacity for bodily awareness enables us to perceive. The space taken up by the arm itself, and other parts of the body, are not merely empty geometrical spaces whose movements and orientation can be tracked. It is widely agreed that if my arm where to be pinched or tickled I would feel sensation and locate it at a point in my arm, and that bodily awareness is what enables me to do this. What is not usually very clear is how we should understand the perception of a pain or tickle in my arm. One suggestion is that the sensation—the pain or the tickle—is not located in my foot at all. Rather what we have is a capacity to perceive *damage* or *disturbance* to our body parts and the content of a pain experience should be thought of as a representation of a part of the body as damaged.[3] This can then be taken to be sufficient as an account of the experience of pain, or in need of supplementation by pain qualia for example. I do not intend to argue the case here, but I think that such an account will in the end prove either phenomenologically implausible, if it does not invoke some sort of non-representational qualia independently of the representational properties it allows itself, or metaphysically problematic in its commitment to qualia if it does. Merely taking pain experiences to be, albeit analogue, representations of damage, disturbance or such like, seems to underdetermine the qualitative aspects of pain experience. But now if such a theorist were to introduce qualia to capture the painfulness of pain and the tickliness of tickles she will be committed to intrinsic mental phenomena which are difficult to explain. Further, such a theorist can reasonably take herself to be proposing a perceptual account of bodily awareness only if she is willing to give a parallel account of perception generally, or willing to show why a parallel account is not required. This would mean that she needs to make plausible the view that a perception of the chair as green, say, involves a representation of the chair and its reflectant properties, a representation that may or may not be accompanied by a non-representational sensation of green.

A second suggestion is to say that bodily awareness not only enables us to perceive our body and body parts and their spatial properties, but

---

[2] See Martin (1995) and (1997a).   [3] See Tye (1995).

that it enables us to apprehend parts of the body in different ways.[4] The idea would be that the same object can be common to different modes of awareness. Depending on the mode of awareness—whether it is pain awareness or tickle awareness—we will take the body part as being painful or tickly. So rather than taking being painful as part of the *content* of what is perceived, being painful is a mode by which the subject relates to the content perceived. We might compare the distinction being invoked here to the distinction, invoked in talk about the ascription of propositional attitude states, between the content of a state and its force.

One not very serious worry about the suggestion is that it invites the thought that there is a different sense corresponding to each sensation type: a dedicated pain-sense, tickle-sense and so on. So, while when we are seeing or hearing we can use the same sense to discriminate a large number of properties, the senses that constitute bodily awareness will be taken to be highly specific. I can see my leg as coloured (red, green, blue etc.). I can hear sounds (loud, sharp, low etc.). However, on this suggestion I will either pain-sense my leg, or tickle-sense my leg and so on. The main worry about the suggestion, however, is that it does not share the feature of other senses identified by claim *B*—there is no commitment to properties of the body perceived and to which I am sensitive, only modes of awareness of body parts.

In response, it is open to the proponent of this view to give a parallel account of perception generally. Perception, she may argue is always the awareness of certain objects in a certain way *w*, where *w* is the mode of awareness rather than anything the subject is aware of. So, on such an account the perception of a green chair should be understood as the awareness of a chair in a particular sort of way—via greenly-awareness. But now we might wonder what account is going to be given of what makes the perception veridical or not. The naïve view is that a perception of an object is veridical if it represents the object as being as it is—if there is a match between content and world. This, most naturally, means that we take the object to have the properties that it in fact has. If we take seeing a green chair as being greenly-aware of the chair, where being green aware does not enter into the content of what is perceived, but rather into the mode of perception, we might wonder what reason we have to take the perception as representing the chair being green. When we become suddenly-aware of the table, say, we do not represent the

---

[4] See Crane (2003) for this view.

table as being sudden. For a sceptic about colour and other secondary properties this might seem to get things about right. However, it would seem to be somewhat perverse for a non-sceptic to introduce modes of awareness corresponding to all the secondary properties there are to be represented given that those properties are there. We can explain our experience as of colour, say, as the representation not just of the object but also in terms of the actual properties of the thing perceived.

This leads to the natural (perhaps naive) suggestion that we avoid taking pains and tickles as the representation of damage, accompanied or not by qualia objects, and avoid taking them as modes of awareness. Rather, we should take them as perceptible properties of parts of our bodies discriminable by bodily awareness. This view involves taking bodily awareness to present us with our arm, say, as a concrete space bearing internal perceptible properties. On this suggestion, the right way to think of what is happening when I feel a tickle or pain in my arm is that I perceive my arm, and perceive it as being tickly or painy at a certain location. This parallels what goes on when I have a visual perception of, say, a green spot on a table. I see the table, located in a space and see it as being green at a certain point. If we take the perception of our bodies via bodily awareness in this way, then we can come to see bodily awareness as satisfying not just *A* above, but also *B*. And for someone who accepts *B*, this must constitute an advantage of the suggestion. Awareness of located sensations—pains, aches, and tickles—can be construed in much the same way as our awareness of familiar secondary properties, as involving awareness of mono-modal secondary properties of our bodies perceptible via bodily awareness.

Although, the above gives us an idea about the right way to understand bodily awareness it cannot be denied that our use of our sensation terms does not parallel our use of other secondary quality terms. While we happily say 'She thought the chair was green, but was wrong' we are less happy about 'She thought her arm was in pain, but she was wrong'. The difference lies, it might be said, in the fact that we are able to distinguish between it appearing to me as if the chair is green and the chair actually being green, but not between it appearing to me that my arm is in pain and my arm being in pain. But in fact there *is* a distinction between it appearing that my arm is in pain and it being the case that my arm is in pain. The possibility of error however, would usually be thought to lie in the fact that it could turn out that I was wrong in taking it to be the case that it was my *arm* that was in pain. It may be insisted that it cannot turn out to be the case that I think I am in pain but not be in pain. And this might be thought to put a distance between the visual model and the bodily awareness model: I can turn out to be wrong that the chair was green but I can also turn out to be wrong about anything being green.

We can I think deal with this difference between the two cases, and retain the model of sensations as perceptible properties of the body. We can, as one strategy, adopt the suggestion that we understand the concept of pain as equivocal. We can use it to refer both to the experience of pain on the one hand and the property perceived as qualifying parts of my body on the other. It would be like taking green to refer both to the green experience—the experience as of greenness—and to the property experienced. It might be said that this cannot be right since in the case of pain there is simply no distinction between the experience of pain and the pain experienced—these are just two ways of saying that same thing. This equation between the two aspects of the concept might be supported by the fact that we commonly disallow the possibility of a subject being wrong about whether she is pain. It is certainly true that, for the most part, we tend to use pain in a way that disallows the possibility that one can be wrong about whether one is pain. It is therefore natural, given the authority it is agreed that we have about whether we are having an experience as of pain, to take our standard use of the term as referring to the experience as of a part of my body being in pain, rather than as referring to a perceptible property of my body.

However, it is in fact relatively common for us to use pain in a way that does allow for error. A person can, for example seem to find out she was so anxious about the possibility of being in pain, because suppose the dentist had told her to expect an injection, that she took herself to have been in pain when she was not. She seemed to have felt the injection before it had been given. We also countenance talk of someone of having such a vivid memory or imagination of being in pain that they feel as if they are in pain when they are not. We seem to allow, in other words, for a subject to have an experience as of being in pain when there is no pain to be felt.[5] Less common is for us to acknowledge the possibility of pains that are not felt, but again it is not unknown. We say things like 'I was working so hard to get to the top of the hill that I did not feel my foot was hurting'. Or I felt the pain in my foot more and more strongly as I came round from the anaesthetic'. In such locutions,

---

[5] See also Williamson's anti-luminosity arguments in Williamson (2000, ch. 4).

where a later awareness seems to give us evidence of a property abiding throughout our not being aware of it, and coming to be aware of it, we seem to leave room for the possibility of unfelt pains.

While, it seems to me that certain features of normal use are consonant with, and indeed explained by, the suggestion made here that we take 'pain' to refer both to the experience as of pain and to a property of the body, we should not think that its acceptability rests on this. Suppose that we concede that we now use the word 'pain' to refer only to the experience as of pain, denying any legitimate use of the term to refer to properties of the body. We are not thereby stopped from claiming that the experience as of pain, what we call 'pain', is an awareness of a perceptual property of part of our bodies. Even if we accept that the experience as of green is the same whether it is a mere appearance of green or a perception of green, and is something we cannot in general be wrong about, this does not stop us from theorising about colour vision as involving a distinction between the perceptible property of the object and the experience of it. It is not clear why the parallel feature of pain should stop us from theorising about pain perception in the same way. It might be that accepting the account of pain perception offered will suggest a reformation, or at least clarification of our use of sensation terms, but that is not enough in itself to militate against it.

It should be emphasised that none of this is going to convince someone who is already a sceptic about *B*, perhaps because they are a sceptic about the properties of colour, smell and sound. If we are inclined to explain colour vision as no more than the occasioning of experiences or intrinsic mental phenomenal properties (qualia) by primary quality causes, then we are likely to be similarly committed to taking pain perception to be the occasioning of pain experiences or qualia in response to physical damage or pressure. In neither case will we accept the need to postulate perceptible secondary properties perceived. Similarly if we deny the existence of colour qualia, as well as that of phenomenal colour properties and take colour vision to be the mere representation of certain primary properties, then we are likely to take pain perception to be the mere representation of damage to the body. The underlying point is that there is no bar to modelling our account of pain perception on our account of colour, or sound perception, whichever account we favour. Therefore, if we think it is plausible to construe vision and audition as involving the perception, by a subject, of secondary quality properties of places and objects, then, I suggest, it is plausible to do so for pain perception also.

It is of interest to ask, why such a model is not more widespread. Why is it so natural to take colours as phenomenal properties of objects that we are able to perceive on the one hand, but so natural to think of pains as merely mental items on the other? The answer I think lies in the fact that the space in which we see colours is public space, the shared arena of inter-subjective coordination and agreement. The space perceivable by means of bodily awareness is a space perceived only by the subject herself. And given this, the judgements a subject makes, grounded in bodily awareness, about whether or not her arm is in pain, cannot be verified by the judgement of another using the same perceptual tools. Those other than the subject have to use other senses—vision, audition and so forth—if they are to perceive that the subject is in pain. This fact means that the subject must, as a pragmatic matter, be taken as the authority of what is going on within her body space, since that is a space to which others simply do not have the same access. The subject relates to her body space via bodily awareness much as we would relate to our visual space if each of us was enclosed in a space to which only we had access via direct vision. In the normal case, the subject must also be taken to be generally authoritative about how things in her body space seem to her, just as she is about how things seem to her in the space around her. Given that, in most cases, the subject's best judgement about how things seem to her with respect to the pain properties of her arm, will be our *only* guide as to how things are with respect to the pain properties of her arm, it is very natural that we tend to collapse the distinction between the subject's state of mind and the state of her body. That said, with advancing technology giving us better access to the goings-on in a person's body space and perceptual mechanisms we are likely to become more used to making a distinction between someone being in pain and her feeling it.

This diagnosis of the nature of our pain ascribing practices may be thought to reveal a problem with the suggestion offered. If we were promoting a primary quality view of colour, holding that colour properties are not essentially phenomenal and can in fact be detected in ways other by seeing them, then it may be that technological advances giving us information about our body space would enable us to make a distinction between real pain and pain sensation—much as we have learnt to make a distinction between heat and heat sensation. But, it may be said, the dis-analogy between sensations and colours identified above is enough to suggest that a realist theory of colours as phenomenal, but external, properties is available while a realist theory of pain as a phenomenal property of the body is not.

Consider an account of colour properties that has it that things have the colours they have partly because of a convergence in the kind of judgements we make about how they seem to us. Such an account has it that the existence of colour properties lies in inter-subjective facts about our judging practices. Now, it can argued, that it is a condition of such an account that different judging subjects have equal access to, and authority over, the properties being judged of. It might be thought that we do not get the practices sufficient to claim the independent existence of the properties taken as manifest unless such a condition is satisfied. The question then is whether holding bodily awareness as giving us perceptual access to a space that others cannot access in that way, means that the condition required for the postulation of independent perceptual properties is not met. It may be that the condition allows us to postulate the existence of colours, sounds and smells, but not of pains, tickles and aches. It is, I think, clear that if we adopt a form of inter-subjectivism that has it that the existence of phenomenal properties depends on the explicit practices and agreements of judging subjects then the fact that only *I* get to sense my body via bodily awareness will mean that we cannot postulate the existence of phenomenal properties relative to bodily awareness. But such a view is not compulsory. Indeed its requirement that there be an actual consensus of judgements made on the same grounds might seem to make it unsatisfactorily idealist. It would for example be committed to the view that for a community with each subject physically restricted to their own space, communicating by walkie-talkie and black and white CCTV, there would be no colour properties.

To propose an adequately defended alternative would require a general account of how we are to decide what properties there really are, a specific account of perceptible properties and an account of perception. Even if I knew how to give such accounts, doing so would take us too far from the present concern. Let me then just suppose that we should identify the properties we are prepared to postulate with reference to the ways our evolved senses stably present the world to us as being.[6] That is we should read off the properties there are from the properties I seem to experience given naturally evolved senses. Then, if we have subjects responding to the same external stimuli in the same ways, describing

---

[6] We might defend this by saying that given a shared evolution in a shared environment it is natural to think that our senses will evolve relative to the properties there are.

their experiences in the same terms, using the same evolved perceptual resources, we have good reason to take them to be responding to the same detectable property, whether or not they have perceptual access to the same space. Given the truth of such a supposition, we would have as much reason to defend the presence of pain properties as of colour or smell properties.

The above discussion has brought out the fact that there are a number of ways we might construe the widely accepted claim that bodily awareness is a perceptual faculty. I have tried to fill out one way of understanding that claim. I have suggested that we construe bodily awareness as a faculty which enables us to perceive properties of our bodies—its shape, location, movement, as well phenomenal pain properties, tickle properties, and the like. Unless one is a sceptic about secondary properties, or has a specific reason for thinking that there could not be phenomenal perceptible properties of our bodies, I think there is no impediment to doing so.

11

Bodily Awareness and Self-Knowledge

1. INTRODUCTION

In the previous chapter I presented a suggestion about how to construe bodily awareness. With that in the background I want now to try to relate the discussion of our knowledge of our own actions to recent discussions about bodily awareness. A number of analytic philosophers have turned to the phenomenon of bodily awareness as an important part of an attempt to give a non-Cartesian account of the self.[1] The attempt to use awareness of our bodies as, in Evans's phrase, an 'antidote to a Cartesian conception of the self' (1982: 220) probably first emerges in the work of Husserl and is explicitly operative in the work of phenomenologists such as Merleau-Ponty and Heidegger, and is there in Strawson. However, it is probably Evans's own suggestion that use of the first-person is grounded in our capacity to pick ourselves out as spatio-temporally located bounded objects via bodily awareness (as well as certain egocentric perceptual information) that has been the crucial *recent* catalyst in this move. Since then there has been much discussion of whether bodily awareness does constitute an awareness of ourselves, and if so, of what kind. In particular it has been asked whether bodily awareness can be construed as a kind of self-awareness that bears the marks of introspection. I have argued that bodily awareness is not needed to ground individual acts of first-person reference and that an account of self-reference grounded in bodily awareness would be inadequate. But we might think that nevertheless bodily awareness does give us a consciousness of ourselves, as selves that are physical beings. I want to argue, however, that bodily awareness does not compete with our awareness of our actions through agent's awareness as a source for self-knowledge. I will suggest that bodily awareness is only one more

---

[1] Cassam (1997) is a singularly systematic and impressive such attempt. But, see also Ayers (1991) and Brewer (1999).

perceptual faculty, and that in so far as perceptual faculties rely upon a subject attaining knowledge of herself via some input, we cannot count it as a primary source for self-knowledge in the way that we can count knowledge of oneself attained via one's output. Our knowledge of our actions, through agent's awareness, has been characterized as knowledge of oneself via one's output, independent of an incoming representation of the action carried out. As such, I want to suggest, it constitutes a primary source for self-knowledge.

1.1 IEM as the mark of self-knowledge?

So, let me go back to the kind of self-awareness I take to ground the first-person and self-knowledge more broadly. What is it about the knowledge we have about our own actions that enables it to play a privileged role? Perhaps the most obvious first attempt in trying to characterize the particularity of knowledge of our own actions on the basis of agent's awareness, that seemed to connect it suitably to the role we are asking it to play in an account of self-consciousness self-reference, is to claim that it is immune to error through misidentification (IEM). To say that our knowledge of our actions, based on our awareness of being the agent of them, is IEM is to say that a failure to know of one's own actions on that basis cannot be due to a misidentification as to *who* the agent of the action is.

Perception and bodily awareness seem to be sources of self-conscious knowledge. However they are phenomena that, it may be said (we will come shortly to reasons for not saying it), admit of the possibility of error through misidentification. Imagine that I am wired up to another person in such a way that I have for a period of time reliable informational access to two disjointed regions of space. (Let us say that a transmitter located in the brain of the other person sends signals that can appropriately structure my retinal imaging). The information given will be of the same type and subjective character as normal visual information from them. Such a case seems to present us with the possibility that I am in the position of having perceptual access—visual access—to two different regions. If that is the right story then we might think that it follows that my perceptual judgements are not IEM with respect to the first person. I can judge that I am in front of a tree when I am not, it is the other chap. We will have a case of quasi-perception. Similarly, we can seem to imagine cases of quasi-proprioception. Imagine a case in which I am able to receive reliable information from, and about, the state of someone else's body which is phenomenologically indistinguishable from the case where I receive information from, and about, my own body. If there could be such phenomena as quasi-perception and quasi-proprioception or bodily awareness, then judgements made on the basis of the relative informational sources do not obviously exhibit IEM.[2]

In contrast we can, *prima face,* make little sense of the notion of being quasi-aware of a voluntary action in the way that I am aware of my own. If I am wired up to someone else in such a way that I receive information about her actions, it seems that the best that can happen is that I am aware of her body moving. It is hard to see what it would be for me to be aware as an agent of moving her body unless that *counted* as me moving her body. In which case, the action ascription would not be mistaken in virtue of a misidentification of the agent. It really does seem that knowledge that I am acting is IEM with respect to the first person.

To claim IEM relative to the first person for first-person judgements about our own actions, based on an agent's awareness in acting, is not of course to rule out the possibility of error in other ways. It does not mean that I cannot be wrong about what I am doing. First, we can distinguish the possibility of error through misidentification relative to the subject and the possibility of error through misidentification relative to the predicate. I can think that 'I am bleeding' because I see a leg with red stuff on it. I can be wrong about whether it is my leg—it may be the leg of the person next to me, or I can be wrong about whether it is blood—it may be ketchup. I am not here claiming that our knowledge of our actions is IEM relative to the predicative element. (For example, as we have remarked above, we can describe our actions in terms of their effects and these we are not authoritative about.) I am however claiming that they are immune relative to the subject. When I judge on the basis of agent's awareness I can be wrong about what I am doing, or I can be wrong about whether I have succeeded in acting at all. But I cannot be wrong about whether it is me, or someone else, who is acting. Secondly, I can act, and for one reason or another—suppression, inattention and so on—and not know that I have. Thirdly, I can take myself to have acted on bases other than agent's awareness and just be wrong that I acted. If someone else moves my arm just after I had some

---

[2] Of course, given Shoemaker's distinction between *de facto* and *logical* IEM we might say that given that such modes of quasi-perception do not exist, our actual judgements based on our actual perceptions are *de facto* IEM.

prior intention to move it, I may through some process of inference from my knowledge of the prior intention and the feedback through bodily awareness have the impression of having moved it. But, even given these possibilities of error, it seems right to claim IEM relative to the first person for first-person judgements about our own actions based on our agent's awareness in acting.

However, the claim of IEM is not in fact sufficient to set our knowledge of our actions apart from our knowledge through bodily awareness. Things are not as simple as the above discussion suggests. As we saw, in our earlier discussion of Evans, in Chapter 3, there is room for dispute over whether the cases of cross-wiring are correctly described when identified as cases that provide the subject with access through vision or bodily awareness to space or bodies other than her own. It has been suggested that we should rather think of the states that we have been tempted to call a visual perception of distal space, or proprioceptive awareness of a body other than one's own, as illusions or informational states of a kind distinct from visual or proprioceptive perception. If such states are illusory, or are not cases of visual perception or proprioceptive awareness, then we cannot take them as cases in which we have a veridical perception of the relevant kind which fails to deliver information about the perceiver. The claim that such perceptions are IEM relative to the subject is then preserved because the cases that appeared to be counter-examples can be best treated either as not perceptions at all, or at least not perceptions of the relevant kind.

Until we consider the merits of such a view all we can do in trying to claim a difference between the way knowledge of our actions and knowledge of our bodies through perception and bodily awareness relate to self-conscious knowledge is to say that one phenomena is such that it is *amenable* to being characterized, or possibly mischaracterised, in a way that makes it *appear* that there can be IEM in one case but not in the other. I do think that *amenability* to such mischaracterisation of knowledge through bodily awareness, as opposed to knowledge through agent's awareness is evidence for a deeper distinction between the two. However, we need to find that deeper distinction. But in order to do so we need to consider the grounds for the claim that it is a mis-characterisation.

In order to try to get clear about what is at issue in the debate concerning whether we can make sense of such quasi-phenomena in general, and in order to disentangle and ultimately trace, the relations between the phenomena of knowledge of one's actions and bodily awareness, I am now going to consider the argument sketched above as it relates to bodily awareness in particular. I will do so under an understanding of bodily awareness as a perceptual faculty in the way characterised above.[3]

As we saw, to take bodily awareness as perceptual is to claim that bodily awareness can be understood as a way of experiencing the body in much the same way that vision is a way of experiencing the space before us and the objects and properties encountered within it. So to feel a pain in my left foot may not be to have a mental object—the pain—and somehow relate it to the left foot. Rather, to have such a pain maybe to experience something, namely, my left foot as having a certain property—that of being hurt. The experience of that object as having that property we call the experience of pain. And this is quite to parallel to my experiencing the chair as being green. If bodily awareness is understood as perceptual, in this way, we should then take the claim that bodily awareness will not ground judgements that are IEM relative to the first person to rest on the possibility of perceiving another's body via the faculty of bodily awareness. That is, we need to work out what is going on in the case described above where there is a reliable information supporting link between myself and another's body. Is that link sufficient to establish that I have bodily awareness of that body or just that I am amenable to certain kinds of illusions and misapprehensions? As Martin puts it, we have to choose between a sole object and a multiple object view:

Bodily sensations, together with kinaesthesia, proprioception, and the vestibular sense, amount to an awareness of one's body that is [necessarily] only of one's own body and body parts. Call this the *sole-object view* . . . [Or] one might claim that it is merely a contingent matter that one comes to be aware only of one's own body parts in this way, and that it is quite conceivable that one could come to be aware of parts of others' bodies in the same way. Call this the *multiple-object view*.[4]

Both views may seem to be consistent with how things stand. *De facto* bodily awareness provides us with knowledge only of body parts *that are part of my body*. However, as Martin stresses, bodily awareness does not simply give us information about body parts that are in fact mine—it seems to give us information about them *as body parts that are part of my body*. There is a sense of ownership of our bodies

---

[3] The argument draws mainly on Martin (1995).   [4] Martin (1995: 273–74).

that the phenomenology of bodily awareness secures. Given that there is such first-personal content to the awareness that bodily awareness provides how can we think that it could provide us with a *veridical* perception of another's body—that would mean that we had a veridical perception of another's body *as* mine—and that could only be so if the other's body *was* mine. We could accept that it was a veridical perception if we held an idealist conception of my body such that a body counted as mine just in virtue of the fact that I was aware of it in a given way. In which case, the situation would be one in which the other body is also my body—my body would just be a rather complex entity. If this option seems implausible, then we must say that I am suffering an illusion. Whichever option we choose, this account concludes, bodily awareness should be understood along the lines of the sole-object view.

This view seems right as long as one thinks that the phenomenology of bodily awareness is *fixed* as first personal. What the multiple object view may try to do in response is to argue that with sufficiently radical changes in our background beliefs and so on, the phenomenology of bodily awareness could change. Given regular reliable connections to another's body, on being aware via bodily awareness that there is a pain in the leg of this body, I may become unsure which body I am aware of. Imagine that sometime in the future baby products manufacturers provide us with the new 'Internal Baby Monitor' (the IBM). In the case of a screaming child, one sticks the device to the baby and to oneself and one is then presented with the baby's body space 'from the inside'. It would be the bodily awareness equivalent of a CCTV. I can feel if the pain is one of hunger or nappy rash and unplug and act accordingly. Given regular use of such a device it is not hard to imagine circumstances when I wake—having gone to sleep with this gadget on—and wonder whether I have my leg bent over, or the baby has, on account of not being sure whether the device was on or off. What the example trades off here is that the perspectival nature of perception (in this case bodily perception from the inside) seems to be something we could come to separate from its being first personal in content as long as we have the necessary background beliefs. Notable, for my purposes, is that we have a very simple way of determining the answer to the questions—is the IBM on or off? As soon as I decide to move my leg, I will know whether or not the body I am aware of in this way is me. If I am aware of a leg moving then it is my body I am aware of, and if not, it is the baby's.

The sole-object view held the thesis that: necessarily, bodily awareness is awareness of one's own body. However we can understand that to mean two things.

1. That one's body is necessarily that which bodily awareness gives us awareness of.
2. That bodily awareness is necessarily awareness *as of* one's own body.

The sole-object view as first presented was committed to (1) and to the claim that that bodily awareness is awareness *as of* one's own body. However, the cases we have presented suggest that we should understand this latter claim only as a *de facto* claim about the contents of bodily awareness, and not a necessary one. This however means that there is scope to acknowledge different strengths of immunity claim with respect to bodily awareness. We have four possibilities:

1. That one's body is *de facto* that which bodily awareness gives us awareness of and bodily awareness is *de facto* awareness *as of* one's own body.
2. That one's body is *necessarily* that which bodily awareness gives us awareness of and bodily awareness is *de facto* awareness *as of* one's own body.
3. That one's body is *de facto* that which bodily awareness gives us awareness of and bodily awareness is *necessarily* awareness *as of* one's own body.
4. That one's body is *necessarily* that which bodily awareness gives us awareness of and bodily awareness is *necessarily* awareness *as of* one's own body.

It can be conceded to the sole-object view that neither 1 nor 3 are the right way to characterise bodily awareness. There is still, however, the question as to whether 2 or 4 is preferable. The discussion above suggests that the sole-object view gives us a reason only to hold that 2 correctly characterises bodily awareness.

Now it may, of course, be conceded by the holder of sole-object view that the presence of sources of information that are phenomenologically very similar to our experiences via bodily awareness could change the phenomenology of bodily awareness. It could be that the bodily awareness comes to give us awareness appropriately characterised as awareness of 'body around here' rather than awareness of 'my body'. Nevertheless, she may say, this does nothing to show that the sole-object view according to which bodily awareness is necessarily awareness of the subject's *own* body is wrong. All it does is show that there may be modes of perception—reliable information gathering links—the deliverances of which are indistinguishable from perception via bodily awareness, and that the presence of such modes of perception might bring about a generalising in the information-bearing content of our existing perceptions. None of that touches the view that bodily awareness necessarily enables me to perceive only one object—my body (however that is configured). It may be that the sole-object theorist is right about this. It is very plausible to suppose that when I use the IBM, I do not experience the baby's hurt leg by means of bodily awareness but rather by means of another kind of perceptual link altogether. However, it now becomes explicit that we are not individuating perceptual faculties by means of their phenomenology, or the essential first-person content, but rather relative to further facts. This means that even if a subject judges 'My leg is bent', on what is in fact awareness through proprioception, it is implausible to claim that she is aware of her leg being bent as *her* leg being bent, and so implausible to claim that she *knows* that her leg, rather than someone else's, is bent on the basis she has. To know that, it seems she would have to discount the possibility that what she in fact has is a perception of someone else's leg (via the IBM) and that she has mistaken it for her own. However, she *does* seem in a position to know on the basis of bodily awareness that someone's leg is bent.

It might be useful to realise that we can have a quite parallel debate with respect to visual perception. We might well argue that visual perceptions are first personal in content and that a judgement does not count as grounded in *visual perception* unless those perceptions are providing information, via the normal faculty of sight, about the egocentric space of the subject. On this view, any information coming in from a distal point in a form that is phenomenologically indistinguishable from visual perception will be the result of a distinct perceptual process and so will not count as visual information. If this was our view we could rightly hold that first-person judgements, such as 'I am in front of a door' that are based on visual information are IEM. However, if in certain circumstances the subject knows that vision-like information from non-visual sources are around, it no longer seems plausible, if it ever was, to suppose that the contents of her visual perceptions are first-personal (rather than perspectival in some more general way: 'door ahead' perhaps). Consequently, although a judgement to the effect that 'I am in front of a door' based on vision will be immune to falsity, and although she might be able to know that 'Someone is in front of a door' it does not follow that she thereby knows that *she* is in front of a door.

There is another case which seems to me to be telling, in which we might imagine the sense of ownership claimed to be characteristic of bodily awareness falling away. Imagine an entirely passive subject: a subject quite unable to move her body and deeply cognizant of this fact—to such an extent that she does not, and cannot, try to move her body. Can we not imagine in such case that the subject's body will become to her much as the space around her has come to her—as a domain around her of which there is a certain kind of perception, but as an object that is not necessarily experienced as hers?

My hope is that the above discussion suggests that bodily awareness, if understood as a kind of perception, is not really in a position to be the primary source of self-knowledge. Even granted that necessarily something only counts as bodily awareness if it is awareness of myself, what we seem to have to acknowledge is the *possibility* that a subject could be quite in the dark as to whether that which she is aware of in a 'bodily-awareness-like-way' is herself, because she might not know whether her current perceptual state is a veridical product of proprioception or of some other perceptual process. We acknowledged that it might be that in normal circumstances for the subject to be aware of her body in a 'bodily-awareness-like-way' is for her to have a perceptual experience of her body with first-person content. Therefore, in normal circumstances, her perception would be veridical only in the case when it is based on bodily awareness. However, I argued that even if we accept the claim that the content of our *normal* proprioceptive perceptions are not merely perspectival, but are first-personal, we have to accept that, given the presence of alternative perceptual sources, the phenomenology of bodily awareness could change from being first-personal in content to being merely perspectival.

I hope the discussion also raises the suggestion that what seems to be necessary to making bodily awareness of a body, awareness of a body *as mine*, is my ability to act with that body. I suggested that, in the absence of action, the sense of ownership could recede. I also suggested that if we have awareness of multiple bodies in a 'bodily-awareness-like way' (awareness which may not be bodily awareness proper) and knowledge of the possibility of such access, we can use our knowledge of which body responds to our wills in order to know which body is ours.

I want now to consider how the above discussion leaves us with respect to the suggestion that IEM is a mark of a primary source for self-knowledge. It will emerge that there are a number of claims that we could be making when we say that a source of knowledge delivers knowledge of a kind that is IEM. Our broad characterisation of the claim that a source for knowledge was IEM with respect to the first person was that, that a failure to know 'I am F', for some relevant F, on *that* basis could not be due to a misidentification as to who the subject was.

If IEM is understood in this way, then bodily awareness, on the sole-object view, will be a source which supports judgements that are IEM. If bodily awareness necessarily gives information about only one object—my body—and I have access to an object through bodily awareness, then first-person judgements such as 'My leg is bent' made on the basis of such awareness cannot be false as a result of my being aware of the wrong object. However, assuming that is sufficient to secure IEM, then the IEM of a subject's judgement seems to be something that can be attained in virtue of facts independent and unknowable by even a reflective subject. Thus a subject's first-personal judgement could be IEM but not a plausible candidate for knowledge as the subject herself might have reasons to question its truth. This suggests that bodily awareness is not a promising source for self-knowledge.

However, IEM has usually been taken to indicate a kind of immunity from error that is stronger than this. Evans says a judgement is IEM if:

When the first component is expressive of knowledge which the subject has of his own states, available to him in the normal way, and not taken by him to be knowledge which he has gained, or may have gained, in any other way, the utterance 'Someone is F, but is it I who am F?' does not appear to make sense. (Evans 82: 216)

My earlier gloss of the notion of IEM suggested that a first-person judgement made on a given basis is IEM, if the judgement cannot be *false* as a result of a misidentification of the bearer of the property being ascribed. As such it indicated *immunity from falsity* of a certain kind. However, the Evans test suggests that IEM calls for more than immunity from falsity, but also from immunity from a certain kind of misconception or mistake. It is somewhat problematic to judge what might or might not make sense for a subject. We could, however, put the condition in terms of what the subject can or cannot know if she knows that 'Someone is F'. We could state our tests for IEM in terms of the following conditionals:

(I-1) If I know, in normal circumstances, in way *w*, that 'Someone (or this body) is F', then, necessarily, I am F.

(I-2) If I know, in normal circumstances, in way *w*, that 'Someone (or this body) is F' then I will *know* that I am F.

If we put things in this way, we can see that there are two further kinds of immunity that may be claimed: one weaker than both of these and one stronger:

(I-3) If I know, in normal circumstances, in way *w*, that 'Someone (or this body) is F', then, normally, I am F.

(I-4) If I know, even in relevant abnormal circumstances, in way *w* that 'Someone (or this body) is F' then I will *know* that I am F.[5]

Suppose a subject is in a circumstance which is such that she is able to know that 'Someone (or this body) has a bent leg' in a way that implies that she, herself, has a bent leg, say, through bodily awareness. If the subject were to judge 'I have a bent leg' in such circumstances her judgement would be true and IEM according to the tests (I-1) and (I-3). It would be immune to falsity of a certain kind because if, in such a case, she can know that 'Someone has a bent leg', then that someone must be the subject herself, because she knows that someone has a leg bent through bodily awareness, which only provides information about her leg. Further, it might be that in normal circumstances her knowledge that someone's leg is bent will be *sufficient* to secure knowledge that *her* leg is bent. If so, then we have IEM in the sense given by (I-2). However, as we have seen, in some abnormal circumstances, she may not know that the person whose leg is bent is indeed her. That is, while

---

[5] Note that the relevant abnormal cases are those in which the subject takes it that her awareness of an instance of F-ness may be awareness via competing phenomenologically similar, but distinct sources. Note that there could be cases, where a subject has been reliably informed of a bare correlation between its seeming to her that she is F, and someone else's being F, where a subject might come to know that someone is F in part by its seeming to her that she is F. If it's seeming to her as if F, in such a case, is counted as a way of her knowing that someone is F, then such a way of knowing will very rarely be sufficient to secure knowledge that *she* is F. (See Smith (2006).) However, we need not count its seeming to her as if F as a way of her knowing that someone is F. Rather, she knows that someone is F by virtue of knowing that it seems to her that she is F, and knowing that there is a correlation between that occurring and something else occurring, something which in this case just happens to be someone else's being F. Her knowledge that something is F does not depend upon her having any reason to believe that she is aware of a genuine instantiation of F-ness.

she can know that 'someone's leg is bent' and while her judgement that 'I have a bent leg' is guaranteed to be *true*, given her basis for it, we cannot say that she knows it. She may not know it because she may not know which of two competing bases for her judgement is in fact operative. This means that she could quite coherently follow her judgement by the thought 'Or perhaps it is not me, perhaps this body who has a bent leg is someone else'.

In contrast, suppose that there is a circumstance in which a subject is able to know that 'X is moving her leg' in a way that implies both that she is moving her leg and that she can know that *she* is moving her leg. If the subject were to judge 'I am moving my leg' in such a circumstance, her judgement would be true and IEM in certain way. It would be immune because in such a case she can know that 'X is moving her leg' and 'X' is the subject herself because X is known in way that assumes that the object known is the knower. However, as is built into the specification of the circumstance, it would also be immune in another way. Her judgement that 'I am moving my leg' would be guaranteed not only to be true given her basis for it, but also to be known to be true. She could not coherently follow up her judgement with the thought 'Or perhaps it is not me, perhaps X who is moving her leg is someone else.'

It seems that sources for knowledge that have the character of the first case can plausibly be seen to secure judgements that are IEM. However, such sources do not seem suited to providing us with the central cases of self-knowledge. If, on other hand, there *are* sources for knowledge that have the character of the second case, sources for knowledge that 'Someone is F' that not only imply that I must be F, but also imply that I must thereby have knowledge that I am F, then they would seem to be sources of knowledge suitable for self-knowledge. Such sources of knowledge would satisfy the test for IEM set by (I-4). We can call such sources for knowledge, sources that ground judgements that are transparently IEM.[6,7]

---

[6] Note that the claim that certain judgements are transparently IEM is not that they are immune to error altogether. In particular it is not the claim that there is no possibility of acting without being aware that I acted, or of thinking I have acted whilst not having done so. Rather the claim is that *if* I have *knowledge* that someone acted directly via agent's awareness, that is, in virtue of having selected that action, then not only can I not know by that means that someone else acted, but I cannot but *know* that it was me that acted, rather than someone else.

[7] Pryor (1999) makes a distinction between immunity to *de re* misidentification and immunity to *wh*-misidentification. The distinction between transparent and non-transparent immunity made here was formulated prior to that one. Nevertheless, it

What the discussion seems to have given us is reason to believe is that bodily awareness can ground judgements that are IEM in the senses identified by (I-1), (I-2) and (I-3). Of these three (I-2) gives us the strongest kind of IEM. If my judgement that someone's legs are crossed is grounded in normal circumstances in bodily awareness, then given that bodily awareness is necessarily of only one object—my body—it is true that my legs are crossed. Furthermore I will know that my legs are crossed on that basis. However, bodily awareness in general does not seem to support judgements that are IEM in the strongest sense identified, that sense identified by (I-4). We have seen that there are cases in which bodily awareness is capable of grounding the judgement that 'Someone's leg is bent' or 'this body's leg is bent' without the subject thereby knowing that *her* leg is bent. Given certain reliable and phenomenologically indistinguishable information being in play (albeit from a different perceptual faculty) if the subject were to judge 'I have a bent leg' on the basis of bodily awareness, then although she is bound to be judging truly we would deny that she had knowledge that her leg was bent. Judgements based on bodily awareness are not *transparently* IEM relative to the first person.

We started with the suggestion that what was distinctive of non-perceptual knowledge of our actions was that it is IEM and does not

helpful to ask what the relation between the two is. Roughly, a judgement that *a* is F rests on a *de re* misidentification if the grounds for it (although, not necessarily the believer's beliefs for it) are that a particular *b* is F and that *a* = *b*, but where *a* is not *b*. A judgement that *a* is F rests on a *wh*-misidentification if the grounds for it are that there is an F, and that the thing which is F is *a*, but in fact the thing which is F is not *a*, but some distinct *b*. In the former case the judger goes wrong in re-identifying the object known to be F, in the later case the judger goes wrong in identifying which thing is F. Immunity to *de re* misidentification and immunity to *wh*-misidentification are identified as different sorts of immunity. Are those sources of knowledge which give rise to judgements which are transparently immune those which gives rise to judgements which are *wh*-immune with respect to the first person? I think so, since in essence those sources which give rise to judgements which are transparently immune just are those for which there is no gap between knowing in a given way that F is instantiated and knowing that I instantiate F. However, it is not obvious that all judgements which are *wh*-immune need be transparently immune. Consider a normal case of bodily awareness which, as was suggested above, provides information with first-personal content. It may be that such a source provides the subject with a way of knowing that 'someone is F', which, given its first-personal content, is such that the subject in this situation could not even take herself to be justified in believing that some *a*, other than herself, was F. Thus her judgement would arguably be *wh*-immune. However, it is not transparently immune, since if in relevant circumstances she received information of this kind she could know that someone is F without her retaining her knowledge that she is F.

admit of quasi-phenomena in the way that other sources of knowledge seem to do. However, we then saw that one might reasonably deny the possibility of quasi-bodily awareness, with the corresponding lack of immunity. We might argue that bodily awareness is a faculty of perception that is necessarily perception of one's own body and that, therefore, does not admit of awareness someone else's body. If we accept this then we must accept that bodily awareness grounds judgements that are IEM. However, having identified a number of distinct tests for what it might be for a source to count as grounding judgements that are IEM we found that there is a kind of immunity that bodily awareness does not seem able to secure. We concluded that bodily awareness does not ground judgements that are transparently IEM. The obvious suggestion then is that what is distinctive of our non-perceptual knowledge of our actions is that is IEM in this sense.

So, we need now to turn to the task of trying to show that our knowledge of our actions is transparently immune in a way that our knowledge of our movements through bodily awareness is not. There are a number of ways in which our non-perceptual knowledge of our own actions is different from our knowledge through bodily movement that gives us reason to be optimistic about the former exhibiting a stronger unity that the latter.

First, it seems plausible to suggest that the body that I act with, the body whose movements are the direct and immediate consequences of my exercising practical reason, is necessarily and constitutively my body.[8] As we have seen, we might argue that bodily awareness is also necessarily awareness of that which is my body. However, such a claim depends upon accepting that we have a robust and independent conception of the limits of the body, which then allows me to identify which perceptual faculty is the faculty of bodily awareness, properly speaking. We then use this prior identification of the body, combined with the constraint that bodily awareness is the faculty suited to gaining information about that body only, in order to explain away the seeming possibility of being able to be aware of someone else's body via bodily awareness. In contrast, we do not seem to have to identify which body is mine before identifying which actions are mine. In fact if we had evidence that the movements of a body were the intended, direct and immediate consequences of my exercising practical reason we would thereby have evidence for its being (or being part of) my body.

---

[8] Shoemaker (1984) articulates a similar view.

Secondly, a critical difference between our non-perceptual knowledge of our actions and the perceptual knowledge given by bodily awareness is that, in the former case, there is no mediating representation on which the self-ascription is dependent, in the latter case, the self-ascription is dependent upon a representation. We can put the point in terms of the distinction between representational dependence and independence introduced earlier from Peacocke. Our knowledge of ourselves based on bodily awareness is representationally dependent self-knowledge, in the way that knowledge such as I am in front of the door is representationally dependent. In contrast our knowledge of our actions, like our knowledge of our thoughts seems to be representationally independent self-knowledge. Given this, there is in the case of action no scope for the subject to take a critical distance from how things are presented as being by a representation. It is this that opens up the possibility, in cases where there is room for doubt about the source of that representation, of the subject knowing that someone has a given property, but not knowing whether it is *she* that has the property. There being no such representation means that we cannot see how we could construct cross wiring cases of a kind which conditions our claim that our knowledge of our actions is IEM, in the way that we could easily construct cross wiring cases that conditioned our claim that our knowledge of our bodies via bodily awareness is IEM.

But, it might be thought, we can in fact appeal to cross wiring cases of the kind we already have in place to undermine the claimed special status of our self-ascription of our actions. Imagine I am linked to someone else's body so I receive information that is phenomenologically indistinguishable from information I receive from bodily awareness. Knowing this, imagine I experience a hand rising when I try to raise my hand. Then I might worry about whether I succeeded in raising my hand or whether what I experienced was in fact the other person's hand rising. Maybe, I think, I tried to move my hand but failed, and did not get evidence of my failure because of the information received from another's body.

What are we to say of such a case? The first thing to note is that the source that the subject is utilizing in this case, that is, her knowledge of her trying and feedback from bodily awareness, is not the source for our knowledge of our actions that we have argued is central. Nevertheless, it might be claimed that the phenomenology involved in the case is similar enough to the phenomenology involved in the normal case for it to serve to undermine immunity in the strongest sense. But in fact that does not seem to be so, for in this case doubt about *who* the subject of the ascription is really does seem to undermine the possibility of knowing that the property is instantiated at all.

Suppose that, in any such case, the subject were to judge that '*Someone raised her hand*, but I am unsure whether it was me'. It seems that the antecedent clause is not a candidate for knowledge given the sources she takes to be available to her. She may be able to know, given her sources and her understanding of them, that someone's hand rose and still be unsure whether that someone was her. However, to know that someone's *hand rose* is not to know that someone *raised her hand*. It seems that in such a situation if the subject comes to doubt that she raised her hand, despite her seeming to be aware of raising it, then she loses her grounds for thinking that someone raised her hand. She might know that 'Either I raised my hand, or I failed to raise it and someone else's hand rose' but such knowledge is not sufficient to undermine the claim that our knowledge of our actions satisfies the test for IEM (I-4). It is not sufficient to undermine such immunity because this immunity is compatible with my failing to know in certain cases that the antecedent is satisfied, that is, with my failing to know that someone is raising her hand. Cross-wiring cases cannot provide the subject with sufficient grounds (although she may have some evidence) for knowledge that someone raised her hand, while leaving it open who did. Whereas the bodily awareness (and other perceptual) case(s) need not of necessity, if I am informed about the possibility of such cross wiring, undermine the existential judgements, but only my known attribution of them to myself. The reason for the asymmetry lies of course in the fact that to know of a bodily movement by agent's awareness, is to know of it as an *action*, and to know it as an action seems to be to know it as *mine*. In contrast to experience an action via some perceptual input, or other, need only be to experience it as a movement of the body.

What consequence does the above have for my capacity to know that I have certain material properties? If I perceive that my arm moved, then my perception depends upon my arm moving as a cause. If I carry out the action of moving my arm, then that implies that my arm moved. If what was claimed above is right then the following conditionals also seem to hold:

1. If I know immediately, and representationally independently, that there was an *action* of arm moving, then necessarily I can know *I* moved my hand.

2. If I know immediately, and representationally independently, that there was a *perception* of arm moving it *does not follow* that I know that *I* moved my hand.

Given the direction of causation, in the case of action, to know immediately that an action had a certain material effect is to know something material about *me*. That is knowledge I am privileged to have in virtue of being the producer, the cause of the action. But in the perceptual case, knowing that the action had a certain effect, namely, my perception of it, is not sufficient for knowing that the action was mine.

I think it has now emerged that the of essence of the distinction between knowledge of oneself via bodily awareness and knowledge of oneself via agent's awareness lies in whether it possible to envisage circumstances in which the subject has knowledge based on bodily awareness or agent's awareness of what is in fact herself without it being sufficient to ground first-person knowledge. Bodily awareness may necessarily be awareness of one's own body, but it does not seem that it is necessarily awareness *as* of one's own body. However agent's awareness, with respect to physical action, is necessarily awareness of one's body, and further it is necessarily awareness *as* of one's own body.

The cases presented seem to provide us with a way of bringing out a difference between the immunity of judgements of bodily movements and of actions. But what the cases also, I hope, suggest is a link between the two things. What appears critical to making bodily awareness of a body, awareness of a body *as mine*, is my ability to act with that body. In the absence of action the sense of ownership can, I suggest, recede, and given multiple access (access which may not be bodily awareness properly so called) and knowledge of the possibility of such access, what will secure for me that the body I am aware of is mine is that this is the body that responds to my will. The possibility of the kind of thought experiments offered have shown that the key to securing the 'sense of ownership' that is claimed to characterize bodily awareness lies in the body I am aware of being the respondent of my will. I would want to argue that what explains that our bodies are experienced as ours is a coincidence between the body I can move with—that which responds to my will, and the body I perceive via bodily perception. If that coincidence is broken then the awareness of my body as mine is weakened.[9]

[9] I think exactly the same is true for the issue of which space is mine. We might have perceptual access to more than one space or we might fail to act in the one space we do

Given that actions are primitive psychological events, and given that actions can provide a role in grounding self-knowledge that bodily awareness does not, we should conclude that the traditional view, that it is our knowledge of the psychological that is the source of self-knowledge, is right. Moreover, given that physical actions are also physical events, we have no reason to take the traditional view to be Cartesian.

have access to. In both cases, in the absence of a capacity to act, the sense that this is where I am will wane. I also think it is impossible to have two bodies as opposed to two non-continuous or disjointed body parts.

Bibliography

Almog, J., Perry, J. and Wettstein, H. (eds) 1989. *Themes from Kaplan*. Oxford: Oxford University Press.

Alvarez, M. and Hyman, J. 1998. 'Agents and their Actions', *Philosophy* 73: 219–45.

Anscombe, G. E. M. 1963. 'Two Kinds of Error in Action', *Journal of Philosophy* 60: 393–401.

—— 1972. *Intention*, 2nd edn. Oxford: Basil Blackwell.

—— 1981. 'The First Person' in her *Metaphysics and the Philosophy of Mind: Collected Philosophical Papers Volume II*. Oxford: Basil Blackwell.

Armstrong, D. M. 1968. *A Materialist Theory of Mind*. London: Routledge & Kegan Paul.

—— 1984. 'Consciousness and Causality' in *Consciousness and Causality*, Armstrong, D. M. and Malcolm, N. (eds). Oxford: Basil Blackwell.

Ayers, M. 1991. *Locke*, 2 vols. London: Routledge.

Barwise, J. and Perry, J. 1981. 'Situations and Attitudes', *Journal of Philosophy* 78: 669–91.

Bell, D. 1979. *Frege's Theory of Judgement*. Oxford: Oxford University Press.

—— 1987. 'The Art of Judgement', *Mind* 96: 221–4.

Bermúdez, J. L. 1998. *The Paradox of Self-Consciousness*. Cambridge Mass.: MIT Press.

—— 2002. 'Sources of Self-Consciousness', *Proceedings of the Aristotelian Society* 102: 87–107.

—— Marcel, A. and Eilan, N. (eds) 1995. *The Body and the Self*. Cambridge, Mass.: MIT Press.

Bilgrami, A. 1988. 'Self-Knowledge and Resentment' in *Knowing Our Own Minds*, MacDonald, C., Smith B. and Wright C. (eds). Oxford: Oxford University Press.

Blackburn, S. 1986. 'Thought without Representation II; What about Me?', *Aristotelian Society Supplementary Volume* 60: 153–66.

Block, N. 1990. 'Consciousness and Accessibility', *Behavioral and Brain Sciences* 13: 596–98.

—— 1995. 'On a Confusion about a Function of Consciousness', *Behavioral and Brain Sciences* 18: 227–87.

Brewer, B. 1992. 'Self-Location and Agency', *Mind* 101: 17–34.

—— 1999. *Perception and Reason*. Oxford: Oxford University Press.

Broadie, F. 1967. 'Knowing That I Am Doing', *Philosophical Quarterly* 18: 37–149.

Burge, T. 1993. 'Content Preservation', *Philosophical Review* 103: 457–88.

Burge, T. 1996. 'Our Entitlement to Self-Knowledge', *Proceedings of the Aristotelian Society* 96: 91–116.
—— 1998. 'Reason and the First-Person' in *Knowing Our Own Minds*, MacDonald, C., Smith B. and Wright C. (eds). Oxford: Oxford University Press.
—— 2003. 'Perceptual Entitlement', *Philosophy and Phenomenological Research* 67: 503–548.
Butterfill, S. 2001. 'Two Kinds of Purposive Action', *European Journal of Philosophy* 9: 141–65.
Campbell, J. Ms., 'Self-Consciousness and 'I''.
—— 1994. *Past, Space and Self*, Cambridge, Massachusetts: MIT Press.
—— 1998. 'Joint Attention and the First-Person' in *Current Issues in Philosophy of Mind: Royal Institute of Philosophy Annual Supplement* 43: 123–36, O'Hear, A. (ed.) Cambridge: Cambridge University Press
—— 1999. 'Schizophrenia, the Space of Reasons and Thinking as a Motor Process', *The Monist* 82: 609–25.
—— 2003. 'The Role of Demonstratives in Action-Explanation' in *Agency and Self-Awareness*, Roessler, J. and Eilan, N (eds). Oxford: Oxford University Press.
Carruthers, P. 1992. 'Consciousness and Concepts II', *Aristotelian Society Proceedings Supplementary Volume* 66: 41–59.
—— 1998. 'Natural Theories of Consciousness', *European Journal of Philosophy* 6: 203–22.
Cassam, Q (ed.) 1994. *Self-Knowledge*. Oxford: Oxford University Press.
—— 1995. 'Introspection and Bodily Self-Ascription' in *The Body and the Self*, Bermúdez, J. L., Marcel, A. and Eilan, N. (eds). Cambridge, Mass.: MIT Press.
—— 1997. *Self and World*. Oxford: Clarendon Press.
Casteñeda, H-L. 1989. 'Direct Reference, the Semantics of Thinking and Guise Theory' in *Themes from Kaplan*, Almog, J., Perry, J. and Wettstein, H. (eds). Oxford: Oxford University Press.
—— 1999. *The Phenomeno-Logic of the I: Essays on Self-Consciousness*. Bloomington, Ind. and Indianapolis: Indiana University Press.
Chisholm, R. 1981. *The First Person*. Sussex: Harvester Press.
—— 1989. 'Why Singular Propositions?' in *Themes from Kaplan*, Almog, J., Perry, J. and Wettstein, H. (eds). Oxford: Oxford University Press.
Cole, J. 1993. *Pride and a Daily Marathon*. Cambridge, Mass.: MIT Press.
Cole, J. and Paillard, J. 1995. 'Living without Touch and Peripheral Information about Body Position and Movement' in *The Body and the Self*. Bermúdez, J. L., Marcel, A. and Eilan, N. (eds). Cambridge, Mass.: MIT Press.
Corazza, E., Fish, W. and Gorvett, J. 2002. 'Who is I?', *Philosophical Studies* 107: 1–21.
Crane, T. 2003. 'The Intentional Structure of Consciousness' in *Consciousness: New Philosophical Perspectives*, Smith, Q. and Jokic, J. (eds). Oxford: Oxford University Press.

Danto, A. C. 1963. 'What We Can Do', *Journal of Philosophy* 60: 435–45.

—— 1973. *Analytical Philosophy of Action,* Cambridge: Cambridge University Press.

Davidson, D. 1973. 'Freedom to Act' in *Essays on Freedom of Action,* Honderich, T. (ed.). London: Routledge & Kegan Paul.

—— 1980. *Essays on Actions and Events.* Oxford: Oxford University Press.

Della Sala, S., Marchetti, C. and Spinnler, H. 1991. 'Righthanded Anarchic Hand: a Longitudinal Study', *Neuropsychologia* 29: 1113–27.

——, —— and —— 1994. 'The Anarchic Hand; a Fronto-Mesial Sign' in *Handbook of Neuropsychology IX,* F. Boller and J. Grafman (eds). Amsterdam: Elsvier, NorthHolland.

Donnellan, K. 1963. 'Knowing What I am Doing', *Journal of Philosophy* 60: 401–9.

Dretske, F. 1997. *Naturalizing the Mind.* Cambridge Mass.: Bradford Books, MIT Press.

—— 1999. 'The Mind's Awareness of Itself', *Philosophical Studies* 95:103–24.

—— 2000. 'Entitlement: Epistemic Rights Without Epistemic Duties?', *Philosophy and Phenomenological Research* 60: 591–606.

—— (forthcoming). 'Knowing What You Think vs. Knowing That you Think It'.

Dunn, Robert 1998. 'Knowing What I'm About To Do Without Evidence', *International Journal of Philosophical Studies* 6: 231–52.

Evans, G. 1982. *Varieties of Reference.* Oxford: Clarendon Press.

Fichte, J. G. 1964. *Gesamtausgabe der Bayerischen Akademie der Wissenschaften, 15 vols.* Lauth, R., Jacobs, H. and Gliwatsky, H. Stuttgart (eds). Stuttgart-Bad Cannstatt: Frommann-Holzboog.

Frege, G. 1977. 'Thoughts' in *Logical Investigations,* Geach, P. T. (ed.) Oxford: Basil Blackwell.

—— 1980. *Translations from the Philosophical Writings of Gottlob Frege* (ed.) Geach and Black 3rd edn.

Gallois, A. 2000. 'First-Person Accessibility and Consciousness', *Philosophical Topics* 28: 10146.

Garrett, B. 1998. *Personal Identity and Self-Consciousness.* London: Routledge.

Ginet, C. 1990. *On Action.* Cambridge: Cambridge University Press.

Haggard, P. 2003. 'Conscious Awareness on Intention and of Action' in *Agency and Self-Awareness,* Roessler, J. and Eilan, N. (eds). Oxford: Oxford University Press.

—— and Eimer, M. 1999. 'On the Relation Between Brain Potentials and the Awareness of Voluntary Movements', *Experimental Brain Research* 126: 128–33.

—— and Magno, E. 1999. 'Localising Awareness of Action with Transcranial Magnetic Stimulation', *Experimental Brain Research* 127:102–7.

Hamilton, A. 1991. 'Anscombian and Cartesian Scepticism', *Philosophical Quarterly*, 41: 39–54.

—— 2000. 'The Authority of Avowals and the Concept of Belief', *European Journal of Philosophy* 7: 20–39.

—— (forthcoming). *Memory and the Body: A Study of Self-Consciousness.*

Harcourt, E. 1993. 'Are Hybrid Proper Names the Solution to the Completion Problem? A Reply to Wolfgang Künne', *Mind* 102: 301–13.

Heal, J. 2002. 'On First-Person Authority', *Proceedings of the Aristotelian Society* 102: 1–19.

Henrich, D. 1982. 'Fichte's Original Insight', trans. Lachterman, D. R., *Contemporary German Philosophy* 1: 15–23.

Hornsby, J. 1980. *Actions*, London: Routledge & Kegan Paul.

—— 1997. *Simple Mindedness*, Cambridge, Mass: Harvard University Press.

—— 2004. 'Agency and Actions' in *Agency and Action*, Steward, H. and Hyman, J. (eds). Cambridge: Cambridge University Press.

Hossack, K. 2002. 'Self-Knowledge and Consciousness', *Proceedings of the Aristotelian Society* 103: 163–81.

Hume, D. 1978. *A Treatise of Human Nature*, (ed.) Selby-Bigge, L. A. and. Nidditch, P. H. Oxford: Clarendon Press.

Husserl, E. 1973. *Logical Investigations*, trans. Findlay, J. N. London: Routledge.

Hyman, J. and Steward, H. (eds). 2004. *Agency and Action*. Cambridge: Cambridge University Press.

James, W. 1890. *Principles of Psychology*. London: MacMillan.

—— 1976a. 'The Experience of Activity' in his *Essays in Radical Empiricism*. Cambridge, Mass: Harvard University Press.

—— 1976b. 'Does 'Consciousness' Exist?' in his *Essays in Radical Empiricism*. Cambridge, Mass Harvard University Press.

Kant, I. 1933. *Critique of Pure Reason*, trans. Kemp Smith, N. London: Macmillan.

Kaplan, D. 1989. 'Demonstratives' in *Themes from Kaplan*. Oxford: Oxford University Press.

—— 1989. 'Afterthoughts' in *Themes from Kaplan*. Oxford: Oxford University Press.

Kripke, S. 1977. 'Speaker's Reference and Semantic Reference', *Midwest Studies in Philosophy* 2: 255–76.

Lawlor, K. 2001. *New Thoughts about Old Things: Cognitive Policies and the Ground of Singular Concepts*. New York: Garland.

Lewis, D. 1979. 'Attitudes De Dicto and De Se', *Philosophical Review* 88: 513–43. Also in his 1983, *Philosophical Papers, Volume I*. Oxford: Oxford University Press.

—— 1983. 'Postscripts to 'Attitudes De Dicto and De Se'' in his *Philosophical Papers, Volume I*. Oxford: Oxford University Press.

Lowe, E. J. 1993. 'Self, Reference and Self-Reference', *Philosophy*, 68: 15–33.

MacDonald, C., Smith B. and Wright C. (eds). 1998. *Knowing Our Own Minds*. Oxford: Oxford University Press.

McDowell, J. 1986. 'Singular Thought and the Extent of Inner Space' in *Subject, Thought and Context*, Petit, P. and McDowell, J. (eds). Oxford: Clarendon Press.

—— 1994. *Mind and World*. Cambridge, MA: Harvard University Press.

McGinn, C. 1982. 'The Structure of Content' in *Thought and Object* (ed.) Woodfield, A. Oxford: Clarendon Press.

Mackie, J. M. 1980. 'The Transcendental 'I'' in *Philosophical Subjects: Essays presented to P.F. Strawson*, Van Straaten, Z. (ed.). Oxford: Clarendon Press.

Malcolm, N. 1979. 'Whether 'I' is a Referring Expression' in *Intention and Intentionality: Essays in Honour of G. E. M. Anscombe*, Diamond, C. and Teichman, J. (eds). Ithaca, New York: Cornell University Press.

Marcel, A. 2003. 'The Sense of Agency: Awareness and Ownership of Action' in *Agency and Self-Awareness*, Roessler, J and Eilan, N. (eds). Oxford: Oxford University Press.

Marcel, A. and Nimmo-Smith, I. (forthcoming). 'Anosognosia for Pelgia: Specificity, Extension, Partiality and Disunity of Bodily Awareness', *Cortex*.

Marcel, A. and Tegner, R. 1995. 'Anosognosia for Plegia', Presented at 11th European Workshop on Cognitive Neuropsychology, Bressanone, Italy.

Martin, M. 1995. 'Bodily Awareness: A Sense of Ownership' in *The Body and the Self*, Bermúdez, J. L., Marcel, A. and Eilan, N. (eds). Cambridge, Mass.: MIT Press.

—— 1997a. 'Self-Observation', *European Journal of Philosophy* 5.2: 11938.

—— 1997b. 'The Reality of Appearances' in *Thought and Ontology*, Sainsbury, M. (ed.). Milan: Franco-Angeli.

—— 2004. 'The Limits of Self-Awareness', *Philosophical Studies* 120: 37–89.

Melville, H. 1972. *Moby Dick*. Lonsdon: Penguin Classics.

Mellor, D. H. 1989. 'I and Now', *Proceedings of the Aristotelian Society* 89: 79–94. Also in his 1991, *Matters of Metaphysics*, Cambridge: Cambridge University Press.

Merleau-Ponty, M. 1989. *Phenomenology of Perception*, trans. Smith, C. London: Routledge.

Millikan, R. G. 1990. 'The Myth of the Essential Indexical' *Noûs* 24: 723–34.

Moore, A. 1997. *Points of View*. Oxford: Oxford University Press.

Moran, R. 2001. *Authority and Estrangement: An Essay on Self-Knowledge*. Princeton: Princeton University Press.

—— 2004. 'The Agent's Point of View and 'What Happens': Anscombe on 'Practical Knowledge'' in *Action and Agency*, Hyman, J. and Steward, H. (eds) Cambridge: Cambridge University Press.

Neuhouser, F. 1990. *Fichte's Theory of Subjectivity*. Cambridge: Cambridge University Press.

Noordhof, P. 2001. 'Believe What You Want', *Proceedings of the Aristotelian Society* 101: 247–65.

—— 2003. 'Self-Deception, Interpretation and Consciousness', *Philosophy and Phenomenological Research* 77: 75–100.

O'Brien, L.F. 1993. "I': An Investigation of Self-Reference', D.Phil. thesis, Oxford University.

—— 1994. 'Anscombe and the Self-Reference Rule', *Analysis* 54. 4: 277–28.

—— 1995a. 'The Problem of Self-Identification', *Proceedings of the Aristotelian Society* 95: 235–51.

—— 1995b. 'Evans on Self-Identification', *Noûs* 29. 2: 232–47.

—— 1996. 'Solipsism and Self-Reference', *European Journal of Philosophy* 4: 176–94.

—— 2003a. 'On Knowing One's Own Actions' in *Agency and Self-Awareness*, Roessler, J. and Eilan, N. (eds). Oxford: Oxford University Press.

—— 2003b. 'Moran on Agency and Self-Knowledge', *European Journal of Philosophy* 11: 375–90.

—— 2005. 'Self-Knowledge, Agency and Force', *Philosophy and Phenomenological Research* 71: 580–601.

Olsen, C. 1969. 'Knowledge of our Intentional Actions', *Philosophical Quarterly* 19: 324–36.

O'Shaughnessy, B. 1963. 'Observation and the Will', *Journal of Philosophy* 60: 367–92.

—— 1973. 'Trying as the Mental Pineal Gland', *Journal of Philosophy* 70: 365–86.

—— 1980. *The Will*, 2 vols, Cambridge: Cambridge University Press.

Peacocke, C. A. B. 1983. *Sense and Content*. Oxford: Clarendon Press.

—— 1996. 'Entitlement, Self-Knowledge and Conceptual Redeployment', *Proceedings of the Aristotelian Society* 96: 117–58.

—— 1998. 'Conscious Attitudes, Attention and Self-Knowledge' in *Knowing Our Own Minds* MacDonald, C., Smith B. and Wright C. (eds). Oxford: Oxford University Press.

—— 1999. *Being Known*. Oxford: Oxford University Press.

—— 2002. 'Three Principles of Rationalism, *European Journal of Philosophy*, 10: 375–97.

—— 2003. 'Action: Awareness, Ownership, and Knowledge' in *Agency and Self-Awareness*, Roessler, J. and Eilan, N. (eds). Oxford: Oxford University Press.

Perry, J. 1986. 'Thoughts without Representation I', *Aristotelian Society Supplementary Volume* 60: 137–51.

—— 1990. 'Self-Notions', *Logos* 11: 17–31.

—— 1993. *The Problem of the Essential Indexical and Other Essays*. New York: Oxford University Press.

Predelli, S. 1998. 'I Am Not Here Now', *Analysis* 58: 107–12.

—— 2002. 'Intentions, Indexicals and Communication', *Analysis* 62: 310–16.

Pryor, J. 1999. 'Immunity to Error Through Misidentification', *Philosophical Topics* 26: 271–304.

—— 2000. 'The Skeptic and the Dogmatist', *Noûs* 34: 517–49.

—— 2005. 'A Defense of Immediate Non-Inferential Justification' in *Contemporary Debates in Epistemology*, Steup, M. and Sosa, E. (eds). Oxford: Blackwell.

Putnam, H. 1975. 'The Meaning of "Meaning"' in his *Mind Language and Reality*, vol. II. Cambridge: Cambridge University Press.

Roessler, J. 1999. 'Perception, Introspection and Attention', *European Journal of Philosophy* 7: 47–64.

—— 2003. 'Intentional Action and Self-Awareness' in *Agency and Self-Awareness*, Roessler, J. and Eilan, N. (eds). Oxford: Oxford University Press.

Roessler, J. and Eilan, N. (eds). 2003. *Agency and Self-Awareness:*. Oxford: Oxford University Press.

Romdenh-Romluc, K. 2002. 'Now the French are Invading England!', *Analysis* 62: 34–41.

Rosenthal, D. 1986. 'Two Concepts of Consciousness', *Philosophical Studies* 94: 329–59.

Rovane, C. 1997. 'The Epistemology of First-Person Reference', *The Journal of Philosophy* 84: 147–67.

Sacks, M. 1989. *The World We Found*. London: Duckworth.

—— 2000. *Objectivity and Insight*. Oxford: Oxford University Press.

Searle, J. 1983. *Intentionality: An Essay in the Philosophy of Mind*. Cambridge: Cambridge University Press.

Shoemaker, S. 1963. *Self-Knowledge and Self-Identity*. Ithaca: Cornell University Press.

—— 1968. 'Self-Reference and Self-Awareness', *Journal of Philosophy* 65: 555–67. Also in his 1984, *Identity Cause and Mind: Philosophical Essays*. Cambridge: Cambridge University Press.

—— 1984a. *Identity Cause and Mind: Philosophical Essays*. Cambridge: Cambridge University Press.

—— 1984b. 'Embodiment and Behaviour' in his *Identity Cause and Mind* Cambridge: Cambridge University Press.

—— 1995. 'Moore's Paradox and Self-Knowledge', *Philosophical Studies* 77, 211–28. Also in his 1996, *The First-Person Perspective and Other Essays*. Cambridge: Cambridge University Press.

—— 1996. *The First-Person Perspective and Other Essays*. Cambridge: Cambridge University Press.

—— 2003. 'Moran on Self-Knowledge', *European Journal of Philosophy* 11: 391–401.

Sidelle, A. 1991. 'The Answering Machine Paradox', *Canadian Journal of Philosophy* 21: 525–39.

Smith, J. 2006. 'Which Immunity to Error?' *Philosophical Studies* 130: 273–83.

Snowdon, P. 1980/1. 'Perception, Vision and Causation', *Proceedings of Aristotelian Society* [Supplementary Volume], 64: 121–50.

Sosa, E. 1983. 'Consciousness of the Self and of the Present' in *Agent, Language and the Structure of the World*, Tomberlin, J. E. (ed.) Indianapolis: Hackett. pp. 131–45.

—— 1991. 'Intellectual Virtue in Perspective' in his *Knowledge in Perspective: Selected Essays in Epistemology*. Cambridge: Cambridge University Press.

Thomasson, A. L. 2000. 'After Brentano: A One-Level Theory of Consciousness', *European Journal of Philosophy* 8: 190–209.

Tye, M. 1995. *Ten Problems of Consciousness*. Cambridge, Mass.: MIT Press.

Velleman, J. D. 1989. *Practical Reflection*. Princeton: Princeton University Press.

—— 1992. 'What Happens When Someone Acts?', *Mind* 101: 461–81.

—— 1996. 'Self to Self', *Philosophical Review* 105: 39–76.

—— 2000. *The Possibility of Practical Reason*. Oxford: Clarendon Press.

Williams, M. 2000. 'Entitlement: Epistemic Rights without Epistemic Duties?', *Philosophy and Phenomenological Research* 60: 607–12.

Williamson, T. 1995. 'Is Knowing a State of Mind?', *Mind* 104: 533–65.

—— 2000. *Knowledge and its Limits*. Oxford: Oxford University Press.

Wilson, G. 1989. *The Intentionality of Human Action*. Stanford: Stanford University Press.

Wittgenstein, L. 1953. *Philosophical Investigations*, (trans.) Anscombe, G. E. M. Oxford: Blackwell.

—— 1958. *The Blue and Brown Books*. Oxford: Blackwell

—— 1961. *Tractatus Logico-Philosophicus*, (trans.) Pears, D. F. and McGuinness, B. F. London: Routledge & Kegan Paul.

Wright, C. 1989. 'Wittgenstein's Later Philosophy of Mind: Sensations, Privacy and Intention', *Journal of Philosophy* 26: 622–34.

—— 1998. 'Self-Knowledge: The Wittgensteinian Legacy' in *Knowing Our Own Minds*, MacDonald, C., Smith B. and Wright C. (eds). Oxford: Oxford University Press.

Index